The United States
and
Revolutionary Nationalism
in Mexico, 1916–1932

The United States
and
Revolutionary Nationalism
in Mexico, 1916–1932

Robert Freeman Smith

The University of Chicago Press

Chicago and London

The University of Chicago Press, Chicago 60637
The University of Chicago Press, Ltd., London

© 1972 by The University of Chicago
All rights reserved. Published 1972
Printed in the United States of America

International Standard Book Number: 0–226–76506–7
Library of Congress Catalog Card Number: 73–182872

To   Fred Harvey Harrington

and to the memory of

William B. Hesseltine

Contents

Preface

An old friend is returning to the public bond market
here this week after an absence of 53 years.
The Government of Mexico plans to sell publicly
Wednesday four bond issues that total $40,000,000
through an underwriting syndicate headed by
Kuhn, Loeb, & Co. and the First Boston Corporation.
The offering would be the first public dollar bond
offering here by Mexico since $20,000,000 of 4 percent
external gold obligations was floated in 1910.
—New York Times, 14 July 1963

Mexico's return to the New York bond market came almost two
months after the final payment had been made for the oil properties nationalized in 1938. The pre-1910 foreign debt—as modified
by agreements in 1922, 1925, and 1942—had been repaid by
1960. The last remnants of the economic debris created by the
pre-1940 Mexicanization of the economy had been cleared away.
As the *Times*'s writer noted: "Mexico's return to the public bond
market here, however, is considered a milestone in that country's
recent financial history, far more important than the borrowing."
In essence, Mexico had completely reclaimed her pre-1910 reputation as the most stable and respectable underdeveloped nation.

Significant changes had taken place in Mexico and in Mexican
relations with the developed, capitalistic nations. Yet the country
still operated within the international order led by the United
States of America. This prompted some writers in the 1960s to
label Mexico's post-1910 experiences as the "preferred revolution." The Cuban Revolution, beginning in 1959, was partly
responsible for this evaluation. But this post hoc judgment is like

looking at the world through the wrong end of a pair of binoculars, since it diminishes the bitter conflicts which characterized the post-1910 history of Mexico and her relations with the United States. For several decades many U.S. officials and businessmen regarded the Mexican Revolution as anything but "preferred." The official and unofficial protests and denunciations of the reforms engendered by Mexican revolutionary nationalism would fill many library shelves and are identical to those used against Cuba since 1959.[1]

The Mexican Revolution was the first important challenge to the world order of the industrial-creditor, and capitalistic, nations made by an underdeveloped nation trying to assert control over its economy and reform its internal system. Since Mexico had little capital and its economy was dominated by foreign interests, any real attempt at redistributing or asserting national control over property would upset the status quo and adversely affect foreign property interests. The developed nations demanded "prompt, adequate, and effective," compensation (meaning gold and the valuation set by the investor) for any interests affected by reforms. The Mexican government was faced with the dilemma of either complying and having no effective reforms, or else unilaterally abandoning the international law of foreign investments. As F. S. Dunn noted in 1933:

It was clearly to the advantage of the United States and other nations having extensive foreign interests to preserve the existing notion of the sanctity of private property intact. On the other hand, a drastic alteration of the local distribution of wealth was of much greater immediate interest to the revolutionary régime in Mexico than was the preservation of the international economic order. The program mapped out under Article 27 involved a vital clash of interests for which the existing international legal system afforded no ready solution.[2]

As the self-anointed enforcer for the Western Hemisphere of the

1. Revolutionary nationalism: a combination of those ideological and emotional elements which involves some significant change in the socio-economic and political power structures; the assertion of national control over the economy and the society; and a movement for national regeneration. The intensity and contours of revolutionary nationalism will vary according to country, time, cultural milieu, and historical experiences.
2. F. S. Dunn, *The Diplomatic Protection of Americans in Mexico* (New York, 1933), 330–31.

legal-economic order of the industrial-creditor nations, the U.S. government readily assumed the "white man's burden" of attempting to force the revolutionary leaders to abide by the rules of that order. In 1906 Mr. Dooley summed up the essential elements of the conflict rather succinctly: "A riv'lution can't be bound be th' rules iv th' game because it's again' th' rules iv th' game."[3]

In the period from the beginning of Mexican revolutionary nationalism in 1915 through its apparent reversal, 1928–32, few U.S. business or political leaders would accept the idea of an underdeveloped country asserting national control over foreign investments or rejecting the hemispheric hegemony of the United States. But all were divided over the question of which tactics would most effectively influence Mexico. Some preferred a flexible, accommodating approach. Others stressed a firm, no-compromise policy. And a few advocated taking over and remaking Mexico. Whatever the tactic, the result was some kind of interference in the internal affairs of Mexico. There was a considerable difference in *modus operandi* and style between the international bankers, represented by Thomas W. Lamont, and the oil companies, represented by such men as Frederic R. Kellogg, Frederic N. Watriss, and Harold Walker, or between officials such as Josephus Daniels and Dwight Morrow on the one hand, and Henry P. Fletcher and James R. Sheffield on the other.

Mexican officials were faced with this problem: to what degree could they implement national control over the economy before the U.S. government resorted to armed intervention? They anticipated military action on several occasions after 1915. But because of various circumstances, such as World War I and the subsequent reaction against war, it is doubtful if any administration could have mounted a major intervention. This question cannot be given a definite answer, but I believe that economic boycotts would have been put into effect·if the Mexicans had nationalized the oil industry. Mexican officials, however, backed away from any substantial enforcement of national control of oil, which was considered the most vital natural resource. Minor gains were made, but from the Carranza decrees of 1916 to the final nationalization of most of the oil companies in 1938, the major producers refused to accept the fundamental laws of Mexico. After

3. Finley Peter Dunne, *Dissertations by Mr. Dooley* (New York, 1906), 130.

each attempt to assert some national control, legal compromises were effected which left the oil companies relatively undisturbed in their control of the industry. President Lázaro Cárdenas finally resolved the question of sovereignty in 1938 and made article 27 of the constitution a fully effective measure. During this period Mexican officials had a little more success in cutting the amount of the foreign debt, recovering land held by foreigners, and asserting some control over aspects of the mining industry. The conflict between national sovereignty and foreign interests was still a long way from a solution by 1933.

In various ways the nonmilitary, anti-expansionist, and authentic self-determination traditions in the United States complicated the problem of controlling an obstreperous underdeveloped nation. The imperial tradition was the strongest, but the others provided some competition, and imposed certain limitations, for the period under consideration. Some church, labor, academic, and peace groups espoused the minority traditions with consistency. Their influence should not be overestimated. Perhaps of more significance for relations with Mexico was the competition of traditions within the more powerful groups and classes in the country. The reluctance to use military force was one of the more important aspects of this competition, and directly influenced the extent and type of control which U.S. leaders were able to exercise in Mexico.

Analysis of the U.S. confrontation with revolutionary nationalism in Mexico gives, I think, some support to the view that attempts, no matter what the intentions, to control and dominate underdeveloped countries produce more ill will and complications than solutions. Military methods are even more productive of hatred and conflict. U.S.-Mexican relations between 1915 and 1933 were filled with conflict and ill will, and military intervention might have had disastrous results. At least the U.S. leaders of that era avoided the worst tactics, and this kept the door open for the diplomatic settlements of the next period (1933–1945). And the general inability or unwillingness of the U.S. leaders to use military force meant that, sooner or later, they would probably have to accept some of the fruits of revolutionary nationalism as the price of continued U.S. economic, political, and ideological influence in Mexico.

Revolutionary nationalism continues to be a major force in the underdeveloped world. The alternative to living with it (and accepting nationalization) is to try to control the countries involved. Since the 1950s these countries are no longer dependent on the capitalistic world order for money, markets, and arms. This has helped to stimulate the increased use of military force to oppose revolutionary nationalism. But the economic and moral costs of military intervention have increased tremendously since the days of Woodrow Wilson.

The United States has faced, and will continue to face, the problem of nationalization in Latin America and elsewhere. Peru, Bolivia, and Chile have recently expropriated foreign oil holdings, mines, and other businesses, and diplomatic complications have resulted. What will happen if they develop a completely revolutionary program and even repudiate the hemispheric hegemony of the United States? As with Mexico in 1910 various nations are also facing a major economic crisis over payments on their foreign debt. The United Nations Economic Commission for Latin America (ECLA) has estimated that in 1966 the overall total for financing services absorbed 33 percent of the total value of Latin American income from exports. The commission predicted that within twelve years several countries will face complete bankruptcy because of the outflow of funds. It seems a safe assumption that this situation will stimulate revolutionary nationalism and produce demands for economic independence and debt repudiation. Such developments could produce crisis after crisis unless the leadership of the United States adopts a policy of complete openness to change and repudiates the idea that revolutionary nationalism is a threat to the United States. We must "mark, learn and inwardly digest" the words of the Mexican novelist Carlos Fuentes:

Do you see, Americans? The world has changed. Latin America is no longer your preserve. The world moves ahead. And you are standing on the rim. . . . Revolutions are going to progress. . . . You will not be able to put out all the fires in Latin America, Africa, and Asia.[4]

4. Carlos Fuentes, "The Argument of Latin America: Words for the North Americans," in Fuentes et al., *Whither Latin America?* (New York, 1963), 22.

I have tried in this book to concentrate on the major issues involved in the confrontation between Mexican revolutionary nationalism and the national interests of the United States *as these were defined* by U.S. political and business leaders. Certain diplomatic issues are not covered, such as the Chamizal dispute. In addition, I have not attempted simply to repeat what other scholars have said about the diplomacy of the period, especially for the 1920s. For studies which cover other aspects of relations between the two countries I would refer the reader to the works of Arthur Link, Howard Cline, L. Ethan Ellis, John W. F. Dulles, Sister M. Elizabeth Rice, Luis Zorrilla, Lorenzo Meyer, and Stanley R. Ross. And I acknowledge my own intellectual debt to their scholarly efforts.

I have chosen the years 1916–32 for coverage because they stand out as a defined period for the basic issues involved in this study. The conflict between Mexico and the United States over the question of revolutionary reform emerged in 1916, during the Wilson administration, and reached a kind of settlement during the Hoover administration. This was the first period of conflict. By the early 1930s the Mexican Revolution appeared to have moved to a much more conservative stage, and the heat had disappeared from the relations between the two nations. Also, by 1932 the International Committee of Bankers on Mexico, one of the most important organizations during this first period, had almost ceased to function. The issue of the foreign debt of Mexico had not been settled, but the economic depression forced the indefinite suspension of negotiations and governmental agitation for a settlement was muted. The revival of revolutionary nationalism, and the reopening of the various economic issues under President Lázaro Cárdenas stands as a "second" period separated from the first by several years of calm. For this period the interested readers should consult E. David Cronon, *Josephus Daniels in Mexico,* and Bryce Wood, *The Making of the Good Neighbor Policy.*

Like all others laboring in the vineyard of historical research, I have been aided by numerous individuals and a few institutions. Among the latter, the Universities of Wisconsin, Rhode Island, Connecticut, and Toledo provided some research funds for this study.

I wish to thank the following persons, who as graduate students shared their research findings with me: Andrew T. Ford, Peter Karsten, David Kivela, Lance Odden, Richard Werking, and Richard Zeitlin (all at the University of Wisconsin); Robert White, S.J. (Cornell); and George Lubick (Toledo). My special appreciation goes to Edward Rice for the work which he did as my research assistant in 1966–67.

The staffs of the various research libraries have been most helpful, and my special thanks are extended to: Robert M. Lovett (Baker Library, Harvard Graduate School of Business Administration), Rena Durkan (Amherst College), Roland Baughman (Butler Library, Columbia University), and Milton O. Gustafson and Ralph Huss (National Archives). For special and friendly assistance while working in the Archivo General de la Secretaría de Relaciones Exteriores de México, I extend thanks to Lic. Aida Moreno Manccinelli and Lic. Mario Vallejo.

For various reasons my deep appreciation goes to Daniel Cosío Villegas (Colegio de México), Richard Davis (Washington University, St. Louis), Henrietta Larson (Northfield, Minn.), the late Thomas S. Lamont (J. P. Morgan & Co.), Richard Scandrett (Cornwall, N. Y.), and Berta Ulloa (Colegio de México).

I would also like to express my appreciation to Lucille Endsley, Sharon Klonowski, and Karen Young (University of Toledo) for typing various parts of the manuscript.

I am especially indebted to my wife Alberta, and my children, Robin and Robert, for their encouragement, patience and love. As usual, Alberta devoted untold hours to typing and proofreading and contributed many helpful suggestions. For these and other reasons this is her book as well.

1   Mexico and Revolution

*He [Porfirio Díaz] said that, so far as the ambassador
was concerned, he was a Mexican, for whom
mañana would do as well as today. As for the
secretary of foreign affairs, he also could wait. But I,
as one of his "collaborators in the development of
Mexico," deserved instant admittance day or night,
for "Mexico herself" waited on me.*

—John Hays Hammond

Economic Background

The foreign observers who came to Mexico City for the centennial
of the Hidalgo rebellion of 1810 were impressed by the apparent
serenity and opulence of this once turbulent country. The well-
scrubbed streets and massive new buildings of the capital city
seemed to symbolize the changed conditions which had taken place
under the firm leadership of Porfirio Díaz. The leaders of the industrial-creditor nations now believed that Mexico was a model underdeveloped country. Peace, order, and stability were maintained,
and foreign investments were protected. As a corollary, the legal
system of Mexico had been reshaped to conform to the international
legal order which the developed nations had constructed for the
protection of trade and investment. The Mexican government
not only accepted the industrial-creditor nations' rules for the
"game" of international economic relations but also followed
internal economic policies which opened Mexico to the full impact
of foreign business expansion.

Changes had taken place under the auspices of the Porfirian
peace. Political turbulence had ended, and older observers could
contrast this with the situation in 1873 which had provoked the

1

editor of the *Army and Navy Journal* to write: "We have stood
enough from Mexico. . . . Come to order she must, or be
punished."[1] The *rurales* (rural police) now maintained order in
the country, and obstreperous elements such as Yaqui Indians
and striking copper-miners were given bloody lessons from the
catechism of law and order.

Economically, Mexico seemed to be fulfilling the prophecy of
Cecil Rhodes: "Mexico is the treasure house from which will come
the gold, silver, copper, and precious stones that will build the
empire of tomorrow, and make the future cities of the world veritable Jerusalems."[2] Early in his presidential career Díaz had
decided that the development of Mexico depended upon large-
scale foreign investments, and he instituted a variety of policies
to make Mexico safe and attractive for foreign business. Low
taxes; physical protection; legal guarantees, coupled with friendly
courts; subsidies; governmental concessions to public lands and
waters—all constituted important elements in the new economic
order. The larger foreign companies also could depend upon the
central government to handle any problems which arose with local
and state authorities.

As a result, some development did take place. This generally was
concentrated in the extractive industries and in satellite areas such
as railroads and electric power. During the period 1891–1910 the
production of copper rose from 5,650 to 48,160 metric tons; gold
from 1,477 to 41,420 kilograms; and lead from 30,187 to 124,292
metric tons.[3] Railroad mileage increased from 416 miles in 1876
to 15,360 miles by 1910. This development produced attractive
profits and such firms as American Smelting and Refining, Phelps-
Dodge, and the Southern Pacific Railway developed extensive holdings. From the infant iron and steel industry of Monterrey to the
sugar plantations of the south, U.S. capital was in a paramount
position. By 1908, the *Wall Street Summary* could report that
three-fourths of the dividend-paying mines in Mexico were owned
by U.S. interests and that these "paid a sum 24 percent in excess

    1. *Army and Navy Journal,* 31 May 1873, p. 668.
    2. Quoted in P. Harvey Middleton, *Industrial Mexico: 1919 Facts and
Figures* (New York, 1919), as epigraph.
    3. Marvin Bernstein, *The Mexican Mining Industry, 1890–1950: A Study
of the Interaction of Politics, Economics, and Technology* (Albany, N.Y.,
1966), 51.

of the aggregate net earnings of all the National Banks in the United States, or about $95,000,000."[4]

In 1901, Edward L. Doheny and his associates brought in the first oil well in Mexico, and by 1903 commercial production was underway. Until then the Waters-Pierce Oil Company (35 percent interest held by H. Clay Pierce and 65 percent by Standard Oil of New Jersey) had a monopoly on shipment of oil to Mexico by virtue of an import concession given by Díaz. After 1903, foreign capital poured into the Mexican oil industry. Two of the pioneer companies, the Huasteca Company (Doheny and Associates) and El Aguila (Mexican Eagle, controlled by Weetman Pearson and Sons of London), were paying substantial dividends by 1911.[5]

The developmental policies of the Díaz regime also were directed at the rural economy. Don Porfirio and his colleagues believed that the small *rancheros* and the Indians were unproductive. The government developed a systematic policy designed to redistribute the land to large holders. Theoretically these owners would either increase agricultural output or sell the land to colonies of productive foreigners. A law passed in 1883, and expanded in 1894, provided the legal basis which the government used to grant concessions to individuals and companies for the purpose of locating and surveying so-called empty lands. In effect these groups had the power to examine the land titles of any holder or village community. If the titles were questionable, or if the required pieces of paper could not be found, the land could be denounced, and the individual or company involved could retain one-third as a reward for "finding" lost national lands. In addition, the "finders" were allowed to purchase the remainder from the government at very low prices.

Political favorites obtained these concessions, and some became very large landowners. Many, however, transferred their concessions to foreign companies. Some colonization was effected as required by law, but most of the land was either held for speculation or became part of the expanding hacienda system. As a result a small number of individuals and companies obtained 72,335,907 hectares (one hectare equals 2.47 acres) of land during the Díaz

4. Quoted in Bernstein, *Mexican Mining Industry*, 77.

5. Cleona Lewis, *America's Stake in International Investments* (New York, 1938), 220–22; J. Vasquez Schiaffino, "Mexico," *Petroleum Magazine* (August 1919), 103–4.

era. This same element also gobbled lands under the pretext of enforcing the reform laws of the 1850s, which originally were designed to curb the corporate holdings of the Roman Catholic Church, and under the law of 1888 which allowed the president to grant monopoly concessions to water rights.

The enactment and utilization of these laws reflected the laissez-faire viewpoint of the ruling elite in Mexico and the foreign businessmen from the industrial-creditor nations. These groups operated on the simplistic belief that government cooperation with private enterprise would automatically lead to progress and modernization. The Mexican elite liked to call themselves *científicos* (scientific ones), since they utilized elements of Positivism to explain or rationalize their policies. They spoke in some detail about the future benefits which would "trickle down" to the rest of the population, but in the short run their actions were almost entirely designed to maximize private profits. The Díaz government did exert some national control over banks and railroads after 1900, but for most of this period regulation was minimal.

The dominant economic philosophy and the reinforcing legal framework of the industrial-creditor nations also were incorporated into the new mining legislation of Mexico. The mining code of 1884 eliminated all prior legislation and expressly removed the government's claim to ownership of bituminous and other mineral fuels and nonmetallic minerals. The ownership of these subsurface deposits was now given to those who owned the land. In spite of the new departures incorporated into the 1884 code, the old cultural-legal traditions of Mexico were not entirely eliminated. Fee simple titles were not granted and retention of titles was still subject to "regular workings" of the mine.[6]

The *científicos* were not completely satisfied with the 1884 code, and in 1892 a commission drafted a much more laissez-faire law. Its object was declared to be: "Facility to acquire, liberty to exploit, and security to retain." As Marvin Bernstein concisely notes, the mining code of 1892 reduced the state to a passive level, and "the mineowner and speculator in Mexico attained a position of almost complete liberty of action."[7] The legal framework of the Mexican economy had been substantially adjusted to the international legal order of the developed nations. This industrial-

6. Bernstein, *Mexican Mining Industry*, 18–19.
7. Ibid., 27–28.

creditor nations' concept of order and stability went beyond the absence of violence to include the kind of protection which the laws and policies of underdeveloped nations provided for foreign enterprise. By this standard, foreign businessmen and government officials considered Porfirian Mexico to be one of the most well-behaved "backward" nations in the world. Indeed, in the light of the rising Populist movement some even believed that property rights were safer in Mexico than in the United States.

Elements of cultural conflict—as symbolized by the different legal traditions of the Anglo-American and Hispanic cultures—remained. The concept of a fee simple title to property did not appear in the mining code of 1892, and later legislation revealed that even the *científicos* had not been completely converted to the legal norms of the Anglo-American economic order. By 1900, some of them had even begun to realize that many of the legal and diplomatic doctrines of the industrial-creditor powers, such as "equality of opportunity" for investors and merchants and rights of aliens, had peculiar meanings when applied to the under-developed areas, meanings which primarily benefited the larger powers in their penetration of economically weak countries.

Control by foreign capital of large segments of the Mexican economy constituted an important facet of the distorted development of the Díaz period. While much of this control was a product of new enterprises, at least some of it was a result of foreign businesses absorbing smaller Mexican enterprises. Not only were the native enterprises overwhelmed by the size of foreign competitors but some also suffered from the favoritism which the Díaz government lavished upon foreign interests. One such example was the concession to an English cotton company of the Nazas River water rights. This action ruined the small Mexican farmers in the region. This is not to argue that Díaz and the *científicos* deliberately conspired to ruin their fellow countrymen, with the exception of the Indians. In fact, after 1900 the government tried to promote more Mexican economic activity, but, in their early haste to promote a "favorable climate" for foreign investments, Mexican officials did practice discrimination and rationalized it with the argument that some short-term sacrifice of indigenous interests would be more than compensated by rapid development. The *científicos* liked to talk about the necessity of "breaking eggs to make omelettes." There is a logic to this insofar as it is an expression of the necessity to force change under some circumstances. The *científicos'* problem, however, was their naive faith that broken eggs automatically become omelettes with little conscious direction.

There are various estimates concerning the exact extent of foreign control of the Mexican economy. All agree that foreign capital held a position of predominance in almost all areas of commerce and industry: approximately 97 percent of mining properties, 98 percent of the rubber and guayule industries, and 90, or more, percent of the petroleum industry. U.S. companies controlled approximately 70 percent of the total foreign investment. The henequen industry of Yucatan was one of the few to remain under Mexican control. Foreign ownership was not as heavy in the rural area, but Frank Tannenbaum notes that, as late as 1923, foreigners owned 20.1 percent of the privately owned lands in Mexico, a development concentrated largely in the northern and coastal states and affecting 42.7 percent of the land in Chihuahua and 41.9 percent in Nayarit. North Americans controlled 51.7 percent of all the foreign landholdings in Mexico in that year.[8]

The predominant role of foreign capital had a mixed effect upon the pre-1910 Mexican economy. Certainly it can be argued that development took place, jobs were created, and export earnings increased—and that all these factors were based on foreign investment. Yet the Mexicans did lose control of much of their economy, and as a result they lost much of their capacity to allocate reinvestment. This could be regained, but it would require extensive regulation of foreign business by the national government, since most of the power over allocation of profits was in foreign hands and Mexican business simply was not able to purchase a decisive share in the economy. Such action would produce

8. Frank Tannenbaum, *Mexico: The Struggle for Peace and Bread* (New York, 1960), 140–41. See also Frank R. Brandenburg, *The Making of Modern Mexico* (Englewood Cliffs, N.J., 1964), 214–15; G. Butler Sherwell, *Mexico's Capacity to Pay: A General Analysis of the Present International Economic Position of Mexico* (Washington, D.C., 1929), 7–24; Bernstein, *Mexican Mining Industry*, 72–77; War Department (Office of the Chief of Staff), "American and Foreign Capital Invested in Mexico," 14 March 1914, National Archives, Records of the Department of State (United States), file number 812.503/19; hereafter cited as SD followed by the file number.

conflict between the government and the foreign investors. The traditional private enterprise system did not recognize the legitimacy of the kind of extensive state action which would be required fundamentally to alter the status quo in economic relations between nations.

Unregulated foreign investment took back an ample share of the profits of development. Economists may argue whether this was a fair or distorted share. Mexico returned to the investing nations approximately 65 percent of her total export earnings (1910) in the form of profit remittances, service on the foreign debt, freight costs, insurance fees, and other charges. This did not include payment for imports.[9]

The Mexican economy was in a deep rut, and while foreign capital was not the only factor responsible, its predominance helped to deepen and limit the prevailing tendencies. In spite of oversimplified generalizations about underdeveloped countries, the early economic growth of Mexico and the United States cannot be compared. Domestic North American capital always retained sufficient control of the U.S. economy, often with government assistance, to be able to influence much of the allocation of profits, and the profit remittances of foreign investments did not divert very much capital from the domestic economy. Foreign investors made money in North America, but they did not dominate the productive enterprises.[10]

The impact of foreign investment in Mexico was conditioned in part by the physical, cultural, and socioeconomic aspects of the country. An archaic social structure, great concentration of wealth, a social value system which gave great prestige to the *hacendado*, and a limited resource base (especially arable land), all constituted important elements of the internal situation. Within this matrix foreign capital tended to reinforce, rather than solve, some of the basic socioeconomic problems of Mexico. As Frank

9. Sherwell, *Mexico's Capacity to Pay*, 7–24.
10. For the United States, the percentage of money earned through exports (including specie) that was returned to Europe as profit on investments, freight, and other costs, not including cost of goods imported, reached a peak of 25 percent in 1865. The percentage had been 12.5 in 1854 and 10.5 in 1860. It was 24 percent in 1872, 21 percent in 1874, and 13 percent in 1880. U.S. Department of Commerce, Bureau of the Census, *Historical Statistics of the United States: Colonial Times to 1957* (Washington, D.C., 1960), 562–64.

Brandenburg has written: "The belief that foreign capital per se would become the panacea of Mexico's economic ills was disproven, for as long as the vicious circle of poverty shackled the economy, foreign capital tended to perpetuate the status quo."[11] By 1900 some of the *científicos* began to see certain implications of foreign capital predominance and advocated a policy of limited regulation.

Porfirian Nationalism, 1898–1910

The intensification of nationalism, the growing concern over unregulated foreign enterprises, and the mounting agitation for reform in all areas of Mexican life characterized the decade from 1900 to 1910. All of these foreshadowed the developments of the revolutionary era. As the Porfirian epoch produced its most luxuriant by-products, the main feeder roots of revolution were reaching maturity.

Distrust of foreign capital and agitation for its regulation had never completely disappeared. The editor of *El Pacifico* lamented in 1881: "The invasion is pacific, and promises happy results for the American sowing his gold broadcast over the entire republic. Railroad enterprises, the purchase of mines and rural property are the means which are employed to cause the autonomy of Mexico to disappear."[12] This distrust of foreign enterprise increased, and its essence was expressed in the popular slogan that Mexico had become "the mother of foreigners and the stepmother of Mexicans."

The impact of foreign capital stimulated concern in the ranks of the governing elite. The *científicos* and their business and landowning compatriots did not necessarily desire foreign economic domination, and some of them began to consider regulatory measures. Under the leadership of the minister of finance, José Ives

11. *Making of Modern Mexico*, 214.
12. James M. Callahan, *American Foreign Policy in Mexican Relations* (New York, 1932), 500. See also Harvey O'Connor, *The Guggenheims: The Making of an American Dynasty* (New York, 1937), 328–29; William Franklin Sands and Joseph M. Lalley, *Our Jungle Diplomacy* (Chapel Hill, N. C., 1944), 143–44. Sands, a foreign service officer who served in Mexico during the latter part of the Díaz period, observed that many intellectuals, including some of the *científicos*, were talking about *el peligro yanqui* (the Yankee peril).

Limantour, the government, between 1903 and 1906, purchased controlling interests in the Interoceanic, Mexican National, and the Mexican Central Railways. By decrees in 1906 and 1907 the government combined these into the National Railways of Mexico. In 1908, the final agreement was signed with the seven foreign banking houses representing the other stockholders, and government ownership of the line was proclaimed. But it was ownership with a limitation. The agreement provided for two independent boards of directors—one in New York and one in Mexico City—with the former having the power to foreclose if the company did not meet the payments on its stock issues.[13]

Proponents of more stringent governmental regulation launched a campaign to change the mining laws. They particularly wanted to place all bitumens and petroleum under special national jurisdiction in order to control foreign corporations. Their arguments clearly indicated that the older legal definitions of ownership of the subsoil had not died. Instead they were gaining a renewed vitality as the proponents of strong regulation turned to them as instruments for the assertion of national control over Mexico's resources. This group demonstrated surprising strength in the vote on the mine law of 1910.[14] They lost this battle, but the stage was set for the regulatory measures of the revolutionary period. Foreign control of the Mexican economy had stimulated a new economic nationalism and a rising tide of anti-U.S. sentiment which even Díaz and the most laissez-faire *científicos* could not ignore.

There were further manifestations of these feelings in the post-1900 foreign policy of the Díaz government. The president and most of his advisers did not advocate an overt anti-U.S. position, or even a major break with past policies; they did indicate some desire to modify the role of U.S. influence in Mexico and to assert a greater degree of independent action in foreign policy matters. The growing predominance of North American capital in the Mexican economy and the expansion of U.S. economic and political power in the Caribbean and Central America stimulated these ideas.

13. John H. McNeely, *The Railways of Mexico: A Study in Nationalization*, Southwestern Studies, vol. 2, no. 1 (El Paso, Tex., 1964), 16–19. The Mexican Southern Railroad was added in 1909.
14. Bernstein, *Mexican Mining Industry*, 80–82.

In 1906 Díaz informed the German minister that Mexico was thinking about military reoganization and compulsory military training. The president also hinted strongly that German officers and equipment would be welcome. During 1906–7, the German government toyed with this subtle invitation, and several Mexican officials let it be known that the military reforms were aimed at U.S. influence. General Bernardo Reyes was considered the leading advocate of German-Mexican cooperation based upon opposition to the expanding power of the United States and its Monroe Doctrine. Most of the German officials—including the kaiser— had reservations about such a course of action, and after some initial enthusiasm the German government decided that it was unwise to provoke the United States over Mexico. Some Mexican officials also had mixed views of this kind of cooperation. Although nothing came of these overtures, the possibility of a German counterweight to the power of the United States did not completely disappear from the foreign policy calculations of some Mexicans.[15]

After 1903 the Mexican government began to play a more active role in Central American affairs. In part, this was due to the growing activity of the U.S. government in the area. Mexican officials hoped to protect what they considered to be Mexican interests and at the same time exercise some restraining influence on U.S. policy. Mexico and the United States generally cooperated in offering mediation and "good offices" in the settlement of disputes between the various countries. This cooperation vanished in 1909 when the U.S. government went beyond such limited tactics in a country which was friendly to Mexico. The increasingly hostile policy of the United States toward the government of José Santos Zelaya in Nicaragua disturbed the Mexicans, since Zelaya had sided with Mexico in her long-standing rivalry with Guatemala. The Mexicans tried to dissuade the United States from military intervention and offered to obtain the resignation of Zelaya. In this way, Mexican officials hoped that Zelaya's party would remain in power to continue its policy of friendship toward Mexico. U.S. officials did not want cooperation which was not subordinate to their objectives, and some even expressed fear of an independent Mexican influence in Central America. Mexican

15. Warren Schiff, "German Military Penetration into Mexico during the Late Díaz Period," *Hispanic American Historical Review* (hereafter *HAHR*), 39 (November 1959): 568–79.

diplomacy failed as the United States pursued its own goals in Nicaragua, but as a final gesture of independence Mexico sent a warship to bring the deposed Zelaya to Mexico, where he was received by Díaz and other officials.[16]

Mexican officials also began to grant more favors to European businesses. One of the best examples of this was the concession-filled contract negotiated with the British oil company El Aguila in 1906.[17] This company received a number of privileges, including a three-kilometer buffer zone around all of its wells. Most tax obligations were eliminated for the life of the contract, and a fifty-year exemption from the export tax added frosting to the concession cake.

In 1910 Limantour made a special trip to Europe in order to obtain new loans and probably tried to bypass the New York banking firms which had handled most of the government's bond issues since 1899. The railway consolidation effort was partly designed to block plans of a U.S. group, sponsored by E. H. Harriman and H. Clay Pierce, to control and consolidate Mexican railroads. The finance minister also took steps prior to 1911 to acquire the largest meat packing concern in Mexico, a North American company which had a virtual monopoly over the industry. Thus, during this prerevolutionary decade, Mexico took the first halting steps to reduce the North American predominance over the economy of the country by means of government control and encouragement of European investment.

Latent anti-Yankee sentiment existed in several strata of Mexican society, and after 1900 it became particularly noticeable among the mining and railroad workers. Lower levels of the Mexican governmental system seemed to be particularly sensitive to the problem of foreign-owned railroads, and prior to 1906 the State Department protested a rising wave of incidents involving the arrest and imprisonment of North American railroad workers.

16. Daniel Cosío Villegas, *La vida política exterior, parte primera*, vol. 5 of *Historia moderna de México: El Porfiriato* (México, D.F., 1960), 620–92. Correspondence in the State Department files for December 1910 and the early part of 1911 reported a possible alliance between Guatemala and Mexico (and perhaps involving El Salvador) which would tend to offset U.S. influence not only in Guatemala but also in Honduras and El Salvador. SD 712.14/70.

17. Copy of this concession enclosed in Harold Walker (Huasteca Petroleum Co.) to Ira Patchin (J. P. Morgan & Co.), 4 April 1923, Thomas W. Lamont Manuscripts, Baker Library, Harvard Graduate School of Business Administration.

Anti-Yankee feeling intensified after the *rurales* aided the North Americans in smashing the Cananea strike in 1906. Consular agents reported spreading antiforeign sentiment, and the State Department received many vivid rumors of antiforeign activity among miners and railroad workers. An incident in November 1910 provided a gauge to the kind of anti-Yankee sentiment which had been developing in the more urban and commercial areas. As word spread that a Mexican, Antonio Rodríguez, had been lynched at Rock Springs, Texas, violence flared spontaneously in Mexico City, Guadalajara, and other population centers. The mob in the former city trampled a U.S. flag and stoned the building of the *Mexican Herald*—the recognized voice of the North American investor and resident.

This type of antiforeign, and especially anti-U.S., feeling was more than a historical hangover from the conquest of the 1840s, or the border troubles of the 1870s. It was directed at property holders as well as other groups which were believed to be cooperating with the Mexican elite.

Revolutionary Ideas

Between 1900 and 1910, the Díaz regime faced a growing opposition from diverse groups with varying interests and ambitions. For most of the period there was not much unity between the opposition groups in terms of either organization or agreement on desired reforms. Several organizations were formed for the purpose of building a coherent political opposition with national platforms which could unify these diverse groups. One of the more significant reform themes was that of asserting national control over natural resources.

A reform group especially important because of its later ideological influence developed under the leadership of Ricardo Flores Magón and his brothers. Ricardo began fighting against Díaz as a student in 1892, and in 1900 he and several others founded the newspaper *Regeneración*. The paper had a sporadic existence, but it was an articulate source for nationalist and reform ideas. As the Flores Magón brothers moved from a legalistic, anti-Díaz to a revolutionary, anticapitalistic position, the newspaper reflected this increasingly militant and anti-Yankee view.

In September 1905, Ricardo Flores Magón formed the organizing committee of the Mexican Liberal party in Saint Louis, and in July 1906 the committee issued a sweeping reform manifesto which foreshadowed many of the points later included in the constitution of 1917. Among other things, the manifesto demanded that Mexicans be given preference over foreigners in economic matters to establish equality of opportunity and that foreigners who acquired economic rights or concessions be treated as Mexican citizens. The eight-hour day for labor, the restriction of the church, and some type of land redistribution (especially of lands "illegally" acquired under Díaz) were also outlined in various parts of the program.[18]

Andrés Molina Enríquez was also one of the most influential and persuasive articulators of reform ideas. His book *Great National Problems*—published in 1909—contained a detailed analysis of the problems of Mexico and a prophetic discussion of the progression of revolution.[19] Molina Enríquez developed in great detail the concept that reform in Mexico had to be based upon the elaboration of an intensive Mexican nationalism and its enforcement upon all aspects of Mexican life. The economy and politics of Mexico were controlled by foreigners, especially North Americans, and their *criollo* allies in the Mexican upper class; Molina Enríquez believed that this power structure had to be broken in order for any real changes to take place in the living conditions of most of the people. His book constituted a significant step in the articulation of revolutionary nationalism in the underdeveloped world, for Molina Enríquez clearly saw that the economic and cultural presence of the developed nations was an integral part of the status quo and that foreign interests were part of the indigenous power structure. But within this system reform and more equitable distribution of wealth would be difficult, if not impossible, to achieve. Any real attempt to change the old order would produce conflict with foreign interests, since their power would be curtailed through the imposition of national controls. Molina Enríquez believed that revolutionary changes in Mexico would have international repercussions.

He also believed that in order for Mexico to achieve its true national independence it would have to expound a particularly

18. Manuel González Ramírez, *Planes políticos y otros documentos,* vol. 1 of *Fuentes para la historia de la Revolución Mexicana* (México, D.F., 1954), 3–29. Antonio Díaz Soto y Gama collaborated in the writing and later became the leading adviser to Emiliano Zapata.

19. Andrés Molina Enríquez, *Los grandes problemas nacionales* (México, D.F., 1909), 312–13, 338–40, 345–46, 357–60.

self-conscious nationalism in all areas of its culture, from articles of everyday consumption to the arts. Only in this manner could Mexico resist the powerful influences from abroad and develop the cohesiveness needed for reform and development.

These views would be interesting but beside the point if they were simply the musings of one man. But Molina Enríquez articulated the ideas and feelings of those reform-minded intellectuals and professionals who would help to make the revolution and shape the policies of the government. Some seven years after writing *Great National Problems*, the author participated in the writing of another document—article 27 of the 1917 constitution.

Revolution, 1910–15

Francisco I. Madero's campaign against the reelection of Porfirio Díaz provided the catalytic agent which drew together most of the opposition in a kind of nebulous unity. A sincere idealist, closely akin to many North American Progressives in his belief that "good government" solved most problems, Madero cut across ideological and group lines with his simple focus on the election issue. Díaz gave his unwitting cooperation by making Madero and the election issue an object of concentrated attack. The beauty of such a simple issue was that men could read into it a variety of reforms—or nothing except the issue of transfer of power within the elite.[20] The slogan "Effective Suffrage, No Re-election" became a temporary rallying cry for a wide variety of reformers, men on the make, and former supporters of Díaz who hoped they could use the movement to maintain their power after the president's demise. The ideas and rhetoric of reform were gaining momentum, and by 1911 all political factions had adopted parts of the paraphernalia of reform; for some, however, the hour was too late and the adoptions too limited.

When Díaz attempted to crush the opposition, revolt flared in various parts of the country. The regime was riddled with corruption and inefficiency, and the Federal Army suffered a series of defeats at the hands of rebel groups led by Pascual Orozco, Abraham González, Francisco "Pancho" Villa, and Emiliano Zapata. The first stage of the Mexican Revolution ended on 25 May 1911,

20. Francisco I. Madero, *La sucesión presidencial en 1910*, 3d ed. (México, D.F., 1911); see especially the conclusion.

when Porfirio Díaz accepted Madero's terms and resigned. His closest colleagues had urged him to do this, with the hope that his elimination would end the revolution without changing the power structure. Very little real violence had occurred, and many in the elite, including some of Madero's supporters, now hoped for a return to business as usual.

An interim president, Francisco León de la Barra (formerly minister of foreign affairs under Díaz) governed Mexico from 26 May to 6 November 1911. Don Porfirio might be gone, but the system remained. The hope for reforms had been unleashed, however, and those Mexicans who thought that the elimination of Díaz would end all agitation were sadly mistaken.

The conservative provisional government was not interested in reform of any kind, but it did make a strenuous effort to crush the Zapatistas. Madero recommended some conciliatory measures and at one point in August he thought that he had successfully mediated a truce. The Mexican conservatives, however, believed that by pushing Zapata into renewed conflict they could split the loose, and already shaky, Madero coalition. Madero was ignored with impunity by the provisional government as Generals Victoriano Huerta and Federico Morales used forces which had been Maderista to fight Zapata. Although Madero acquiesced not only in this conservative manipulation but also in the more than five months of national drift, the coalition was not completely disrupted. Zapata still had some hope that Madero would push land reform when he finally assumed the presidency.[21]

By the time Madero took office in November 1911, the hopes and frustrations of some of the reform elements, especially the agrarian, were producing demands for immediate and effective action. At this stage, Madero still had a rather limited understanding of the various problems which produced these hopes and frustrations. He considered the agrarian problem to be primarily a case of promoting the ranchos, and this—in spite of the warnings of Luis Cabrera and others—did not seem to him to be an urgent problem.[22] When Zapata wanted to know when the land would be returned to the villages, Madero talked about the com-

21. John H. McNeely, "Origins of the Zapata Revolt in Morelos," *HAHR* 46 (May 1966): 160–63.
22. Jesús Silva Herzog, *El agrarismo mexicano y la reforma agraria* (México, D.F., 1959), 164–65.

plicated nature of the problem and offered him a gift of several haciendas. Convinced now that Madero was just another politician, Zapata returned to the hills of Morelos with an ominous warning: "Be it known to Señor Madero, and through him to the rest of the world, that we will not lay down our arms until we have recovered our lands." To the despoiled men of Morelos, justice was not a complicated problem. Expectations of change soared in other sectors. Strikes broke out in various mines, as the miners demanded 25 percent wage increases and the abolition of company secret police. They were not treated as they had been under Díaz, but federal police were still allowed to break strikes. Other groups pushed the demand for control of foreign enterprise, and in the Congress one deputy sounded the theme "Mexican oil lands for Mexicans."

The Madero government was soon faced with conflict. Negotiations with Zapata broke down, probably because the military leaders wanted to crush the movement. Madero had some difficulty in controlling the army, and when General Casso López attacked Zapata while negotiations were still in progress, the president quietly accepted the renewed conflict. Zapata now considered Madero the leader of the *hacendados*, and on 28 November 1911 the Zapatistas proclaimed the Plan of Ayala, in which the sense of betrayal was clearly stated: "The nation is tired of deceitful and traitorous men who make promises as liberators but who, upon reaching power, forget their promises and become tyrants."[23] The Plan presented one of the most advanced programs of agrarian reform yet written, and one that would have eliminated much of the hacienda system quite rapidly. In this regard it was also a radical plan for changing the economic system, since it would have confiscated all the land of those *hacendados* who resisted the expropriation program. With the Plan of Ayala, a rapid solution for the agrarian question was clearly delineated for the first time, and the various shades of reform began to separate as a prism separates the color spectrum.

The agrarian question and the Zapata conflict plagued Madero for the duration of his administration. He did try to effect some reforms, but his belief in patience, gradual evolution, and strict adherence to parliamentary rules limited both the speed and the

23. McNeely, "Origins of the Zapata Revolt," 166. See González Ramírez, *Planes políticos*, 73–77, for the text of the Plan.

effectiveness of his reform program. Reform plans were under consideration by the legislative and executive branches when the Madero government was overthrown by General Huerta in February 1913.

Because of the nature of his death at the hands of the old officer corps, Madero became a kind of unifying martyr for the forces which quickly gathered in opposition to Huerta.[24] On 26 March 1913, Venustiano Carranza, the governor of Coahuila, proclaimed the Plan of Guadalupe and marched against Huerta. Zapata continued his fight in the south, and by fall Pancho Villa's Division of the North was ready for action. Although Huerta wanted to restore the Porfirian system, he had little time for anything except trying to suppress the opposition. Yet he managed to hold power for a year and five months.

With conflict in various parts of the country, the economy of Mexico and the finances of the government deteriorated. The U.S. government contributed to this situation by blocking most of Huerta's attempts to obtain loans from Europe and by seizing the important entrepôt of Veracruz. The opposition forces were winning battles and steadily expanding the area under their control. In June 1914, Villa's forces marched south from Torreón toward Mexico City as the Zapatistas moved north and the Carranza forces pushed west from Tampico. On 14 July, Huerta resigned and fled into exile.

Even before Huerta's defeat the revolutionary coalition began to split. This was particularly evident when Villa defied Carranza's instructions to remain in Torreón. Representatives of the Villa and Carranza forces drafted an understanding (Pact of Torreón) in July 1914, but Carranza rejected it. By September the rupture was complete, and Zapata joined a loose coalition with Villa after the Revolutionary Convention of Aguascalientes in October. By November these two coalitions were openly at war. Fortunately for Carranza, two important generals, Pablo Gonzales and Alvaro Obregón, had decided to follow his leadership. Obregón had been working for a compromise between the various groups, and possibly he and other generals would have dropped Carranza if they

24. In like manner, Huerta became the chief demon and was accused of personal responsibility for the murder of the Madero brothers. A recent study questions this: William L. Sherman and Richard E. Greenleaf, *Victoriano Huerta: A Reappraisal* (México, D.F., 1960).

had been able to formulate some kind of unity at the Aguascalientes Convention (October-November 1914). When the convention did not become a "third" force and Carranza clearly emerged as the symbolic center of opposition to the views and ambitions of the Villa and Zapata forces, Obregón and a majority of the generals at the convention decided to renew their support of his leadership.[25]

Why did this rupture take place? Personality conflicts and the desire for power were involved, but this says everything, and nothing. The various leaders had their own concepts of Mexico's future, and each believed that his policies would provide the best solution. Power was the only way to put these into operation and block the supposed "unwise" or "venal" plans of others. The revolutionary forces had always been a heterogeneous collection of groups and motives. Opportunism and ambition certainly explains the allegiance, and shifts in allegiance, of some leaders. But the motives of the key figures—central leaders such as Villa, Carranza, Zapata, and Obregón—cannot be explained solely in these terms.

The leaders split into two fairly distinct factions in part because that had come to personify different orientations and interests. The Villa-Zapata group had a pronounced agrarian flavor, and its leaders had close ties with the illiterate, poverty-stricken peon. Although Villa did not formulate any detailed programs of reform, such as emanated from Zapata and his advisers, he nonetheless stood for more than violence. The correspondent John Reed wrote about the "passionate dream—the vision which animates this ignorant fighter."[26] This was the vision of agrarian reform which Villa tried to communicate to Reed and which was the main topic of the "law" promulgated by Villa at Aguascalientes in the fall of 1914. This rural, lower-class orientation also helps to account for Villa's and Zapata's general suspicion of men with urban, educated backgrounds. Villa believed that Carranza was surrounded by "chocolate drinkers and sweet-scented friends" and that this *hacendado* had little sympathy for the poor.[27] John

25. Robert E. Quirk, *The Mexican Revolution, 1914–1915: The Convention of Aguascalientes* (Bloomington, Ind., 1960), 68–126.
26. John Reed, *Insurgent Mexico* (New York and London, 1914), 145.
27. Martín Luis Guzmán, *Memoirs of Pancho Villa*, trans. Virginia H. Taylor (Austin, Tex., 1965), 145, 477–78. The "law" was written by Don Miguel Díaz Lombardo. Daniel Moreno, *Pancho Villa y Emiliano Zapata: La causa de pobre* (México, D.F., 1960), 5–6, 21–26.

Womack, Jr., describes Carranza as seen through the eyes of the people of Morelos: "Rebel and revolutionary he might now be, but in another world—an established and civilized world of clean linen, breakfast trays, high politics, and ice buckets for wine."[28]

In comparison with Carranza's group, the Villa-Zapata element tended to be more regional in outlook, and less concerned with building the nation-state. They had little interest in building institutions or worrying about the administrative details of government and viewed politicians and the political structure with suspicion. To the leaders with their immediatist focus the bureaucratic mechanics of administrative reform and the complicated arguments about legislative and judicial processes seemed to be excuses for delay or even denial of reform. The Zapatistas gave vivid expression to these views in the August 1914 Declaration of Milpa Alta, which concluded that regardless of elections, suffrage, free press, or the "democracy of Madero," the people had not benefited: "Their portion is bitterness. They continue to suffer poverty and humiliations without end."[29]

The Carranza coalition was much more politically oriented, and placed great stress on the development of the power and the administrative mechanisms of the nation-state. The title "Constitutionalist" was a symbol of this focus. Beginning in 1913 Carranza emphasized his assumed role of national leader and opposed the strong, regional leaders. An intense nationalist, he desired in his own way to build a Mexico which could deal with the powers of the world on an equal basis. This was important to the influential men who gravitated to the coalition because of their ambitions for the commercial and industrial development of Mexico. They believed that national programs and national control of the economy, especially the resources, were essential for the development they sought. These men therefore emphasized reforms which were concerned largely with regulation of foreign enterprise and the promotion of domestic business interests. As Charles W. Anderson notes, many of these economic advisers to Carranza were "products of the rudimentary capitalistic structure of Mexico City" who wanted economic modernization.[30] The

28. John Womack, Jr., *Zapata and the Mexican Revolution* (New York, 1969), 210.
29. Quirk, *Mexican Revolution*, 65.
30. "Bankers as Revolutionaries," in William P. Glade and Charles W. Anderson, *The Political Economy of Mexico: Politics and Development*

assertion of a degree of national control over the economy produced conflict with some foreign enterprises. When combined with the insistence that foreign governments treat Mexico as an equal and refrain from gratuitous advice and intervention, this emphasis on economic independence produced charges that Mexican nationalism was based primarily upon hatred of foreigners. Hatred and resentment were involved. But, for the most part, the operative, as distinct from the rhetorical, nationalism of the Carranza coalition assumed an antiforeign coloration only in reaction either to the active opposition of foreign governments and foreign enterprise to Mexican governmental policy or to their interference in the internal affairs of the country.[31]

No neat division produced by a historian is absolute; there were overlapping interests and views between the factions. In spite of the more cautious, gradualist orientation of the Carranza group, there were dedicated reformers with agrarian sympathies within the fold who believed that the Constitutionalists offered the best hope for unity and reform. On the other hand, a few old-line Porfirians appeared in the ranks of the other group.

The more astute politicians of the Carranza coalition, such as Obregón, recognized the need to broaden their base of support by expanding their reform program. They worked to develop some unity among the various reform-minded groups of the coalition in order to pressure Carranza to accept reform ideas beyond those of Madero. In 1914–15 the political fate of the Constitutionalists and all of their interests seemed, with some justification, to depend upon a wider appeal. Reform plans and decrees being issued by states and individual generals usually dealt with debts of peons, petroleum lands, land reform, and minimum wages. In October 1913, Pastor Rouaix, the provisional governor of Durango, had published the first agrarian law which could be

---

Banking in Mexico (Madison, Wis., 1963), 114, 112–15. My discussion of these groups is in part derived from the ideas of Octavio Paz, *The Labyrinth of Solitude: Life and Thought in Mexico*, trans. Lysander Kemp (New York, 1961), 142–46.

31. See Carranza's conversation with John Reed, *Insurgent Mexico*, 276–77. The nationalism of the Carranzistas is described in detail in Antonio Manero, *Mexico y la solidaridad Americana: La Doctrina Carranza* (Madrid, 1918). See also Antonio Manero, *Qué es la Revolución? Breve exposicion sobre las principales causas de la Revolución Constitutionalista en México* (Veracruz, México, 1915), especially Carranza's manifesto of 11 June 1915, xxvii–xxxvii.

considered revolutionary, since it provided for expropriation.[32] To the national-oriented Carranza supporters, such actions seemed to be leading to a confused assortment of reform actions which could threaten the establishment of national authority and loyalty. Perhaps there was also some fear that state and local action would produce a more radical array of reforms.

Carranza's lack of interest in, and opposition to, most reform programs had cost him support. He had rejected the Plan of Torreón with its demands for hacienda lands to be given to the peons, and Zapata seemed to have completely monopolized the support of agrarian reform when the Plan of Ayala was adopted by the Aguascalientes Convention. In order to counteract their growing antireformist image, General Obregón and Dr. Atl formed a group of ten civilians and ten soldiers in November 1914 to develop the principles of a "social movement." Rafael Zubarán Capmany, A. J. Pani, Roque Estrada, and Jesús Urueta were some of the prominent men appointed to this *Confederación*. The "conservatives" in the coalition were alarmed by the movement and tried to influence Carranza against it. The *Confederación*, however, did succeed in getting Carranza to promulgate the Veracruz decrees of 6 January 1915 and to take a public stand for some kind of reform program. At a banquet on 9 January, Carranza shocked the "conservatives" with his opening statement: "Hoy empieza la revolución social" (Today the social revolution begins).[33]

Historians generally agree that Carranza had little if any interest in agrarian and labor reform, and these gestures of 1915 are described as having no significance.[34] The Veracruz decrees were rather limited and vague in meaning, but they did represent the first efforts of the reform bloc to give some additional reform

32. Pastor Rouaix, *Génesis de las articulos 27 y 123 de la constitucion política de 1917* (Puebla, México, 1945), 54–56.

33. Dr. Atl [Gerardo Murillo], "Obregón y el principio de renovación social," in Ruben Romero, Juan de Dios Robledo, et al., *Obregón: Aspectos de su vida* (México, D.F., 1935), 67–73. Dr. Atl was a prominent writer and painter. The other civilians were professional men (lawyers, engineers, etc.). The Veracruz decrees instituted limited steps for the distribution of land to the villages. On 14 December 1914, Carranza had issued a general declaration on economic and political reforms.

34. See Quirk, *Mexican Revolution, 1914–1915*, 152. My analysis is derived in part from Frank Tannenbaum, *Peace by Revolution: Mexico after 1910*, 2d ed. (New York, 1966), 161–63.

emphasis to the Constitutionalist position beyond the Madero program. During 1915–16, a very limited amount of land was redistributed under these provisions of the decrees.

In February 1915, Obregón—in conjunction with Zubarán Capmany—made another major contribution to the broadening of the coalition when he negotiated a pact between the Constitutionalists and the Casa del Obrero Mundial. Carranza had little interest in labor and no concept of its potential power, but Obregón's action added both muscle and prestige to the coalition. The Casa organized six "Red Battalions" to fight under Constitutionalist leadership and agreed to try to influence foreign labor groups, especially the American Federation of Labor. If this succeeded, Obregón and his colleagues hoped that the AFL would be able to persuade the Wilson administration to recognize the Constitutionalist group as the legitimate government of Mexico.[35]

These steps to broaden the base of support undoubtedly helped the Constitutionalists in their struggle for power. Control of the revenue-producing seaports, the tactical and supply problems of Villa and Zapata, and the ability of General Obregón also strengthened them. They began to win vital battles in 1915, and after Obregón's victory over Villa at Celaya in April the forces of the north began to disintegrate. On 2 August 1915, the Constitutionalists took Mexico City for the last time.

The U.S. government extended de facto recognition to the Carranza government in October 1915. Villa and Zapata harassed the new government for several years, but their main effort had been broken. Many of their followers gave up the struggle and some joined the victorious coalition.[36] Now the Carranza government could begin to develop national policies and programs which went beyond mere survival. The revolution had entered a new stage and the first fruits would soon produce complications with foreign governments.

35. Harvey A. Levenstein, "The United States Labor Movement and Mexico, 1910–1951," Ph.D. diss., University of Wisconsin, 1966, 21–30. Dr. Atl, "Obregón y el principio de renovación social," 81–82.

36. From 1915 to 1920 Zapatista control of Morelos varied according to the amount of effective military pressure from the Carranzista forces. It was a mixed picture of retreat and advance. After the victory of Obregón in 1920, the Zapatistas became part of the new power structure; Womack, *Zapata*, chaps. 8–11.

2 The Problem of the "Backward" Nation

> *An ever-present menace to the peace of the world, and a present trouble, is the insecurity of life and property in backward countries, leading to intervention by foreign powers and to actual war. . . . The present insecurity of life and property in Mexico in connection with the hundreds of millions of dollars which foreigners have invested there may force the United States . . . eventually to intervene and put an end to present conditions.*
> —Theodore Marburg, 1912

The Idea of the "Backward" Nation

A combination of material interests and ideas about the conduct and status of so-called backward nations shaped the reaction of the United States to the upheaval, nationalistic aspirations, and reforms of the Mexican Revolution. Prior to 1910, North American officials, intellectuals, and businessmen had articulated, and begun to act upon, a multidimensional conception of the "backward," or underdeveloped, areas. This, in turn, became an integral part of their ideas on economic expansion and the strategic necessities imposed by the new frontiers of interests and ambitions. Woodrow Wilson stated these views in very clear terms when he wrote:

Since trade ignores national boundaries and the manufacturer insists on having the world as a market, the flag of his nation must follow him, and the doors of the nations which are closed against him must be battered down. Concessions obtained by financiers must be safeguarded by ministers of state, even if the sovereignty of unwilling nations be outraged in the process. Colo-

23

nies must be obtained or planted, in order that no useful corner of the world may be overlooked or left unused.[1]

The most important elements of this world view were: (1) the resources of the underdeveloped countries must be made available to developed nations to provide the raw materials for their industrial and military systems; (2) the markets of these same countries must be open to the exports of the developed nations; (3) investments must be protected, since these are vital elements in trade expansion and overall national prosperity; (4) order and stability (meaning no upheavals and friendly treatment of foreign interests) are necessary for the expansion of trade and investment, which in turn reinforces these conditions; and (5) the industrial-creditor nations have the right and the duty to police the underdeveloped areas in order to secure their version of order and stability.

These elements were often mixed with the emotional rhetoric of expansionist ideology, which spoke in terms of a "civilizing mission," the "white man's burden," and "protecting rights." Racism combined with these rather well, since most of the inhabitants of the underdeveloped world were non-white. Thus a belief in the racial inferiority of the peoples concerned seemed to give added justification to policies of economic penetration and political control. This combination of beliefs and myths provided the emotional dynamic for the material ambitions of the United States. As the Reverend Josiah Strong wrote in his layman's guide to the theology of empire: "The world is to be Christianized and civilized. . . . And what is the process of civilizing but *the creating of more and higher wants*? Commerce follows the missionary."[2]

The industrial-creditor nations' conception of order and stability included much more than the prevention or suppression of violence. Underdeveloped countries also were expected to follow policies which effectively opened their economies to foreign penetration. In effect, they were to treat U.S. businessmen according to the economic views and legal principles of the United States, except in cases where the prevailing custom—such as concessions

1. Quoted in William E. Diamond, *The Economic Thought of Woodrow Wilson* (Baltimore, 1943), 141.
2. *Our Country: Its Possible Future and Its Present Crisis*, rev. ed. (New York, 1891), 28.

—provided even more favorable treatment. This principle of extra-territoriality, whether in treaty form or not, imposed the protective legal arrangements for private property of the industrial-creditor world upon the underdeveloped countries. When enforced, this meant that foreign businesses had extraterritorial "rights" exempt-ing them from the operation of those laws and policies which might *effectively* restrict their activity. This was especially the case when regulation, taxation, or protective measures (for the citizens of the underdeveloped country) were involved. The Chinese shrewdly noted the basic realities of this development when they devised their term for "rights" by combining two words which mean "power" and "interest."[3]

The State Department reaction to a proposed court of arbitra-tion demonstrated the practical application of these concepts. The officials involved believed that questions of foreign investments would constitute the "chief work" of such a court, and the policy memorandum noted:

Every American investor who puts money into a foreign enterprise does so under the influence of certain legal principles which he regards as fundamental to all business undertakings, for example the inviolability of contracts, that property shall not be taken without due process of law (which to his mind includes a hear-ing), and that private property shall not be confiscated without compensation.

The memorandum concluded that the countries and "systems of laws" which provided the bulk of foreign investments should not join any court which distributed the judgeships on the basis of population or which "recognized the unqualified equality of states."[4]

The commonly accepted legal norms and economic practices of the industrial-creditor nations were called "International Law" and referred to as the "accepted practices of international con-duct." One of the leading international legal authorities of this

3. A. P. Thornton, *Doctrines of Imperialism* (New York and London, 1965), 157. Whitelaw Reid said much the same thing in 1899, *Problems of Expansion, as Considered in Papers and Addresses* (New York, 1900), 155–56.
4. "Memorandum: Concerning a Court of Arbitration," n.d., Philander C. Knox Papers, Library of Congress, Washington, D.C.

era, Edwin Borchard, gave the following commentary on the subject:

In addition, they [national states] must manifest their power to exercise jurisdiction effectively and . . . to assure foreigners within it of a minimum of rights. This minimum standard below which a state cannot fall without incurring responsibility to one or more of the other members of the international community *has been shaped and established by the advance of civilization and the necessities of modern international intercourse on the part of individuals.*[5]

Borchard noted that if the laws of a state were "out of harmony with the standard of civilized states," or if the administration of the laws "transgresses the prescriptions of civilized justice,"·then the "personal sovereignty of the home state reasserts itself." In such cases even foreign control of another state was justified. He also stated frankly that the use of this "protective right" was most often used by strong states against weak states, and by "European type" against non-European type states. Borchard was objective enough to realize that this "protective right" had "often" served to give resident aliens "a privileged position, not enjoyed by natives or the nationals of weak countries."[6]

Borchard wrote in the symbolic terms used by developed nations to justify their policies, and he—as well as other authorities in the field—basically accepted this industrial-creditor view of world order. But, after all, what did the term "civilized state" really mean? Who determined the interpretation of "patent injustice"? Was China or Mexico less civilized than Germany or the United States? Did restrictions on foreign business activity represent a greater "patent injustice" than the miserable wages paid to Mexican mine workers? Such questions are far from rhetorical; they reflect the issues raised by the underdeveloped nations.

In spite of its concern over the effects of turmoil and minor restrictions on economic penetration and order, the United States —and the other developed nations—did not have to contend with any fundamental challenges to the industrial-creditor conception

5. Edwin Borchard, *Diplomatic Protection of Citizens Abroad; or, The Law of International Claims* (New York, 1915), 27; italics added. See also C. Neale Ronning, *Law and Politics in Inter-American Diplomacy* (New York, 1963), 33–35.
6. Borchard, *Diplomatic Protection of Citizens Abroad,* 346–47.

of property rights until the reformist nationalism of the Mexican Revolution began to affect government policies. Prior to this, however, several Latin American nations had tried to gain some protection from the police power of the developed nations by asserting two international doctrines of their own. The Drago Doctrine stated that powerful nations did not have the right to collect by force the foreign debts owed to their citizens. Luis Drago, the Argentine foreign minister, hoped that this would become a "corollary" of the Monroe Doctrine, which would prevent such intervention by all countries. This was not what the United States meant in the "Roosevelt corollary." Secretary of State Elihu Root did not want to antagonize the major Latin American nations by completely rejecting the Drago Doctrine, and he persuaded the Second Hague Conference to adopt a modified version. This still sanctioned intervention as a last resort, and Drago voted against it.[7] The United States maintained its "right" to police and continued to exercise this as it saw fit.

The Calvo Doctrine was much more extensive, involving not only intervention but also the basic questions concerning the "rights" of resident foreigners. Carlos Calvo, an Argentine diplomat and commentator on international law, began with the premise of the equality of states and attacked the extraterritorial concepts of the powerful states. He wrote:

It is certain that aliens who establish themselves in a country have the same right to protection as nationals, but they ought not to lay claims to a protection more extended. . . .

The rule that in more than one case it has been attempted to impose on American states is that foreigners merit more regard and privileges more marked and extended than those accorded even to the nationals of the country where they reside.[8]

Calvo argued that foreign residents were subject to the same laws and to the same judicial processes as the citizens of the country. Foreign businesses had no right of appeal to another legal system (extraterritoriality principle) and were to be treated

7. Arthur P. Whitaker, *The Western Hemisphere Idea: Its Rise and Decline* (Ithaca, N.Y., 1954), 101–4. Drago made his proposal in 1902.

8. Quoted in Donald R. Shea, *The Calvo Clause: A Problem of Inter-American and International Law and Diplomacy* (Minneapolis, 1955), 18. Calvo's ideas were developed in his six-volume study of international law which went through five editions between 1868 and 1896.

as if they were owned by citizens of the country. All questions of economic policy involving foreign resident business would be domestic questions only, not subject to interference by foreign governments. In short, the international rules of the developed nations would no longer be the overriding mechanism through which they controlled the treatment of their citizens by under-developed countries.

The Calvo Doctrine was a nationalistic assertion of equal sovereignty and the right of a state to control its own internal situation. These principles had already been asserted by the developed nations in their relations with other countries. European creditors had discovered that they were not able to sue for, or collect by any means, the defaulted internal improvement debts, stemming from the 1830s, of various states of the United States. Not only did most of the states regulate foreign residents and their property but many also imposed additional restrictions which did not apply to citizens. Legislation by the state of California in 1913, 1920, and 1923, effectively barred Japanese residents from owning real property and imposed a variety of other restrictions on their economic activities. Minnesota barred aliens from acquiring more than 90,000 square feet of land, and Missouri required aliens to sell lands—which they could acquire under limited cir-cumstances—within six years. Every state in the United States placed restrictions on the jobs which aliens could hold. New York led the pack with twenty-seven restricted occupations. Aliens could not "pull" boats in Oregon, inspect boilers in New Jersey, run a pool hall in Arkansas (or three other states), embalm a corpse in Connecticut, sell poison in South Dakota, shoe horses in Illinois, or breed fish in California. All restrictions on aliens applied per-manently to Orientals, since they were not allowed to become U.S. citizens.[9]

Thus, as Calvo, Drago, and others indicated, the United States and the other developed nations were not defending a uniform system of international law which applied equally to all states. Instead, the industrial-creditor nations were defending a peculiar set of rules designed to implement their predominance in the underdeveloped areas. But the Latin American nations, and

9. Milton R. Konvitz, *The Alien and the Asiatic in American Law* (Ithaca, N.Y., 1946), 156–61, 171–209, 114–15. The first bar fell in 1943 when Chinese were permitted to become citizens.

Mexico especially, would struggle for years to implement the Calvo Doctrine in one way or another.

Until the Mexican Revolution, discussions concerning the Calvo Doctrine were largely academic. No country had attempted a major implementation of it, and the leaders of the Latin American nations still accepted the basic premises and policies of capitalism. What would happen if new leaders came to power asserting doctrines of revolutionary nationalism which threatened to make fundamental changes in the economic system or the relations, both economic and political, between their country and the developed capitalist nations? Such fears, though vague, did exist in the United States. In 1897 Captain Alfred Thayer Mahan wrote about the possible threat posed by the "backward" nations:

There will be seen, on the one hand, a vast preponderance of numbers, and those numbers, however incoherent now in mass, composed of units which in their individual capacity have in no small degree the great elements of strength whereby man prevails over man and the fittest survive. Deficient, apparently, in aptitude for political and social organization, they have failed to evolve the aggregate power and intellectual scope of which as communities they are otherwise capable. This lesson too they may learn. . . . But men do not covet less the prosperity which they themselves cannot or do not create,—a trait wherein lies the strength of communism as an aggressive social force. Communities which want and cannot have, except by force, will take by force, unless they are restrained by force; . . . [10]

Long before the cold war, Mahan was urging the United States to contain the forces of revolutionary nationalism in the underdeveloped world.

The contemporary ideas, beliefs, and prejudices of the developed nations shaped the reaction of the United States to the Mexican Revolution throughout the entire period from 1916 through 1932. Influential North Americans, in and out of government, generally agreed that internal order and stability must be maintained in underdeveloped nations in order to protect and advance their interpretations of the national interest. In addition, the underdeveloped countries must carry out their economic policies within

10. A. T. Mahan, *The Interest of America in Sea Power Present and Future* (Boston, 1898), 252–53.

the bounds of the system of industrial capitalism and the legal framework which had been erected to protect the property relationships of this system. The struggle to achieve these goals constitutes a basic unifying factor behind the Mexican policy of the administrations of Woodrow Wilson, Warren Harding, and Calvin Coolidge.

The basic dilemma, however, was how to achieve these goals, especially in a larger, and more belligerent, underdeveloped country such as Mexico. Thus the major controversies concerning the Mexican policy of the United States were over the tactics or methods to be used in restoring order and stability to Mexico and in keeping the reforms of the revolution within the bounds of the international legal order of the industrial-creditor nations.

Specific issues such as control of subsurface minerals, foreign debts, and agrarian reform complicated the task of developing tactical policies. Even within administrations, ideas about methods varied, and one of the key variables was the definition of the point at which a law or regulation passed from "legitimate" regulation to nationalization—that is, when a tax or the size and number of federal mineral reserves or the definition of subsurface claims became "confiscatory." Closely related to this definition was each policy maker's view of the Mexican Revolution. Those who believed that it was a devious conspiracy, either of radicals or corrupt politicians, tended to be dogmatic in their evaluation of Mexico's laws and to advocate a more uncompromising policy. On the other hand, those who viewed the revolution as a complex, tumultuous stage in Mexico's historical evolution tended to have less anxiety over every jot and tittle of Mexican law and to concentrate on establishing a working relationship with key officials of the Mexican government. These same variations existed among the representatives of the various private groups with economic interests in Mexico. The variegated array of informal working relationships between these men and government officials with similar views provided another element in the policy making process.

But the ideas, interests, and beliefs of the Mexicans also would influence the policies and actions of North Americans in various ways. Mexico was not Haiti or the Dominican Republic, and the "wind that swept Mexico" was far more than a "golpe de estado" or the aimless violence of "backward" Indians and sadistic *bandidos*.

Woodrow Wilson and the "Backward" Nations

When Woodrow Wilson took office on 4 March 1913, he confronted a revived revolution in Mexico with all the attendant dangers to foreign lives and property. The new president was a firm believer in the industrial-creditor concept of order and stability, and he emphasized the role of Anglo-American political institutions in establishing these conditions. In his view, revolutions occurred either because bad men were trying to usurp power through unconstitutional means or because the people were unable to vote in free elections. Revolutions would not occur when elections were held, constitutional provisions were obeyed, and bad men were eliminated. Granting recognition to men who seized power or who did not follow correct constitutional practices would only encourage revolutions, since only bad men would refuse to support a government which held elections. Constitutional provisions should protect private property and all rights legitimately acquired—that is, under a correct legal system. In addition, Wilson's constitutionalist concept of freedom and democracy was intimately linked to his views on capitalism and private property; he noted, "If America is not to have free enterprise, then she can have freedom of no sort whatever."[11] He believed that the right kind of institutions and laws—which were equated with the terms freedom and democracy—would eliminate instability and revolutions and that the end product would be a condition of "constitutional order" where legitimate business would flourish and the doors would be open to commerce.

Wilson shared the world view of those who believed that the mission of the United States was to spread the institutional prerequisites of order and stability to the underdeveloped world as a necessary concomitant of economic penetration. He sounded very much like Mahan when he expressed this theme in an *Atlantic Monthly* article in 1901:

The East is to be opened and transformed . . . the standards of the West are to be imposed upon it; nations and peoples who have stood still the centuries through are to be quickened, and to be made part of the universal world of commerce and of ideas which has so steadily been a-making by the advance of European power from age to age. It is our peculiar duty, as it is also Eng-

11. Quoted in William Appleman Williams, *The Tragedy of American Diplomacy* (New York, 1962), 52; for a detailed analysis see ibid., 86–96.

land's, to moderate the process in the interests of liberty: to im-
part to the peoples thus driven out upon the road of change . . .
our own principles of self-help; *teach them order and self-control
in the midst of change.*[12]

Wilson, and almost all others in positions of authority, continually said that the teaching of order and self-control, through
the inculcation or imposition of North American political institutions, was not based upon selfish interests but upon the desire to
help the peoples concerned. These officials sincerely believed that
what was good for the United States was good for others—especially for the underdeveloped and backward peoples. But in this
context freedom and self-determination meant specific conditions
of order and the right kind of laws and policies.[13] Wilson was a
true believer in the righteousness of this policy, but the rhetoric
of morality should not obscure what actually happened. Robert
Lansing, who was either more cynical or less concerned with
moral justification, pointed out this situation to Wilson on one
occasion when the president had prepared a glowing defense of
the U.S. regard for freedom and self-determination in its relations with Mexico. The secretary wrote in the margin, "Haiti,
S. Domingo, Nicaragua, Panama?" This particular speech was not
delivered.[14]

President Wilson did place much emphasis on rule by good
men—which in practice meant men who followed constitutional
procedures, enforced law and order, and were friendly to the
United States. When Sir William Tyrrell, in November 1913, asked
Wilson to explain his Mexican policy, the president replied: "I am
going to teach the South American republics to elect good men."[15]
Perhaps one could also note that a good man was one who agreed
with Wilson, and faced with the rising intensity of Mexican nationalism Wilson saw himself as a veritable Demosthenes bearing the
lantern of North American truths in search of a just Mexican.

12. Quoted in Diamond, *Economic Thought of Woodrow Wilson,* 137.
13. For a penetrating analysis of Wilson's use of "free elections" see
Theodore P. Wright, *American Support of Free Elections Abroad* (Washington, D.C., 1964), 84–90.
14. Ray Stannard Baker, *Woodrow Wilson: Life and Letters,* 8 vols.
(Garden City, N.Y., 1927–39), 6: 78.
15. Quoted in Burton J. Hendrick, *The Life and Letters of Walter H.
Page,* 3 vols. (Garden City, N.Y., 1923–25), 1: 204–5. Tyrrell was the private secretary to Sir Edward Grey, the British foreign secretary.

Wilson also applied the criterion of good and bad to businesses. He was firmly convinced that some bad businessmen stirred up revolutions and exploited people through dishonest practices. In addition, bad businessmen were those who called for an all-out invasion of Mexico—those who wanted limited intervention were not necessarily classified as bad. The president repeatedly stressed that his Mexican policy was not designed to protect property rights. In one sense this was true, since Wilson's primary concern was not the physical protection of each and every holding in Mexico, especially if this involved extensive military efforts. But one of the major emphases of his policy was to insure the kind of order and legal structure in which business could flourish. In fact, the Wilson administration went beyond this general point and did make numerous representations for specific interests. On the basis of the historical record, the Wilson administration did as much as—if not more than—the administrations of Taft, Harding, and Coolidge to protect North American property interests in Mexico. The Mexicans certainly recognized this, for they were constantly being reminded of it. For example, as Wilson said on one occasion:

We should let every one who assumes to exercise authority in any part of Mexico know in the most unequivocal way that we shall vigilantly watch the fortunes of those Americans who can not get away, and shall hold those responsible for their sufferings and losses to a definite reckoning. That can be and will be made plain beyond the possibility of a misunderstanding.[16]

Some have argued that the real test of Wilson's idealistic policy was his refusal to go to war with Mexico. Taft, Harding, and Coolidge also refused to step into this abyss, and they did not

16. Address of 27 August 1913, *A Compilation of the Messages and Papers of the Presidents,* 20 vols. (New York, 1922), 16: 7888. For Mexican views (both at the time and later) see Eduardo Luquin, *La política internacional de la revolución constitucionalista* (México, D.F., 1957), 104, 224–26; Isidro Fabela, *Historia diplomática de la Revolución Mexicana,* 2 vols. (México, D.F., 1958–59), 2: 331–34. Wilson and Bryan took the same position in regard to U.S. economic interests in China; see Noel Harvey Pugach, "Progress, Prosperity, and the Open Door: The Ideas and Career of Paul S. Reinsch," Ph.D. diss., University of Wisconsin, 1967, 7–8. The contradiction between rhetoric and action on the part of Wilson and U.S. policy makers in general is ably presented by Luis G. Zorrilla, *Historia de las relaciones entre México y los Estados Unidos de America, 1800–1958,* 2 vols. (México, D.F., 1966), 316–19, 324.

have to contend with the complications of a European war and the struggle for a peace treaty. All these administrations evidenced the combination of ideals and interests which was a part of their commonly shared world view. The economic penetration of the underdeveloped world and its defense by nonmilitary means, if at all possible, were basic elements of this world view. Secretary of State William Jennings Bryan succinctly expressed this combination of economic and idealistic expansion in the Western Hemisphere when he wrote in 1913 that these would "give our country such increased influence . . . that we could prevent revolutions, promote education, and advance stable and just government. . . . we would in the end profit, negatively, by not having to incur expense in guarding our own and foreign interests there, and positively, by the increase of our trade."[17]

Wilson and the Mexican Revolution, 1913–15

During the summer of 1913 the Wilson administration began its campaign to eliminate the Huerta government. Various tactics were employed: offers of mediation, ultimatums, threats of force, loan proposals, and the occupation of the port of Veracruz (April 1914). The British government feared that this policy would not bring order to Mexico and might jeopardize British economic interests. Wilson sought to reassure British officials. After a conference in November 1913 with Sir William Tyrrell, the president wrote him a letter outlining U.S. policy. In it he said: "I beg that you will assure Sir Edward Grey that the United States Government intends not merely to force Huerta from power, but also to exert every influence it can exert to secure Mexico a better government under which all contracts and business concessions will be safer than they have been."[18] Wilson also noted his hope that Grey could convey this message to British and Canadian investors.

The president forcefully reiterated this position in his "international note" of 24 November, which was sent to fifteen European states, Brazil, and Japan. This note provided a clear statement of the industrial-creditor concept of order, as well as Wilson's

17. Quoted in Williams, *Tragedy of American Diplomacy,* 62–63.
18. 22 November 1913, Woodrow Wilson Papers, Library of Congress. For details see, William S. Coker, "Mediación británica en el conflicto Wilson-Huerta," *Historia Mexicana* 18 (October–December 1968).

belief that the continued rule of Huerta was a fundamental threat to this concept:

> Usurpations like that of General Huerta menace the peace and development of America as nothing else could. They not only render the development of ordered self-government impossible; they also tend to set law entirely aside, to put the lives and fortunes of citizens and foreigners alike in constant jeopardy, to invalidate contracts and concessions in any way the usurper may devise for his own profit, and to impair both the national credit and all the foundations of business, domestic or foreign.
>
> It is the purpose of the United States, therefore, to discredit and defeat such usurpations whenever they occur.

In the meantime, Wilson promised that every effort would be made "that the circumstances permit to safeguard foreign lives and property."[19]

The oil fields around Tampico were already being watched over by the U.S. Navy. Admiral Frank F. Fletcher warned the Constitutionalist forces not to attack the property of Lord Cowdray or to levy taxes on foreign oil producers.[20] In reply to a request for protection by H. Clay Pierce, Secretary Bryan stated that the department would instruct its representatives to extend "all possible and proper protection."[21]

The Huerta government had more staying power than Wilson or his advisers realized. By February 1914 the Constitutionalist forces had been halted by a resurgent Huerta. President Wilson now abandoned his plans for a provisional government and decided to give complete support to the Constitutionalists, at least until they had eliminated Huerta. This decision was aided when Luis Cabrera, Carranza's agent in Washington, provided satisfactory answers to questions concerning the future treatment of foreign interests. Cabrera stated that although radical social and economic reforms were planned, these would be accomplished by constitutional and legal means which would respect property

19. "Our Purposes in Mexico," 24 November 1913, John Bassett Moore Papers, Library of Congress. This note also asserted the principle of the open door.

20. Navy Department to Admiral Fletcher, 19 and 23 November 1913, in Admiral B. Fiske to Counselor, State Department, 9 April 1914, SD 812.6363/103.

21. Pierce to Bryan, 2 December 1913, Bryan to Pierce, 27 January 1914, SD 812.6363/19.

rights, including "just and equitable concessions." Confiscation and anarchy would not be tolerated.[22] The U.S. government then lifted the embargo on arms shipments to the Carranza forces, an act which the State Department counselor John Bassett Moore called "the first of the series of measures for playing off one Mexican military 'chief' against another."[23]

The United States seized Veracruz in April 1914, and shortly thereafter Argentina, Brazil, and Chile offered their services as mediators between the United States and Mexico. But Wilson intended to use the mediation conference—which convened at Niagara Falls, Canada, in May 1914—to do far more than ease tensions. As Arthur Link succinctly describes it: "He [Wilson] meant to use the A.B.C. mediation, first, to eliminate Huerta, and, second, to establish a new provisional government in Mexico City that he could control."[24]

The Constitutionalists, however, refused to fall into a trap which would make them in any way dependent upon or under obligation to the U.S. government. Carranza refused the mediation of the conference, and his representatives informed the U.S. delegates that Mexico would settle its own problems without interference from any source. Wilson, however, clearly intended to exercise some influence over Huerta's successors and was not eager to see either Villa or Carranza become president.[25]

Shortly after the triumph of the Constitutionalists in July 1914, Wilson dispatched a detailed set of instructions for proper behavior to Carranza. Three "matters of critical consequence" were listed: "First, the treatment of foreigners, foreign lives, foreign property, foreign rights, and particularly the delicate matter of the financial obligations, the legitimate financial obligations, of the government now suspended. Unless the utmost care, fairness and liberality are shown in these matters, the most dangerous

22. Arthur S. Link, *Wilson: The New Freedom* (Princeton, N.J., 1956), 388–89.

23. Comments by John Bassett Moore on Lincoln Steffens's article in *Everybody's*, September 1916; Moore MSS.

24. Link, *Wilson: The New Freedom,* 407. For the Veracruz occupation see Robert E. Quirk, *An Affair of Honor: Woodrow Wilson and the Occupation of Vera Cruz* (Lexington, Ky., 1962).

25. Secretary of State to the Special Commissioners, 27 May 1914, *Papers Relating to the Foreign Relations of the United States, 1914* (Washington, D.C., 1928), 509–10.

complications may arise."[26] The other two dealt with the generous treatment which Carranza was expected to display toward political and military opponents and the Roman Catholic Church. In short, there was to be no revolution, since adherence to all these prescriptions would prevent any basic changes in the socioeconomic structure of Mexico. Carranza did state that foreigners would be protected and all legitimate—a term most productive of controversy—contracts and obligations respected. But he refused to give assurances about the opposition, and Wilson then sent a note hinting at the "fatal consequences" which might follow if his advice were spurned.[27] Revolutionary nationalism and U.S. hemispheric hegemony now had completely locked horns.

For the next fifteen months the U.S. government followed a most tortuous and oft-times contradictory course in its attempt to mold Mexican political developments. The process of playing off one military chief against another became almost ludicrous as the opinions of U.S. officials seemed to shift with every contradictory report from the south. All agreed that Mexico should be stabilized under pro-U.S. leadership, but they held various opinions concerning which leader or coalition would most effectively accomplish this goal. The Wilson administration increasingly stressed a new coalition of the factions. By mid-1915, it seemed that the Villistas met the pro-U.S. requirement but held little promise in regard to stable leadership. Conversely, the Carranzistas appeared to offer the best hope for stability, but Carranza's intensely nationalistic posture rejected U.S. influence. The civil war between the factions made this dilemma even more complex, especially after April 1915, when the Carranza forces increasingly gained the ascendancy.[28]

26. Secretary of State to Vice Consul Silliman, 23 July 1914, *Foreign Relations, 1914,* 568–69.

27. Isidro Fabela to J. R. Silliman, 27 July 1914; Secretary of State to Silliman, 31 July 1914, *Foreign Relations, 1914,* 575, 577.

28. The official dilemma is presented in DuVal West, "Partial Report and Impressions Received at Veracruz (March 24, 1915–April 5, 1915)," 5 April 1915, SD 812.00/20721. West was a special representative of President Wilson. Report of DuVal West's visit to Zapata, 16 April 1915, sent in Bryan to Wilson, 18 May 1915, SD 812.00/24272a. For attempts to obtain the recognition of Villa, General Hugh Scott to James R. Garfield, 11 September 1915; Nelson O. Rhoades to Garfield, 13 July 1915; Rhoades to Scott, 18 August 1915; James R. Garfield Papers, Library of Congress. Garfield and Rhoades were Washington representatives of the Villa faction; Garfield was the son of former President James A. Garfield.

In May 1915 Colonel House developed a plan for mediation by the A.B.C. powers and the United States, which was part of his overall concept for a pan-American peace system. House wanted Wilson "to use the A.B.C. powers to bring about a government in Mexico that could be supported by themselves and ourselves, then compel the Mexican people to live under that government, whether or no."[29] House presented this plan to the president in late June, and it meshed with the campaign which Wilson had begun earlier that month. In his 2 June 1915 statement to the people of the United States—which was given extensive distribution throughout Mexico—he had called upon the various factions to unite, and warned of possible (unspecified) actions by the United States if the fighting continued. Both sides quickly rejected this suggestion.[30] Subsequently, Wilson asked Lansing to find "some direct but unofficial channel" through which Carranza could be given the "impression," "that it was within the possibilities that we might recognize him . . . but that he need not expect us to consider that course seriously unless he went to the full length of conciliation and conference with all factions with a view to the accommodation upon which the opinion of the whole world now insists."[31] Accommodation, however, did not apply just to factions in Mexico. As Wilson noted in another letter, it also meant some accommodation to the offers and suggestions of the United States—"he must win our confidence, at least in some degree, if he hopes for ultimate recognition."[32] On 5 July, Lansing also proposed that the A.B.C. powers and the United States call a conference of the "lesser chiefs," for the purpose of creating a coalition government which would set aside the top leaders.[33] Yet, on 11 July, Lansing noted in his diary several policies to frustrate the work of German agents in Latin America, and one stated: "The maintenance of friendly relations with Mexico. To do this it will be necessary to recognize Carranza's

29. The Diary of Edward M. House, 11 May and 3 June 1915, Edward M. House Papers, Yale University Library.

30. Ibid., 24 June 1915; *Papers Relating to the Foreign Relations of the United States, 1915* (Washington, D.C., 1934), 694–95.

31. Wilson to the Secretary of State ad interim, 17 June 1915, *Papers Relating to the Foreign Relations of the United States: Lansing Papers, 1914–1920*, 2 vols. (Washington, D.C., 1940), 2:535.

32. Wilson to Lansing, 18 June 1915, ibid., 535–36.

33. Lansing to Wilson, 5 July 1915, ibid., 538–39.

faction which seems to be the stronger."[34] Both Wilson and Lansing wanted a compromise government, but both reluctantly were beginning to face the prospect of a Carranzista victory. The A.B.C. conference seemed to be the last chance to achieve a unified coalition without Villa or Carranza, and Wilson became engrossed in a speculative search for the most acceptable leader of the new coalition. The construction of a revised leadership structure for Mexico would require careful action. As he calculated the methods of appealing to all factions, Wilson wrote, "We must play these men as they are."[35] Thus, the A.B.C. conference was to be a peculiar political chess match with a new rule—both kings had to be checkmated. The game was still "playing off one chief against another."

The conference convened on 5 August, and at the first session Secretary of State Lansing spelled out the ground rules: (1) the revolution had triumphed in 1914; therefore any existing conflicts were due only to "personal ambitions and personal greed"; (2) no single faction represented the revolution; (3) therefore, a new government must be formed to unite the greater part of all factions. The conferees agreed, and decided to invite all factions to an "immediate conference." If this failed they proposed "to work out a plan of selecting a government to be recognized by the countries represented." In any event, Carranza was to be eliminated and another man anointed, "who would draw the secondary chiefs to him."[36]

The mounting wave of Constitutionalist victories, however, undermined all the coalition proposals. During August, several last-ditch attempts were made at "playing off" the chiefs. Because of severe financial problems, Villa levied heavy taxes on cotton growers and copper-mining companies. He also seized from foreigners whatever goods he needed, ordered the mining companies to produce copper, and took over the light and power company of Chihuahua. Lansing informed President Wilson that these actions would interfere with the plans to hold a conference, and he suggested that General Scott be sent to El Paso to meet

34. Robert Lansing, Private Diary, 11 July 1915, Robert Lansing Papers, Library of Congress.
35. Wilson to Lansing, 8 July 1915, *Lansing Papers,* 2:540–41.
36. Lansing to Wilson, 6 August 1915, ibid., 543–44.

with Villa.[37] At this point Lansing was playing a peculiar game in his attempt to hold some form of club over Carranza. The secretary proposed that Villa be aided in marketing cattle in the United States by establishing a special inspection facility on the border and arranging with the Cudahy Packing Company for a processing plant in Juárez. As Lansing explained it, this would relieve Villa's financial dilemma and thus take the pressure off foreign business.[38]

A rather confused president approved the plan, but questioned its relationship to the proposed conference. Lansing explained:

We do not wish the Carranza faction to be the only one to deal with in Mexico. Carranza seems so impossible that an appearance, at least, of opposition to him will give us an opportunity to invite a compromise of factions. I think, therefore, it is politic, for the time, to allow Villa to obtain sufficient financial resources to allow his faction to remain in arms until a compromise can be effected.[39]

By early September, the Constitutionalists had taken a commanding lead in the struggle for control of Mexico. Lansing was still trying to maneuver the chiefs into a coalition. On 1 September, he queried the National City Bank of New York concerning a rumor that the bank was considering a loan to Carranza. The secretary wanted to prevent any such loan. The rumor, however, was false.[40]

Within two weeks, Lansing faced the reality of Carranzista power and informed Wilson that he had "almost reached the conclusion that they are so dominant that they are entitled to recognition." The secretary still hoped to obtain some gesture from Carranza that would acknowledge the role of the United States in settling the Mexican situation. Thus, he suggested that Carranza's representatives be invited to Washington to discuss the possibility of recognition with the A.B.C.-U.S. representatives.[41] The other problem was that of converting the peace con-

37. 6 August 1915, SD 812.00/24277a.
38. Lansing to Wilson, 6 and 7 August 1915, *Lansing Papers,* 2:545–47; Rhoades to General Scott, 18 August 1915, Garfield MSS.
39. Lansing to Wilson, 9 August 1915, *Lansing Papers,* 2:547–48.
40. Lansing to Frank Vanderlip, 1 September 1915; Vanderlip to Lansing, 2 September 1915; Frank Vanderlip Papers, Columbia University Library.
41. Lansing to Wilson, 12 September 1915; Wilson to Lansing, 13 September 1915; *Lansing Papers,* 2: 550–52. A secret agent sent to interview

ference into a surrender session for those who had accepted the invitation.

The ministers conference resumed on 18 September, futilely debated which course to follow, and finally decided on 9 October to recognize Carranza. In all probability this decision was prompted by U.S. pressure. The Constitutionalists still remained aloof from the proceedings.

The Wilson administration had retreated from its previous position. In his diary, Lansing noted that this shift was dictated by "Our possible relations with Germany." As he explained this:

Germany desires to keep up the turmoil in Mexico until the United States is forced to intervene; *therefore, we must not intervene.*

Germany does not wish to have any one faction dominant in Mexico; *therefore, we must recognize one faction as dominant in Mexico.*

When we recognize a faction as the government, Germany will undoubtedly seek to cause a quarrel between that government and ours; *therefore, we must avoid a quarrel regardless of criticism and complaint in Congress and the press.*[42]

European complications influenced the decision to recognize Carranza. Wilson and Lansing wanted to concentrate their attention on Europe, and this created pressure for some type of settlement of the conflict in Mexico and the establishment of formal relations with a Mexican government. But there is another side to the coin. Both wanted a settlement which would reflect some degree of U.S. influence, and they exhausted every possibility short of intervention to achieve such a result. The strength of the Constitutionalists and the stubborn nationalism of Carranza threatened all these maneuvers. The United States was presented at last with a *fait accompli*—any settlement would have to be with the Constitutionalists and on their terms.

Lansing had noted in July that German activities in Latin America meant that the United States should recognize "Carranza's *faction.*"[43] But for almost two more months he tried a variety of

Carranza in August reported on 1 September Carranza's promise of complete triumph within a month or six weeks if interference from the United States would stop; Canada (Consul) to Secretary of State, 1 September 1915, Lansing to Wilson, 3 September 1915, SD 812.00/16187½.

42. Lansing, Private Notes, 10 October 1915, Lansing MSS.
43. Lansing, Private Diary, 11 July 1915, Lansing MSS; italics added.

schemes to implement a coalition settlement which would force Carranza to make some gesture toward recognizing the predominant position and influence of the United States. The recommendations in Lansing's diary entry of 10 October 1915, represented a change in position and were influenced strongly by Carranza and the Constitutionalists. The United States had not been able to force its solution on Mexico, and the German situation was only part of the dilemma.

The United States extended *de facto* recognition to the Carranza government on 19 October 1915. But the Wilson administration still tried to qualify this acceptance of Carranza. *De facto* recognition was a sort of "half-way house." The idea at this time was to withhold full *de jure* recognition until the new government demonstrated its "good behavior." The meaning of this behavior was spelled out in detail in a memorandum prepared by Leon J. Canova, head of the Division of Mexican Affairs, at Lansing's request. Some modifications were made, and the document was handed to Eliseo Arredondo when he presented his credentials to the State Department. He was instructed to use the memorandum when he saw Carranza, since these were matters which must be handled properly and effectively. Seven of the eighteen points in the document dealt with protection of foreign economic rights in Mexico—loans, property, and trade. The others concerned questions of religion, elections, and the treatment of the opposition—necessary accouterments of peace and order in the official U.S. view. Basically, this was an extended version of the U.S. demands of July 1914.[44]

The U.S. government had made a limited, tactical withdrawal in the face of Carranza's strength. It had not given up the attempt to influence the Mexican Revolution, however. To U.S. officials, the revolution had ended and Mexico must now return to the ranks of the stable, well-behaved underdeveloped nations. But the stage was already set for renewed complications. As Wilson and Lansing soon discovered, the nationalism of the revolution was not a force which could be tamed simply by *de facto* recognition. The instructions for proper behavior were just as unpalatable to Carranza after 19 October as they had been in July 1914—perhaps more so, since he was now the victor.

44. Memorandum for E. Arredondo, 19 October 1915, SD 812.00/16546½. See note 26 above for note of July 1914.

3 The U.S. Punitive Expedition of 1916–1917

Supinely we sit, and we let dumdums go
to blood-drunken, desperate, red Mexico.
—"The Dumdum," 1916

Regulation and Intervention

Reviewing the history of U.S.-Mexican relations from 1913 to 1926, the chief of the State Department's Mexican Division stressed their consistently tense nature. In his memorandum of 17 December 1926, R. C. Tanis explained the matter: "This state of affairs has resulted from the persistent efforts of Carranza and succeeding executives of Mexico to deprive American citizens of properties legally acquired by them under the Mexican laws in effect at the time of purchase, and from the fact that the Government of the United States has consistently opposed such efforts."[1] Tanis then traced the history of U.S. protests over reforms and policies affecting the property of North Americans. The almost steady stream of protest notes reflected the steadily increasing importance of the second stage of the unfolding revolutionary process: the development of a reform impetus stressing national control over the resources of the country. For a time this process was entangled with the effect which disorder and violence had upon foreign lives and property. In terms of U.S. protests and policy these two aspects to a limited degree would remain en-

---

1. "Memorandum of the Political Relations between the United States and Mexico and the Effect thereon of Mexico's Policy of Confiscation and Repudiation since 1913," 17 December 1926, SD 711.12/817. Fabela, *Historia diplomática,* 2:296–97, stresses the same point. Luis Cabrera divided the revolutionary process into two periods, 1910–17 (destruction), 1917–27 (legislation), *Veinte años despues* (México, D.F., 1937).

43

tangled until 1920. But after 1915 the Mexican reforms and policies affecting foreign economic interests became one of the major problems in U.S.-Mexican relations, and by mid-1920 it was the paramount issue.

Between 1913 and 1916 the State Department received numerous reports and statements about the possibility of national and state reform legislation. Many of these dealt with the possible nationalization of petroleum, but this problem seemed to be relatively insignificant—at least as compared to some other problems faced by foreign property owners—until early in 1915.[2] At that time the State Department received information that Carranza had issued a decree requiring the oil companies to obtain the permission of the Constitutionalist government in order to continue operations. This government approval would be issued after the companies agreed to abide by the new petroleum laws which were being prepared. To the State Department and the oil companies this seemed to be an attempt by the Constitutionalists to obtain advance acceptance of a kind of Calvo Doctrine regulation.[3] The Carranza government did not push the issue, but it did expand its regulatory functions. Complaints by foreign businesses increased —as did rumors of nationalization. In part, the eighteen-issue memorandum of October 1915 reflected these rumors and reports.[4]

In January 1916 the first attempts at asserting Mexican control over the oil industry sparked a lengthy and acrimonious debate between Mexico and the United States. The Departamento de Fomento (Development) canceled the contract of concession by which the Compañía Petrolera Maritima, S. A. (Maritime Oil Company) explored and exploited the oil and gasses in river beds and banks in Veracruz and Tamaulipas. The concession had originally been granted to various Mexican nationals in 1912, and they had transferred it to the North American company in 1913, after Huerta came to power.[5] In his protest to the State Department, the company president presented an argument which would

2. In September 1913 a Mexican deputy proposed a law for the nationalization of petroleum with compensation; *El Imparcial,* 26 September 1913; it was not enacted.
3. John Osborne to Frederic Kellogg, 16 January 1915, SD 812.6363/ 148. Osborne was an oil company lawyer.
4. SD 812.00/16548½; see also Memorandum by Leon Canova, 13 October 1915, /16546½.
5. Lansing to John R. Silliman, 19 January 1916, SD 812.6363/205a.

be repeated many times by U.S. businessmen and government officials.

> . . . these contracts are the only protection of the vested property rights and interests in Mexico and other Latin-American countries of American citizens who are conducting enterprises there, and . . . they protect hundreds of millions of dollars of American investments in all the republics and states of the Western Hemisphere. Therefore if our government shall permit the Mexican government arbitrarily to repudiate these contracts, it will cast a cloud upon the title to all American investments, not only in Mexico, but in Central and South America.[6]

Secretary Lansing agreed, and instructed the special agent John R. Silliman, "You will request Carranza to take appropriate steps to suspend the decree of forfeiture and to protect property of company against seizure or interference."[7]

This Mexican action seemed to confirm the growing tide of rumors about oil nationalization. At the request of Boaz Long of the State Department's Latin American Division, Lansing sent a warning for Silliman to deliver to Carranza. According to the secretary, the department had been "reliably informed" that the Mexican government planned to issue a decree for the nationalization of petroleum. Silliman was instructed to point out to Carranza the "dangerous situation" which might result.[8]

More intimately acquainted with the thinking of the Mexican officials, Silliman reported the official denial of nationalization plans and then delivered a lecture to the officials in Washington. "It is most respectfully suggested," he wrote, "that the Department adopt appropriate measures to protect itself from the imposition of such absurdly untrue information as that upon which its instructions January 19, 4 P.M. was based."[9] Lansing's sharp rebuke to the special agent revealed several interesting things about the attitudes and point of view of those officials, such as Lansing, Long, and Canova, who were directly connected with

6. J. A. Vincent to Lansing, 7 January 1916, SD 812.6363/218.
7. 19 January 1916, SD 812.6363/205a; the Maritime Oil Company was represented by Judge Delbert Haff, who had been involved in the 1913 negotiations between Huerta and the U.S. government, with the railroad companies acting as intermediaries.
8. 19 January 1916, SD 812.6363/202a; warning prepared at the request of Boaz Long.
9. 21 January 1916, SD 812.6363/203–4.

Mexican relations. The secretary informed Silliman that department officials "have had personal knowledge that for more than a
year such a measure was contemplated." Lansing stressed the
urgency of the matter, and bluntly informed the special agent that
the department did not approve the implication in his message
"and expects hereafter you will be careful *to adopt a very different
tone* when you have suggestions to make."[10] Lansing, and other
officials, already had decided that the Mexicans intended to
nationalize the oil industry, and most subsequent acts by the
Mexican government aimed at regulating or asserting some degree
of national control over the industry would be interpreted as pre-
ludes to confiscation. Much of this information, or knowledge,
which Lansing mentioned came from private sources, and Silliman
was not supposed to question its veracity, especially when such
information confirmed the secretary's preconceptions.[11]

Shortly thereafter, Canova recommended Silliman's removal. In
addition, Canova submitted to Lansing an extensive catalog of
things that Carranza had done and failed to do, especially in
regard to the protection of North American lives and property.
One point of concern was the "harmful decrees" against North
Americans issued by various state governors. Canova attributed
these to Carranza's permissiveness, but he was utterly unable to
understand the nationalistic elements involved.[12]

Various governors, and the national government, had begun to
assert more authority over the oil industry. In January 1916
General Candido Aguilar (governor of Veracruz) issued a decree
requiring the consent of the state government for sales, leases, and
transfers of oil lands. The decree also stipulated that all persons
participating in such contracts "shall be considered as Mexicans
whatever their nationality and may not in any case allege the
defense of foreign citizenship, nor ask protection or aid from

10. 22 January 1916, SD 812.6363/204; "to show greater deference"
was crossed out and the italicized words inserted.
11. The State Department received a large amount of undigested gossip,
rumors, and bits of information from consuls as well as attorneys for U.S.
companies and members of the American colony in Mexico. Ambassador
Fletcher reported his conversation with Harold Walker (Doheny oil interests) concerning confiscation in Fletcher to Polk, 29 January 1916, SD
812.6363/205.
12. "Confidential Memorandum for use at the Conference with the Secretary and the Counselor," 14 February 1916, Frank Polk Papers, Yale
University Library.

foreign diplomatic or consular officers, nor from the Government of their country, nor have any rights other than laws concede to Mexicans." The consul at Veracruz believed that this Calvo Doctrine provision would have a "disastrous effect on foreigners owning oil lands and leases."[13] In November 1915 the national government had issued a regulatory decree requiring all oil companies to file an inventory of their properties. This was expanded a month later to require the use of the Spanish language and the metric system in all documents sent to the government and on all signs and notices at company facilities.[14]

These initial regulatory actions were quickly overshadowed by Pancho Villa. The Santa Isabel massacre of fifteen North Americans on 10 January 1916 set the stage. Then, on 9 March, the Villistas attacked Columbus, New Mexico, in search of arms, ammunition, and booty.[15] Ironically, Wilson's tortuous attempts to bring "order and stability" to Mexico helped to create this crisis. Villa felt that he had been used badly by the United States, and General Hugh L. Scott had predicted some reaction. "His bridle is off," Scott wrote to James R. Garfield in October 1915. Garfield prophetically replied, "Your expectations of trouble will be more than fulfilled."[16] Indeed, when Villa needed arms and supplies it was only natural that he head north. Anger was involved, but U.S. meddling in Mexican affairs also helped to remove any inhibitions which Villa may have had concerning such a raid.

Hardline interventionists now clamored for military action, and even less militant persons attacked Wilson's Mexican policy. Wilson found himself in a dilemma. He had intervened at Veracruz in 1914 over a lesser pretext, and his consistency was being questioned in an election year. To Wilson and Lansing, Europe was now the main event. Mexico constituted an important problem, but the Villista raids were not considered the major element in it. They were an unpleasant side show that stole the headlines and

13. Thomas H. Bevan (consul) to Secretary, 25 January 1916, SD 812.6363/205.
14. Bevan to Secretary, 18 January 1916, SD 812.6363/210. The oil companies did not submit to these regulations and most of them were not enforced.
15. Haldeen Braddy, *Pancho Villa at Columbus: The Raid of 1916* (El Paso, Tex., 1965), 36–37.
16. Scott to Garfield, 14 October 1915, Garfield to Scott, 16 October 1915, Garfield MSS.

diverted attention from the basic issues. But the national soil had been invaded, and some North Americans were peculiarly touchy about foreign forces inside their own country. Without enthusiasm —but perhaps in the belief that he would avoid demands for the complete Cubanization of Mexico—Wilson ordered General John J. Pershing to pursue Villa into Mexico.

Prior to the actual order, the U.S. government requested Carranza's consent. The Mexican leader now faced a major problem. He had no love for the Villistas, but he was reluctant to approve a Yankee expedition. After the United States promised to recognize Mexican sovereignty and to discuss the old border-crossing treaty, Carranza did acquiesce in a very qualified permission.[17] It soon became apparent, however, that the two administrations had differing ideas concerning the nature and extent of bandit-chasing expeditions. Most Mexican officials opposed the Pershing expedition from the beginning and hoped to limit the scope of its operations to the border areas. Two days after Pershing crossed the Rio Bravo (16 March) the Mexican government submitted a new border treaty to the United States. The proposals reflected the mixture of nationalistic resentment and fear felt by the Mexican leaders as they viewed the 6,000-man army marching south. The Mexican treaty would grant reciprocity of border crossings, establish a zone (60 kilometers on both sides) beyond which troops could not proceed, and limit any expedition to 1,000 men for five days. This force could consist only of cavalry with a limited heavy-weapons group.[18]

Mexican officials feared that either the bandit-chasing expedition was a subtle way of getting an army of "pacification" into the country or under political pressure the force could be easily given

17. Correspondence and commentary concerning these operations are in Comisión de Investigaciones Históricas de la Revolución Mexicana, under the direction of Josefina E. de Fabela, *Documentos históricos de la Revolución Mexicana*, 12 (México, D.F., 1967): 13–94; Luquin, *Política internacional*, 171–73.

18. Discussion of expedition based upon correspondence in Fabela, *Documentos históricos*, 12: 116–19; Candido Aguilar to Eliseo Arredondo, 18 March 1916, in *Labor internacional de la revolución constitucionalista de México (Libro Rojo)* (México, D.F., 1960), 137–40 (1st ed. published 1918); Luquin, *Política internacional*, 173–79. Acting Secretary of State to Wilson, 20 March 1916, *Lansing Papers*, 2: 555–56. General Obregón cooperated with the expedition until April; Haldeen Braddy, *Pershing's Mission in Mexico* (El Paso, Tex., 1966), 23–24. The expedition grew to approximately 10,000; ibid., xvii.

this additional mission. At first, most officials probably leaned toward the latter view, since they were quite aware of what the interventionist newspapers and some Republicans were saying about cleaning up Mexico.[19] The *Wall Street Journal*—which had not been hardline interventionist—talked about the expedition as an "invasion" aimed as much at Carranza as at Villa and advocated a complete blockade to back up this "commitment."[20] The Mexican officials took these militant pronouncements at face value. This reinforced the belief that the punitive expedition was more than a bandit-hunting force. The U.S. rejection of the proposed treaty and Pershing's continued march south added to this belief.

During the latter part of March, Wilson considered terminating the expedition. Secretary Lansing and Secretary of War Newton D. Baker supported such a move, but a clash at Parral (12 April) between U.S. troopers and Mexican civilians and soldiers stifled this development. Carranza now formally requested the removal of all U.S. troops from Mexican soil. Wilson proposed a conference between Generals Scott and Obregón, and at a meeting at El Paso these military leaders formulated a secret agreement for the gradual withdrawal of U.S. forces.

At this juncture two incidents occurred which, to the Mexicans, seemed to have serious implications. A guerrilla, or bandit, force raided Boquillas and Glen Springs, Texas, and a fresh U.S. force was ordered to pursue them into Mexico. Carranza believed that this bandit group had been organized on the North American side of the border by his enemies who were trying to provoke a war or lower the prestige of the Mexican government. He then ordered Obregón to terminate his talks with Scott.[21]

19. Mexican fears reported in Arredondo to Aguilar, 23 March 1916, *Labor internacional;* on 10 March, the *El Paso Morning Times* reported that Senator Fall had introduced a bill to recruit 500,000 men for intervention; Braddy, *Pershing's Mission,* 8. Reports on the size and nature of the expedition in Andres G. Garcia (consul, El Paso, Tex.) to General Candido Aguilar, 10 April 1916; Archivo General de la Secretaría de Relaciones Exteriores de México, Ramo 119, "Revolución Mexicana, 1910–1920," L-E-800, Leg 16 (2); hereafter cited as SREM followed by volume number (800) and file number (Leg 16); the letters L-E- apply to all volumes.

20. Editorial, "Muddling Through," *Wall Street Journal,* 14 March 1916.

21. Carranza to Obregón, 7 May 1916, *Labor internacional,* 179–80. The impact of these raids on the Mexican government is discussed in Zorrilla, *Historia de las relaciones* 2: 290–91; for other U.S. offensive actions in May and June, ibid., 292–93, and Andres G. Garcia to Carranza, 8 May 1916, SREM 800, Leg 16 (2).

Carranza advised Obregón that he wanted to avoid a conflict with the United States, but he was convinced that the threat to his government had become much more serious. The Mexican government clearly elaborated its feelings in its 22 May note to the United States. In it General Aguilar spoke of the "new invasion" which followed the attack on Boquillas and stated that if this force were not withdrawn the Mexican government would consider it an invasion and act to defend itself. Aguilar also charged that the "Columbus Expedition" had become a movement to limit the independence of Mexico. Why, he asked, were infantry and artillery units included in the expedition when everyone knew that cavalry forces were best suited for pursuing bandits? Then Aguilar linked the U.S. protests over the protection of North American interests to the expeditions. To the Mexican government all were now seen as part of a common effort to influence the revolution.[22] The accusations in this note represented the maturing of suspicions which had been developing since March. To Mexican officials the policies of the Wilson administration increasingly seemed to be influenced by the militant interventionists because of the presidential election campaign.[23]

The U.S. government did not reply to the Mexican note for almost a month, but in the interim the Mexican government began preparations for a possible conflict with Pershing's expedition. Reports and rumors concerning impending war, raids, and intrigue poured into the State Department. Some of these cited German or Japanese involvement, and one ominous note reported that a small group had "invaded Texas . . . with a red flag and a can of kerosene oil." Pershing was ordered to "act conservatively," so that the responsibility for any incident would rest "beyond question on the Carranza troops."[24] General Jacinto B. Treviño informed

22. Note of 11 May 1916, *Labor internacional,* 192.
23. Opinion expressed in Aguilar to Lansing, 22 May 1916, ibid., 196–210, and Alberto Salinas Carranza, *La Expedición Punitiva* (México, D.F., 1936), 244. Reports from secret agents of steady streams of soldiers, artillery, and supplies moving through Columbus, New Mexico, are in letters of Consul Garcia during May and June; SREM 800, Leg 16 (2).
24. Consul Garrett to Secretary, 12 June 1916, *Papers Relating to the Foreign Relations of the United States, 1916* (Washington, D.C., 1925), 573; Funston to Pershing, 29 May 1916, ibid., 566–67. The Mexican government firmly refused the services of two German navy pilots, with an airplane; General Obregón to Secretaría de Relaciones Exteriores, 25 April 1916, SREM 798, Leg 13.

Pershing on 16 June that the movement of U.S. troops in any direction except north would be met with armed resistance.[25] Five days later, units of the Mexican army blocked the movement of two troops of U.S. cavalry at Carrizal and a small battle ensued. On 18 June the National Guard of the United States was called up for border duty, and the War Department now planned to occupy the northern states of Mexico "in case the Mexicans refuse to make any terms."[26] Leon Canova advocated hitting the Mexicans "as hard and fast as it is possible for us to hit . . . until they are utterly demoralized, and have the fear of God and of the American people driven into their hearts."[27]

The Mexican government notified the other Latin American nations of the possibility of war between Mexico and the United States. The Mexican note bluntly stated that the basic reason for U.S. intervention was opposition to the Mexican policy of eliminating the privileged treatment of foreign capital. In conclusion, the Mexican government declared that the "foreign invasion" must be repulsed and Mexican sovereignty be respected.[28]

The Wilson administration now realized that the United States stood on the brink of a full-scale war with Mexico, but it would be a war caused by an incident which was clouded by questions of responsibility. Wilson and his advisers regarded the border incursions as "a symptom of the deeply rooted internal disturbances" which had been aggravated by the economic policies and problems of the Carranza government.[29] The Wilson administration had dispatched the Pershing expedition not only to eliminate this symptom by catching Villa, but also indirectly to pressure the Carranza government to maintain order and stability. The latter

25. Pershing to Funston, 17 June 1916, *Foreign Relations, 1916,* 577.

26. Frederick Palmer, *Newton D. Baker: America at War,* 2 vols. (New York, 1931), 1:22.

27. Memorandum, Submitted to the Secretary of State by the Mexican Division, LJC [Canova], 28 June 1916, Henry P. Fletcher Papers, Library of Congress.

28. Aguilar a los Señores Secretarías de Relaciones Exteriores de los paises Indohispanos, 27 June 1916, *Labor internacional,* 245–48. Fabela, *Historia diplomática,* 2: 277–79, concerning Mexico's decision for war; ibid., 290–91, for note to Latin American nations.

29. "Draft of Statement Setting Forth the Policy of the Government of the United States," October 1916; and Franklin K. Lane, John R. Mott, George Gray, to Wilson, 10 October 1916, Albert B. Fall Papers, Henry E. Huntington Library, San Marino, California. Lansing to Wilson, 4 May 1916, SD 812.00/24290c, discusses underlying causes of conflict.

point was based upon the assumption of the Wilson administration that Mexican officials in fact had the capability to do this but refused to act because of their opposition to foreigners. The U.S. reply (20 June) to the Mexican note of 22 May explicitly stated these points:

The Government of the United States has viewed with deep concern and increasing disappointment the progress of the revolution in Mexico. . . . For three years the Mexican Republic has been torn with civil strife; the lives of Americans and other aliens have been sacrificed; vast properties developed by American capital and enterprise have been destroyed or rendered non-productive; bandits have been permitted to roam at will through the territory contiguous to the United States and to seize, without punishment or without effective attempts at punishment, the property of Americans.

The Mexican government was further informed that recognition had been granted with the expectation that the government would speedily restore order, to provide the "Mexican people, and others . . . opportunity to rebuild in peace and security their shattered fortunes." The United States had ignored repeated provocations to restore order by force in northern Mexico and had "sought by appeals and moderate though explicit demands to impress upon the *de facto* Government the seriousness of the situation and to arouse it to its duty to perform its international obligations toward citizens of the United States who had entered the territory of Mexico or had vested interests within its boundaries." In conclusion the U.S. note stated that the protection of American lives and property in Mexico was, first, the obligation of Mexico and, second, the obligation of the United States. Thus, the United States declared that it was "duty bound" to maintain its "national rights" and warned Mexico that an "appeal to arms" would lead to the "gravest consequences."[30]

In the note of 20 June Wilson and Lansing placed just as much emphasis upon protecting U.S. interests in Mexico as upon preventing raids across the border. In addition, they clearly indicated

30. Secretary of State to the Secretary for Foreign Relations (Mexico), 20 June 1916, SD 812.00/18450. Wilson thought that the note was excellent: "They might as well know at once *all* that they will be up against if they continue their present attitude"; Wilson to Lansing, 18 June 1916, *Lansing Papers*, 2:557.

that the basis of conflict was the Carranza government's attitude and policies toward foreign lives and property. The Pershing expedition would remain in Mexico until Carranza provided concrete evidence that these had been altered to meet U.S. specifications. Raids across the border now were linked to internal questions of order and the protection of foreign interests. The original decision to send troops into Mexico may have been based solely upon Villa's attacks across the border, but by June 1916 the Pershing expedition had become a lever to induce changes in Mexican policy.

Wilson did not want to engage in a major war to pacify Mexico, although he did not dismiss the possibility; yet a limited conflict to prevent the expulsion of the Pershing expedition could quickly escalate to such an extensive campaign.[31] If Pershing were driven out of Mexico, or if the United States immediately withdrew the expedition under pressure, the Mexican government might be encouraged to defy the United States on all issues. The dilemma of the Wilson administration was how to avoid a war and still settle the problems of safeguarding the border and protecting foreign interests in Mexico. The Mexican government also faced a dilemma—how to remove the Pershing expedition from Mexican soil without a major war and without accepting the dictates of the U.S. government in regard to internal policies or the legitimacy of its asserted "policing role in Mexico."

The atmosphere may have been tense in June 1916, but both sides were looking for some type of peaceful accommodation. Prior to the clash at Carrizal some U.S. officials had discussed the possibility of forming a joint U.S.-Mexican commission to settle the various problems which affected relations between the two nations. As part of his efforts to make the American Federation of Labor an influential group in U.S. official circles and in the Mexican labor movement, Samuel Gompers worked actively for labor representation on such a commission.[32] On 22 June, he

31. Baker, *Wilson: Life and Letters,* 6: 73–75.
32. Samuel Gompers to William B. Wilson, 10 June 1916, Samuel Gompers Papers, State Historical Society of Wisconsin, Madison, Wisconsin. Gompers was interested in getting the AFL into the councils of national power and also in exercising some influence over the labor movement in Mexico; he was especially anxious to destroy the influence of the Industrial Workers of the World (IWW); Memorandum, 7 July 1917, ibid.; see also Levenstein, "United States Labor Movement and Mexico," 45–49.

conferred with President Wilson and stressed the mediating role which he believed the AFL could play in U.S.-Mexican relations. The day before, Gompers and Judge Charles A. Douglas, a Carranzista lobbyist in Washington, had discussed this policy (and the commission) with Frank Polk, counselor in the State Department, and Polk had suggested the conference with the president.[33] Gompers called Wilson's attention to Carranza's reference to possible arbitration, and to the contacts which the AFL had with the Carranza government. Wilson indicated that he would give "serious consideration" to any Mexican proposals for a conference. After this meeting Judge Douglas sent a telegram to Carranza, with Gompers's approval, stating that a suggestion of arbitration would be "received with favor" by President Wilson.[34]

In conversations with Gompers, President Wilson, Secretary of Labor William B. Wilson, and Frank Polk had stressed the cautious policy which the administration was following in regard to the Carrizal incident and the larger question of war with Mexico. The Mexican government communicated with Gompers in the hope that the AFL might help avert war. Secretary of Labor Wilson met with Gompers and Colonel Edmundo Martinez, a representative of the Mexican government, and stressed the desire of the administration for a peaceful solution. The secretary also stated that if U.S. troops had caused the Carrizal clash, then the United States would have to bear the responsibility.[35]

These indirect contacts may have helped prepare the ground for the Mexican note of 3 July 1916 stating that country's desire for a peaceful settlement. The Mexican government noted that several Latin American countries had offered friendly mediation and asked whether the United States was disposed to accept these or negotiate directly with Mexico. On 7 July, Secretary Lansing accepted the latter suggestion, and the Mexican government then proposed the establishment of a commission composed of three

33. Memorandum, 21 June 1916, Gompers MSS.
34. Memorandum, 22 June 1916, ibid.
35. Ibid.; Memorandum, 24 June 1916, ibid. Gompers claimed much credit for the recognition of Carranza and the fact that there was no intervention in 1915. He sent copies of his 1915 Wilson correspondence (urging no intervention and recognition) to Carranza and added, "You may draw your own conclusions as your judgment may direct"; Gompers to Carranza, 8 March 1916, ibid.

men from each country.[36] With the agreement to convene the six-man American-Mexican Joint Commission, the crisis atmosphere rapidly subsided.

The Mexican government appointed as commissioners Ignacio Bonillas (a prominent lawyer), Alberto J. Pani (Minister of Industry), and Luis Cabrera (Minister of Finance). Woodrow Wilson appointed Secretary of the Interior Franklin K. Lane and Louis Brandeis, but the latter suddenly withdrew in mid-August.[37] Wilson then completed the commission with Judge George Gray and John R. Mott, secretary of the YMCA. Colonel House suggested the appointment of a Catholic, if one could be found who "was more of a Wilson man than a church man."[38]

Secretary Lane exemplified in many ways the attitudes and ideas of the Wilson administration, and as chief negotiator for the U.S. government he articulated clearly the Mexican policy of the administration. Thus, the negotiations between the U.S. and Mexican commissioners provided a revealing picture of the fundamental issues involved in U.S. policy and the frustrations which plagued U.S. efforts to shape the actions of a nationalistic revolution.

Characteristically, Lane knew very little about Mexico except that "Carranza is obsessed with the idea that he is a real god and not a tin god, that he holds thunderbolts in his hands instead of confetti, and he won't let us help him."[39] The last sentiment in this sentence was a common complaint in official circles. In this context, "helping" meant instructing Mexicans in the most "practicable" economic and political policies. As Lane explained, "nation building" involved "the development of its opportunity, the education of its people, the establishment of its finances, and the *opening of its industries in the establishment of its relations with other countries.*"[40] In July 1916 he summarized Wilson's

36. Aguilar to Arredondo, 3 and 7 July 1916, *Labor internacional,* 258–61. See also Luquin, *Política internacional,* 257–58.

37. Franklin K. Lane to James Harlan, August 1916, in Anne Lane and Louise Wall, eds., *The Letters of Franklin K. Lane: Personal and Political* (Boston and New York, 1922), 223.

38. Edward M. House to Frank Polk, 10 August 1916, Polk MSS.

39. Lane, *Letters of Franklin K. Lane,* 225; see also 223.

40. Lane to Alexander Vogelsang (acting secretary of the interior), 29 September 1916, ibid, 226; see also Lane to Frederick J. Lane, 29 September 1916, ibid., 227.

Mexican policy by citing Rudyard Kipling's poem "The White Man's Burden" and concluded:

There is a great deal of the special policeman, of the sanitary engineer, of the social worker, and of the welfare dictator about the American people. . . . It is one of the most fundamental instincts that have made white men give to the world its history for the last thousand years.[41]

Lane, as spokesman for the Wilson administration, was not only to "instruct" the Mexicans in matters of internal economic and political policy but also to settle these "vital questions" (especially as they affected U.S. interests in Mexico).[42] The U.S. government informed the Mexicans that the powers of the commission should be broad in order to consider the "other matters which affect relations."[43]

The Mexican government, however, clearly discerned the nature of U.S. strategy. Settlement of the border issue and the withdrawal of Pershing's expedition were to be based upon Mexico's accepting the U.S. formula for Mexican domestic policy. Carranza therefore gave his commissioners explicit instructions. The main object of the negotiations was to obtain evacuation of U.S. troops and to draft a treaty for the protection of the frontier—which would also prevent future expeditions. All actions of the commission were to be sent to Carranza for final acceptance, and nothing could be considered definite until presidential authorization had been given. When these basic objects had been obtained, and when U.S. forces had departed, then other matters concerning "friendly relations" might be discussed if given prior approval by the "First Chief."[44] With these ironclad instructions, Carranza

41. "The President's Mexican Policy: An Interview by Franklin K. Lane," *New York World,* 16 July 1916; copy in Franklin K. Lane Papers, Bancroft Library, Berkeley, California.
42. "Recommendations of President Wilson Regarding the Policy to be Followed by the American Members of the American and Mexican Joint Commission; made to John R. Mott on October 8, 1916 by President Wilson at Shadow Lawn," Lane, Gray, Mott to Wilson, 10 October 1916, Fall MSS.
43. Polk to Aguilar, 28 July 1916, *Labor internacional,* 263–64.
44. "Instrucciones de C. Primer Jefe del Ejército Constitucionalista, Encargado del Poder Ejecutivo de la Unión, para la Comisión Diplomática formada por el señor licenciado Luis Cabrera, y por los señores ingenieros Ignacio Bonillas y Alberto J. Pani," 3 August 1916, ibid., 265–66. For later instructions see Fabela, *Historia diplomática,* 2:316–46, 356–61.

intended to prevent his commissioners from being cajoled or pressured into signing an agreement dealing with domestic issues. For the Carranza government the vital issue of national sovereignty was at stake.

The Joint Commission began negotiations on 6 September 1916 at New London, Connecticut. Arriving by yacht, President Wilson attended the first meeting and tried to impress upon the Mexican commissioners the importance of protecting lives and property. Then the Mexicans were informed that an agreement for the withdrawal of Pershing's troops could be negotiated as soon as their government gave "formal assurance" that it accepted the basic U.S. proposals. According to the U.S. commissioners, the most important of these was the protection of the life and property of foreigners—which must be adequate to allow foreigners to resume operation of mines or other industries. Closely associated with this was the next "vital matter"—the recognition of property rights ("all property rights heretofore acquired by foreigners, in accordance with the established laws of Mexico, shall be regarded as valid"). The other elements in this proposed agreement were the establishment of a claims commission, religious toleration, the elimination of disease and the relief of starvation, and the enforcement of the neutrality laws by the United States. Wilson and the American commissioners stressed the point that this program would lead to the rehabilitation of Mexico and an era of cordial cooperation.[45]

From the very beginning of the conference, however, the Mexican commissioners insisted that the actual withdrawal of U.S. troops was the basic issue. The U.S. group, led by Secretary Lane, became rather irritable. Referring to the "revolutionist's standpoint" of Luis Cabrera and the other Mexican commissioners, Lane wrote: "They will not admit any obligation as superior to the success of the revolution, nor will they agree at this time to

45. Details of meetings in Lane, Gray, Mott to Wilson, 10 October 1916, Fall MSS; discussion of proposals in Memorandum of American Commissioners, 3 October 1916, *Labor internacional,* 270; Fabela, *Historia diplomática,* 2:314–15; quoted portions of agreement in "Memorandum Embodying Principles of Agreement Submitted by the American Commissioners to the Mexican Commissioners, Friday, October 27, 1916," Fall MSS; Luis Cabrera wrote to Carranza on 12 October, reporting the U.S. concern over "confiscatory measures"; Fabela, *Historia diplomática,* 2:332–36.

discuss such questions as the arbitrary forfeiture of mining claims until we are out of Mexico."[46] Revolutionary nationalism had once again collided with U.S. efforts to "instruct," guide, and influence Mexican developments.

When the conference reached a deadlock early in October 1916, President Wilson summoned John Mott to Shadow Lawn, New Jersey, where he informed him that he wanted the Mexicans to give "official assurances" that as soon as the troop withdrawal and border protection plan was adopted the commission would consider "these other matters which are so vital to establishing and maintaining right relations between the two countries." In addition, the Mexicans were to be told that U.S. friendship, and possibly even continued recognition for Carranza, were at stake.[47]

The Mexican commissioners did not accept Wilson's slightly revised formula, and in late October the U.S. commissioners again tried to obtain Mexican agreement to the basic U.S. plan through a change in wording. The 27 October "Principles of Agreement" divided the proposals into two parts. Part I provided for border control and the withdrawal of troops over a ninety-day period (provided that no raids took place within seventy-five miles of the border). The latter provision seemed to be a modification of the U.S. position to meet the Mexican objections. But the U.S. proposal also stated that pending ratification the Mexican government would give "formal assurance that it will agree, in principle, to the other proposals contained in this memorandum [Part II], and which are to be considered an integral part of the agreement."[48] In order to get the ninety-day withdrawal, the Mexicans would have to accept the original U.S. points concerning the "vital questions."

The Mexican commissioners quickly rejected the agreement

46. Lane, Gray, Mott to Wilson, 10 October 1916, Fall MSS. At the time, the State Department was engaged in a controversy with the Mexican government over a decree requiring mining companies to resume operations and increasing taxes on mines; *Foreign Relations, 1916,* 734–40.

47. "Recommendations of President Wilson Regarding the Policy to be Followed by the American Members of the American and Mexican Joint Commission . . ." 8 October 1916; attached to this was "Draft of Statement Setting Forth the Policy of the Government of the United States," Fall MSS; Lane, Gray, Mott to Wilson, 3 January 1917, SD 812.00/24325.

48. "Memorandum Embodying Principles of Agreement Submitted by the American Commissioners to the Mexican Commissioners, Friday, October 27, 1916," Fall MSS.

because of the conditions attached to withdrawal and bluntly stated that they had not come to the United States to abandon the sovereignty of Mexico.[49] Leo S. Rowe, an adviser to the U.S. commission, displayed a common reaction when he blamed the "destructive attitude" of Cabrera for the Mexican position. Rowe believed that Pani and Bonillas would be willing to accept the U.S. proposal, and he seems to have been working to split the Mexican commission. Cabrera adhered steadfastly to the instructions of Carranza and was accused of having a "negative and destructive attitude." Presumably, Mexican officials were not supposed to be loyal to their government's policy, especially when this involved "the consideration of the vital questions in which the American commissioners were particularly interested, such as the protection of life and property, the resumption of industry, the establishment of a claims commission etc."[50]

In mid-November Rowe tried to break the deadlock by proposing that the six-point program be divided into two classes: (1) those admitting of immediate effective action by the Mexican government, and (2) those which can be left to "gradual" action. At the top of the list in the immediate action class was the modification or repeal of a number of federal decrees "which constitute a menace to foreign investments." Rowe stated that the following decrees and taxes required "immediate action": (1) operation of mines decree of 14 September 1916, "providing for the forfeiture of mining concessions in all cases where work is suspended continuously for a period longer than two months" (a supplementary decree had extended the period for resumption of operation to 14 January 1917); (2) decree of 15 August 1916, "requiring foreigners who may acquire real estate, water, oil, or fishing rights to consider themselves Mexicans so far as these rights are concerned and to renounce the right of appeal to their respective governments for protection" (repeal to be "strongly urged"); (3) Pertenencia Tax decree of 1 May 1916 (mining claims); (4) metal export tax of 1 May 1916, levying an increased rate on gold and silver and instituting a tax of 5 percent *ad valorem* on copper, lead, and zinc; (5) oil operations decree of 7 January 1915, ordering work suspension on new wells until legislation could be

49. "Reply of Mexican Commissioners to Memorandum Submitted by American Commissioners, October 27, 1916," ibid.
50. Rowe to Secretary of State, 12 November 1916, SD 812.00/24214.

enacted; (6) metal reserves of banks-of-issue decree of 15 September 1916, eliminating the privilege of issuing bank notes by the Banco Nacional and the Banco de Londres y México (private banks). Rowe was convinced that early action on these matters was needed, especially since the Mexican constitutional convention was at work and there was a "grave danger" that the obnoxious decrees might become constitutional or statutory law. The other items in this first classification were the repeal of state decrees concerning taxation, the claims commission, and the relief program.[51]

A protocol dealing with withdrawal and border control finally was signed on 24 November, after Lane had conveyed to the Mexicans a virtual ultimatum from President Wilson. Carranza objected to the protocol and especially to Lane's accompanying letter, which demanded consideration of the internal issues, and on 18 December he rejected both documents. The Mexican commissioners submitted a series of amendments to the protocol, but the U.S. commissioners rejected these.[52]

The U.S. commissioners then recommended to President Wilson the withdrawal of all U.S. forces from Mexico. As they stated in their report of 3 January 1917:

. . . the proceedings of the Constitutional Convention now in session at Querétaro indicate a fixed and settled purpose to place in the organic law of the Republic provisions which tend to make the position of foreigners in Mexico intolerable, which open the door to confiscation of legally acquired property and which carry with them the germs of serious international friction.

It is this grave menace that creates in us the deepest anxiety and a desire no less insistent to have these matters taken up with the least possible delay.[53]

The commissioners recommended that Ambassador Henry P. Fletcher be sent to Mexico to deal directly with Carranza and to try to prevent the "insertion in the new constitution of Mexico of

51. Leo S. Rowe, "Constructive Program: Confidential Memorandum Submitted to the American Commissioners: The American and Mexican Joint Commission," SD 812.00/24318 (internal evidence indicates a date in mid-November 1916; the note was filed in June 1920).

52. Fabela, *Historia diplomática*, 2:361–68; Arthur S. Link, *Wilson: The New Freedom* (Princeton, 1956), 331–32.

53. Lane, Gray, Mott to Wilson, 3 January 1917, SD 812.00/24325.

provisions of a confiscatory character which are evidently aimed at foreign investments and foreign property rights." They were convinced that these questions could not be negotiated as long as the Pershing expedition stimulated a growing anti-U.S. sentiment. In their report to the State Department the commissioners concluded:

> . . . it is evident that the Carranza government will not take up any of the larger questions until the withdrawal has been completed. Irrespective, therefore, of the excellent impression which such withdrawal will make on the public opinion of Mexico, the American Commissioners deem such withdrawal necessary in order to place the United States in a position to deal with the basic questions. They are not unmindful of the fact that immediate withdrawal is likely to give to Villa and his followers control of the greater part of Chihuahua, but feel that this is a risk that can well be taken in view of the larger purposes to be attained. In any case, should intervention become necessary, it is important that the United States make clear to the world, and particularly to Latin America, that the punitive expedition was not a first step toward intervention.[54]

Woodrow Wilson was in a rather petulant mood when the U.S. commissioners presented their report on 3 January 1917. They had prepared a press notice justifying the withdrawal of Pershing's force, but Wilson "very flatly declined to permit the issuance of this statement." Gray and Mott were angered by what they considered to be such shabby treatment, and both felt that the president no longer represented a spirit of generosity toward Mexico.[55] In all probability Wilson was suffering from acute frustration because a major attempt to shape the Mexican Revolution had so obviously failed. In late December 1916, Rowe had told Lane that the trouble with so many Mexicans was that "they talk as

54. Leo S. Rowe, the American and Mexican Joint Commission to the Secretary of State, 4 January 1917, SD 812.00/24323. Rowe's recommendations to the commissioners stated that withdrawal would provide a "necessary prerequisite" for three possible developments: (1) strengthen the Carranza government to a point where it could fulfill some of its international obligations, (2) lead to the rise of a new leader, (3) prepare the way for armed intervention; "The American and Mexican Joint Commission: Memorandum submitted to the American Commission by L. S. Rowe, January 1, 1917," sent to Henry P. Fletcher on 2 January; Fletcher MSS.
55. Lane to Lansing, 4 January 1917, SD 812.00/24733.

if their country is a fully organized, highly developed sovereign state, dealing on a plane of equality with the other nations of the earth."[56] Carranza seemed to have converted this talk to reality by refusing to accept anything but unconditional evacuation. The war in Europe and the deteriorating state of U.S.-German relations strengthened the Mexican position, especially since Wilson believed that a war with Mexico would involve at least 500,000 troops. Wilson had to choose priorities in January 1917, and at this point Europe took precedence over Mexico. The president was obviously irritated over the further assertion of Mexican independence, but, to give him due credit, he was realistic enough to see that under the circumstances he had little choice but to concede to Mexico a diplomatic victory. In addition, Wilson feared that a massive Mexican intervention (and war) would turn the other Latin American nations toward Europe for leadership, thus opening the way for "round-about flank movements" upon the "regnant position" of the United States in the hemisphere.[57] On 28 January, the War Department formally announced the withdrawal of the punitive expedition, and by 5 February the last of the saddlesore troopers had crossed the Rio Bravo. On the same day the new Mexican constitution was promulgated, and the issue of foreign interests in Mexico moved into a new phase.

Election of 1916 and the War Issue

During 1916 the Mexican government feared that the Wilson administration might be pushed into a broader conflict by election year pressures. Some interventionists (who favored Cubanizing Mexico) and the Republican party did try to make the Mexican situation a campaign issue, but neither group had much success (the interventionists least of all). Theodore Roosevelt and the

56. Rowe to Lane, 26 December 1916, Fall MSS.
57. Baker, *Wilson: Life and Letters*, 6:75; Fabela, *Historia diplomática*, 2:376–78. John Bassett Moore warned Wilson about Latin American reaction to intervention in 1913 and reported that the President "seemed to be surprised, even startled, by the suggestion of such a possibility which obviously had never before occurred to him"; "Memorandum: Conversation between Woodrow Wilson, and J. B. Moore, October 31, 1913," Moore MSS. For Wilson's expression of this fear see the speech of 27 January 1916, Ray Stannard Baker and William E. Dodd, eds., *The Public Papers of Woodrow Wilson: The New Democracy (1913–1917)*, 2 vols. (New York and London, 1926), 2:9.

Progressive party called for the United States to settle the Mexican situation "as we so successfully did in Cuba."[58] When the Progressives returned to the Republican fold in 1916 one area of agreement was the use of the Mexican problem generally as a campaign issue.

The clash at Carrizal set the stage for the election campaign. The congressional debates over Wilson's policy followed party lines. The Republicans filled the air with verbal fireworks and doggerel verse. In "The Dumdum" Wilson was accused of allowing the outlawed bullet to be shipped to Mexico. "Adair of Carrizal" appealed to the national honor:

> And the blood you shed, how red, how red!
> Cries like a bugle from Carrizal.[59]

The Republicans, however, were extremely reluctant to advocate a war with Mexico. Most of them criticized various aspects of Wilson's policy, such as lifting the arms embargo, and asserted that a "firm insistence" upon American rights would settle the problem without war. The Republican presidential candidate, Charles Evans Hughes, followed this approach, which also stressed the theme that the real danger of war would come when France and Great Britain decided to pacify Mexico. To uphold the Monroe Doctrine, the United States must control Carranza:

We can control Carranza only by arms, if President Wilson shall be re-elected. . . . President Wilson has ceased to be a moral factor in influencing Mexican affairs. . . . A new administration might have such moral weight with Carranza that he would yield to its peaceful representation in behalf of foreign interests. President Wilson can accomplish nothing with Carranza except by a general war of subjugation.[60]

58. Speech by Roosevelt entitled "National Duty and International Ideals," 29 April 1916, in Progressive National Committee, "The Progressive Party, Its Record from January to July 1916 (1916)," Garfield MSS; Draft of the Progressive National Platform, 1916, ibid.

59. *Congressional Record,* 64th Cong., 1st sess., 1916, 53, pt. 12: 11833.

60. Speech by Charles Evans Hughes, *New York Sun,* 4 October 1916. See also John Maynard Harlan, *Woodrow Wilson's War: In Wilson's Defeat Lies the Only Hope for Peace,* 36–37; Louis E. Rowley, *Wilson's Policies Menace to Nation;* and Albert B. Fall, *What Future May Bring United States on This Hemisphere,* three pamphlets issued by the Republican party, 1916.

One persistent theme in the Republican campaign was that Wilson had not promoted foreign trade because he had failed to protect investments. As Hughes expressed it:

What is the use of this administration talking to American businessmen with respect to the advancement of American enterprise when those who had their investments in Mexico were unable to work their properties and had to flee at their own risk because their own government would not see them protected in their known rights?[61]

Senator Albert B. Fall also concentrated on the theme that trade follows investments and warned that if the United States did not "take Mexico in hand" and protect American enterprises, the nation would lose control of "the richest, underdeveloped country not only upon this continent, but in the world."[62]

Republicans such as James R. Garfield believed that the party "ought to be able to win" in 1916 on the Mexican issue alone, but such a view vastly exaggerated the impact of Mexican problems on the electorate and ignored the general reluctance to plunge into war. Garfield expressed some concern over the latter factor when he told Roosevelt: "It is curious to see how many people are willing to temporize for the sake of the false security offered by Wilson's policy."[63] An illustration of what Garfield feared was provided by one of Secretary Lansing's friends, who confided:

Until the time of the calling out of our National Guard, I feel that local sentiment was perhaps adverse to our policy, but when the Watertown Company went out, it brought home in a very vivid manner, the seriousness of the situation and the probability of conflict. From that time on, I have heard less criticisms and there now seems to be a well defined sentiment that any policy which will keep us out of conflict with Mexico or with any other nation, is warranted and approved.[64]

The editor of the *Chicago Herald* informed Lansing that he had found in the Middle West little interest in Mexico, coupled with

61. *New York Sun,* 4 October 1916.
62. Fall, "What Future May Bring United States on This Hemisphere," Fall MSS.
63. Garfield to Roosevelt, 25 September 1916, Garfield MSS.
64. A. Raymond Cornwall to Lansing, 13 September 1916, Lansing MSS.

the strong belief that any intervention would be in the interest of "Wall Street financiers and land owners like Hearst."[65]

Antiwar sentiment was also expressed in the numerous letters which Wilson received from church groups and peace societies.[66] The business community was clearly divided over the issue. In May 1916, Theodore H. Price surveyed 1,500 businessmen in all sections of the country. In reply to the question whether foreign trade could be extended without adequate government protection for American lives and property, 1,086 voted no, and 566 said yes. The next question was: "Are the people in your section generally in favor of military intervention by the U.S. in Mexico?" The replies were 596 yes and 566 no. Price reported that he found a greater divergence of opinion on Mexican intervention than that on any other question.[67] The *Wall Street Journal*, though quite hostile to Carranza, generally expressed a cautious attitude concerning intervention.[68] The *Commercial and Financial Chronicle* flatly stated that war with Mexico would be a calamity, "even if American investors are in danger."[69]

Authentic, hardline interventionist pressure was a quite limited phenomenon in 1916, and Wilson definitely exaggerated its strength. He believed that border-state groups, led by Senator Fall, and North Americans in Mexico were trying to "stir up war"—see his famous list of twenty-four "American Plotters and Liars in Mexico."[70] Some of these men did want intervention, but others did not. One North American resident in Mexico explained that he opposed such action because it not only would lead to the destruction of mines and oil wells but also would result in a U.S. "carpetbagger" occupation.[71] This type of rule would mean higher taxes, higher wages, and possible regulation of business. In addi-

65. 14 November 1916, ibid.
66. These can be found in the Wilson MSS. John R. Mott was a leader in the Church Peace Union, and his appointment to the Joint Commission was hailed by Protestant publications; *The Missionary Voice* (Nashville, Tenn.), October 1916, 439.
67. "Preliminary Report Made by Theodore H. Price on Business and Political Conditions in the United States at the Instance of Harris, Winthrop & Company, May 9, 1916," Wilson MSS.
68. Based on a survey of editorials printed in 1916.
69. "Mexico and the United States," *Commercial and Financial Chronicle,* 24 June 1916, 2288–89.
70. Baker, *Wilson: Life and Letters*, 6:72.
71. Mr. Spellacy to Senator Lewis, 3 July 1916, enclosed in John Bassett Moore to Franklin K. Lane, 24 August 1916, Moore MSS.

tion, during the fall of 1916 a group of smaller investors organized the Mexican Property Owners Nonintervention League, which worked for the reelection of Wilson.[72] In November 1916, various U.S. companies with property in Mexico formed an association to promote the protection of their interests, but the large oil companies did not actively participate at first because, as they privately told the other interest groups, they had no complaints against the Mexican government.[73]

Wilson's critics did not form a united front, unless one accepts support of the Republican party as constituting such a coalition. Even then, few critics advanced specific proposals and most spoke generally about the need for a more firmly consistent policy. In spite of the ambiguity of rhetoric, the Republican leadership did not advocate war with Mexico. Senator Henry Cabot Lodge believed that such a war would be an "unmixed evil," and William Howard Taft agreed.[74]

The peace emphasis, which the Democrats developed during the campaign, proved to be highly popular, even though Wilson feared the possible impact of the Mexican problem upon the election. In October he became alarmed over rumors that "influences" on the U.S. side of the border were trying to promote another raid from Mexico. The administration issued a statement criticizing the attempts of Mexican refugees to influence the election, and pointedly stating that "it was unthinkable that any American could be so unpatriotic and heartless as to participate in a plot for political purposes, which if carried out would result in the loss of American lives." As Lansing noted, this statement would have the double effect of deterring the plotters and "of preventing hostile sentiment to you politically in case an attempt was made to carry out the plan."[75]

72. Memorandum of conversation between Gould Harrold (Mexican Property Owners Nonintervention League) and Samuel Gompers, 3 February 1917, Gompers MSS. The sheriff of Cochise country, Arizona, wrote to Wilson attacking the "untruthful statements" of Senator Fall, 3 April 1916, Wilson MSS.

73. Frederic N. Watriss to Frank Polk, 21 November 1916, Polk MSS. The Guggenheim mining interests were advancing gold to Carranza to aid his attack on Villa; O'Connor, *Guggenheims,* 337.

74. Palmer, *Newton D. Baker,* 16; William H. Taft, *United States and Peace* (New York, 1914), 34–35.

75. Wilson to Baker, 26 October 1916; Lansing to Wilson, 27 October 1916, *Lansing Papers,* 2:564–65.

Wilson's opposition claimed that this statement was an example of the Democrats playing politics with the Mexican issue.[76] While this charge was not accurate, Wilson did have a tendency in his public and private utterances concerning Mexico (and other issues) to oversimplify dramatically and to exaggerate the opposition's position as well as his own—peace-loving Wilson guarding Mexico from the terrible pressure of warhawk Republicans. This stance had its political uses. The president's affinity for painting his own lily and exaggerating the pressure for intervention also may have had its roots in his Calvinistic heritage. Politics aside, he may have been trying to justify his policy in the face of criticism by defining the positions as "good vs. evil." In reality there was not much difference between Wilson and the bulk of his critics. They all wanted to manipulate the Mexican Revolution by means short of war if at all possible (this excludes the minority of hardline interventionists). If Wilson's Republican critics had won the election of 1916, their definition of a policy of firm consistency might have led to intervention and war; but Wilson admitted that his own policy could produce the same thing.[77] To an extent, however, the historian can evaluate the rhetoric of Hughes and leading Republicans by their actions when they did win national power in 1920.

Another sidelight of the 1916 campaign was the effort of some Wilson supporters to use anti-Catholic sentiment against the Republicans. The Publicity Bureau for the Exposure of Political Romanism, a group with headquarters in the Masonic Hall, New York City, promulgated the thesis that the Roman Catholic Church was actively crusading for intervention and that the Republican party had joined forces with it to defeat Wilson. The bureau called upon the electorate to defeat this coalition of Catholicism and "Big Business" and thereby insure freedom in the United States and peace with Mexico.[78] It is difficult to measure the impact of this anti-Catholic, peace-with-Mexico argument, but some Protestant missionary groups did publish similar

76. "Mexico and Wall Street," *Wall Street Journal,* 30 October 1916.
77. Baker, *Wilson: Life and Letters,* 6:74.
78. C. Bradway, *Stupendous Issues: The Case Stated and Evidence Presented by the Publicity Bureau for the Exposure of Political Romanism* (New York, 1916).

arguments.[79] Although there is no evidence that Wilson condoned or supported this line of attack, there is also little evidence that he opposed it. Wilson was not entirely free of anti-Catholic bias as he revealed in 1917 when he told Colonel House that the Catholics were trying to control the government.[80]

The Democrats made good use of the campaign slogan, "He Kept Us Out of War," which had implications for Mexico as well as for Europe. But, if there had not been a major war in Europe, would Wilson have eventually led the country into a war with Mexico? The war-connected deterioration in relations between the United States and Germany played an important role in the Wilson administration's Mexican policy from mid-1915. Secretary Lansing explained to an old friend that investigation of German activities meant "it was necessary to take every precaution in dealing with the Mexican Government," and he continued:

This was a decided factor in our Mexican policy, I might say, a *controlling* factor. Yet it could not be explained. We had to accept in silence the criticism of recognizing Carranza, of not acting vigorously, of withdrawing Pershing without accomplishment, of vacillation etc., and this had to be done while a presidential campaign was in progress because the national welfare demanded that our lips should be sealed.[81]

Lansing oversimplified administration policy, but officials did have to weigh any discussion for extended military operations in Mexico against the possibility of involvement with Germany. U.S. forces were spread extremely thin in 1916. In July the Navy Department stated that it could not authorize the landing of forces from ships to protect property in Mexico under any conditions, since this type of "occupation" duty could only be entrusted "to trained soldiers, and the only trained soldiers under naval control (the marines) are now, for the most part, employed in active service in Santo Domingo and Haiti."[82] Recruiting for the army had fallen below expectations, and the 104,000 National Guards-

79. *The Standard* (Chicago), 15 July 1916, 1435 (published by the Northern Baptist Convention); *The Missionary Review of the World* (New York), August 1916, 618 (published by the Methodist Episcopal Church).
80. House Diary, 9 September 1917, House MSS.
81. Lansing to Edward N. Smith, 3 March 1917, Lansing MSS.
82. Polk to J. H. Byrd (Byrd Contracting Co.), 10 July 1916, SD 812.6363/240.

men on the border fell far short of the 500,000-man army which Wilson believed necessary for a Mexican intervention.[83] Without a declaration of war, followed by conscription, the United States would not have enough military power to subdue a nation such as Mexico, and such a conflict would preclude any strong measures against Germany. The Germans understood this and realistically hoped to see the increasingly pro-Allied United States bogged down with Mexican complications.[84] Considering Germany to be the main U.S. problem, Lansing and House wanted to prevent an escalation of military efforts in Mexico, even if this meant unconditional withdrawal and postponing a settlement of the "vital questions" concerning internal Mexican policies.[85]

If the European complications had not existed and, in this context, if Carranza had pressed for the expulsion of Pershing's expedition, the United States might have escalated the conflict into a major intervention and war. Other Carrizals could have replaced the U-boat attacks in the view of U.S. officials and served the same purpose. In addition, the national control features of the 1917 constitution would have added other explosive elements to the situation. As Boaz Long expressed it:

But for the European war, the Mexican situation would have been one of the foremost foreign issues of our time, for many reasons. Not the least powerful one being that it involved the basic question of giving opportune protection to Americans who left good homes to seek their fortunes in foreign fields not solely to advance their own interests but to extend the business of their country by doing constructive good in other countries.[86]

83. Phillip H. Lowry, "The Mexican Policy of Woodrow Wilson," Ph.D. diss., Department of History, Yale University, 1949, 163, 173; Baker, *Wilson: Life and Letters*, 6:75.

84. Clarence C. Clendenen, *United States and Pancho Villa* (Ithaca, N.Y., 1961), 296–304.

85. House Diary, 3 June 1915, House MSS; Howard F. Cline, *United States and Mexico*, rev. enl. ed. (New York, 1963), 179. General Frederick Funston (commanding general, Southern Department) recommended in late August that the expedition be withdrawn; Braddy, *Pershing's Mission in Mexico*, 78–79. The *Wall Street Journal* on several occasions warned that the Mexican situation should not be allowed to hamper U.S. preparedness for the "world situation"; editorials of 21 January, 23 June 1916.

86. "Memorandum and Arguments Relating to Constructive Steps Which Should Be Taken in Central America before the Close of the European War," 15 February 1918, SD 711.13/55.

Several of Wilson's cabinet members displayed interventionist sentiments until the German problem became predominant. David F. Houston (Agriculture), William Gibbs McAdoo (Treasury), and Franklin K. Lane (Interior) provided the best examples. In 1914 Houston noted: "It is possible that we may have to go into Mexico. We are not dealing with people who think in our terms or in those of most nations with which we have many dealings."[87] Given all of these factors, and the "ifs" cited above, Wilson might have led the nation to war against Mexico in much the same manner as he did against Germany. On several occasions the president did say that he did not want a Mexican war; but he had said the same thing about the war in Europe.

87. David F. Houston, *Eight Years with Wilson's Cabinet, 1913–1920,* 2 vols. (Garden City, N.Y., 1926), 2:118.

4 Revolutionary Nationalism in Mexico and the Wilson Administration

> Oh beautiful Guadalupe
> Sacred and beloved Virgin
> You must not let the gringos
> Consume the blood of your children.
> —Mexican *Corrida*, 1916

Constitution of 1917 and the Carranza Doctrine

The Mexican constitution of 1917 represented an amalgamation of diverse views about reform and the nature of the revolution. Nationalism provided the bond which held the package together. It was of necessity a tough, yet flexible, bond, since it had to provide a source of unity for the conflicts, aspirations, and ideals which had emerged since 1910.

The election of delegates to the constitutional convention took place on 22 October 1916 and preliminary sessions began at Querétaro on 21 November. During these sessions three general groups could be distinguished: (1) the "Renovadores," who had served in the federal legislature during 1912–13, were old-line political liberals and represented Carranza's position; (2) the "Jacobins," also called "Obregón radicals," were much more committed to various kinds of reform; and (3) the independents, who drifted between the other two groups.[1] The "Jacobins" attacked

---

1. Ward M. Morton, "The Mexican Constitutional Congress of 1916–1917," *Southwestern Social Science Quarterly* 33 (June 1952): 11, 15. Aarón Sáenz, "Alvaro Obregón," *Historia mexicana* 10 (October–December 1960): 309. Juan de Díos Bojórquez says that only two groups existed, the Carranza classical liberals (25 percent) and the Obregonistas or "Jacobins" (70 percent or more); "El Espíritu Revolucionario de Obregón," in Romero, *Obregón: Aspectos de su vida*, 156–57.

the "Renovadores" as hand-picked deputies of Carranza whose function was to push through the Carranza project and thus obscure the regime's regression to a basically conservative position. In turn, the "Renovadores" charged the "Jacobins" with being the front men for Obregón's drive to power (he was not a member of the constitutional convention).

Thus, the lines of conflict over social reform had been drawn prior to Carranza's presentation of the proposed constitution on 1 December. This document was basically the constitution of 1857 with a few changes, and none of these included the social reforms which had been decreed in 1915.[2] Most of the delegates did not oppose the political elements of the proposed constitution, but many wanted to include extensive sections concerning socioeconomic reforms (especially for land, labor, and education) and national control of resources. As a result, two committees on constitutional reforms were elected to draft the reformist additions. Ward Morton has summarized the end product:

> The Constitution of 1917 is substantially a repetition of the Constitution of 1857, with a few minor reforms, but with four great revolutionary additions. The general machinery of government remained virtually unchanged, with agrarian reform, anti-clericalism, anti-foreign economic imperialism and labor reform added.[3]

The reforms of the new constitution were nationalized expressions of the variety of plans, programs, and decrees promulgated since 1910 and issued by the Constitutionalist government, states, and generals. They cut across factional and ideological lines and proclaimed the aspirations of agrarians, workers, and development-oriented professionals.[4]

Some of the reforms provoked heated debate. Luis T. Navarro defended the Zapatistas as "honorable revolutionaries," and Rubén

2. Felix Fulgencio Palavicini, *Historia de la Constitución de 1917*, 2 vols. (México, D.F., 1938), 1:11–51. The *Mexican Review* (January 1917) printed Carranza's speech; it filled four pages (four columns per page), and economic aspects were covered in a little more than one column.

3. Morton, "Mexican Constitutional Congress," 16.

4. For earlier documents and decrees see González Ramírez, *Planes políticos*, 69–77, 123–27, 165–96. Struggles of the convention discussed in Germán List Arzubide, "La Rebelión Constituyente de 1917," *Historia mexicana* 1 (October–December 1951): 227–50.

Martí sarcastically stated that he would like to have them identified so that he would not have to kill them when he began military operations in Morelos. Navarro countered, "There are revolutionary Zapatistas more honorable than deputy Martí."[5] Other basic differences appeared during the arguments over the anticlerical aspects of article 3 and the antiforeign elements of article 27.

Most of the reform articles involved varying degrees of compromise. General Francisco J. Múgica, chairman of one of the committees on constitutional reform, later said that the "soldiers wanted . . . to socialize property," but finding all of the "learned" men (lawyers) opposed, they accepted article 27 as a compromise.[6] Compromising, at least in principle, Carranza accepted the revised constitution and emphasized that its primary function was to build a unifying, national mystique. Carranza may not have been very interested in the agrarian and labor reform sections, but the task of developing a revitalized Mexican nationalism did provide a unity of purpose for the various factions.

The constitution of 1917 contained several provisions which—if enforced—would alter the status of foreign investments in Mexico. Various articles discussed foreigners and foreign interests, but the famous article 27 contained the most explicit formulation of the drive to assert national control over the economy—and especially the natural resources—of the country. This lengthy article has been summarized as follows:

The ownership of lands and waters in Mexico was vested in the nation which could and did transmit its title to private persons but under what limitations it pleased. Direct ownership of all subsoil was vested in the nation. Only Mexican citizens might own land or obtain concessions to exploit the subsoil; or if foreigners received the same right they must agree to be considered Mexicans in respect of such property and not to invoke the protection of their government in respect of the same. Religious institutions had no power to acquire real property. All places of public worship were the property of the nation. The surface of the land was to be disposed of for the public good, expropriated

5. Cámara de Diputados, *Diario de los debates del Congreso Constituyente*, 2 vols. (México, D.F., 1917), 2:782.
6. Tannenbaum, *Peace by Revolution*, 167.

owners receiving compensation. All measures passed since 1856 alienating communal lands were to be null and void.[7]

Two of the most significant principles embodied in this article were the assertion of national ownership (*dominio directo*) of the subsurface "minerals or other substances," and the application of the Calvo Doctrine. Both were basic elements in the attempt to "Mexicanize" the economy, and would be the focal point for much of the intensive legal debate between Mexico and the industrial-creditor nations.

The authors of article 27 went back to the pre-Díaz legal traditions of Mexico for their basic definition of the ownership of natural resources. The Spanish law of reversion (as embodied in the *Ordenanzas de Minería* of 1783 for New Spain) provided one of the most significant legal foundations for national control of resources. As Harlow S. Person notes, the concepts of ownership and possession in the law of reversion corresponds "more nearly to the concept of perpetual conditional custody and enjoyment of usufruct, and the right to sell and transfer these as conditioned."[8] The oil companies asserted the right of absolute ownership of both surface property and subsurface resources, and as a corollary the right to determine the proper use of these properties. The nationalistic leaders of the revolution were convinced that the future of the nation lay in Mexico's ability to determine the policies for effective development of subsurface resources, policies based upon Mexican evaluation of developmental necessities and not on the international oil companies' worldwide juggling of production and profits. Since, by purchase, lease, or concession, the foreign oil companies controlled vast portions of the oil-bearing lands of the nation, the revolutionary leaders realized that the only way they could assert effective control over resource utilization was by replacing the nouveau-legal concept of absolute ownership with the older concept of ownership "vested in the nation." The principles of the Calvo Doctrine now became vital to obtain the compliance of the foreign oil companies with the revised legal order and their future participation in a Mexican-

7. Arnold Toynbee, ed., *Survey of International Affairs, 1925,* 2 vols. (London, 1928), 2:417.
8. Harlow S. Person, *Mexican Oil: Symbol of Recent Trends in International Relations* (New York and London, 1942), 13; see also 12–13, 37–38.

oriented program of development. The other alternative was complete nationalization, by either expropriation or confiscation, which would have resolved the problem of forcing foreign companies to abide by Mexican laws and policies.

At the end of the convention, Deputy Juan de Díos Bojórquez stated: "The true work of the Revolution begins now—the Revolution is not over; now it ought to become most revolutionary, most radical, most unyielding."[9] The ideals and aspirations had been codified; now the question became one of implementation and enforcement by the Carranza government. The president, however, was not very sympathetic with some of the reforms and did little to implement the agrarian and labor sections, although he had to make a few concessions to the agrarians. Carranza was a dedicated nationalist, however, and this provided a link with those men who were oriented to national control of resources and economic development. He understood the relationships between national control of the economy and the development of the strength and independence of the nation. Carranza and his advisers hoped to secure for Mexico a larger share of the wealth produced by the country, through increased taxation of foreign enterprises and policies aimed at promoting more Mexican participation in commerce and industry. In addition, they hoped to reduce foreign influence over the economic and political affairs of the country.

From 1917 to 1920, the Carranza government tried to implement national control of the economy in various ways. This policy reflected the growing importance of the "national development" group in the shaping of the economic programs of the government. Analyzing the continuing influence of this group, Charles W. Anderson notes:

The work of the Querétaro delegates in drafting the new constitution has a parallel in the activities of the economic advisers to the Revolutionary governments in the years from 1917 to 1934. Led by Secretary of Hacienda (Treasury) Alfredo [Alberto] Pani, this group saw their mission as that of reconstructing the institutional machinery of the Mexican national economy, which had been devastated by the Revolution. They sought to re-establish the nation's foreign-trade position, restore confidence in the monetary system, and get channels of domestic trade and commerce operating once more.

9. *Diario de los debates,* 2:784–85.

These economic advisers had not emerged from the new Revolutionary elites. Rather, they were largely products of the rudimentary capitalistic structure of Mexico City which had been developing during the long regime of Porfirio Díaz.[10]

This group had its ideological roots in the economic nationalism of the latter part of the Díaz period, and Carranza, who had been a leading political figure during this period, agreed with many of its economic concepts.

These Mexicans were not anticapitalistic per se, although they could use the rhetoric when it supported their goals, and most wanted to control—not eliminate—foreign enterprises. They especially wanted to reduce the role of U.S. interests in the economy, since these constituted the principal elements of foreign influence. As a result, to the Americans the policies of the Mexican government appeared to be based primarily on anti-Yankee sentiment. The officials in the development group did not act simply out of blind hatred for the United States. Antagonism and some dislike, as well as traditional suspicions, did prevail in official circles, but this was provoked more by the reaction of the U.S. government and investors to the policies of the Mexican government than by any congenital xenophobia. In his April 1917 speech to the Mexican Congress, for example, Carranza praised the "discretion" and "spirit of cordiality" of the "great republic of the north," and blamed Mexican exiles for the acts which had caused difficulties with the United States.[11] Foreign interests would have a place in the Mexican economy, but it would be defined by Mexicans as a necessary ingredient of true national independence.[12]

Within the framework of domestic economic policy the national development orientation was relatively orthodox in terms of both methods and objectives, although foreign interests considered the

10. Glade and Anderson, *Political Economy of Mexico,* 113–14.

11. Venustiano Carranza, *Address Delivered by President Venustiano Carranza to the Mexican Congress on April 15, 1917* (México, D.F., 1918), 30, 41–42. See also statements by Carranza and Isidro Fabela praising Wilson and the U.S. government (5, 10 July 1914) enclosed in Canova to Secretary of State, 10 July 1914, SD 812.6363/126; Manifesto of Carranza, 11 June 1915, in Antonio Manero, *Qué es la Revolución?* xxvii–xxxii.

12. Roberto V. Pesqueira, "Mexico Wants Oil Developed," *Mexican Review,* September 1920, 14–16; Antonio Manero, *La Revolución bancaria en México, 1865–1955* (1957), 139–42; Zorrilla, *Historia de las relaciones,* 2:349.

assertion of national control to be quite radical. In 1913 Carranza had called for the creation of a bank to control currency issue and credit. The constitution of 1917 provided the legal basis for such a national bank, and various speakers called it a "necessity for national independence."[13] As Anderson notes about its proponents, "the function of the central bank was not to replace private banking but to re-establish it on a sound basis, within an effective monetary system, so that it could contribute to the mobilization of capital resources required for the fulfillment of the Revolutionary program."[14]

In his opening speech before the constitutional convention, Carranza placed much emphasis upon "individual liberty"—a rather orthodox element of nineteenth-century liberalism. Alberto Pani followed the same tradition when he told the First National Congress of Merchants (1918) that the remedy for the class struggle was the "formation and encouragement of an autonomous Middle Class." He concluded: "The revolutionary tendency is not directed towards a utopic socialistic levelling: its social ideal is to permit every man to obtain from the aggregate sum of wellbeing acquired by the whole community, a part proportionate to his personal contribution of labour, intelligence and economy."[15]

Carranza stressed financial orthodoxy when he told the Congress in April 1917 that the government did not shirk the recognition of all legitimate financial obligations (loans) contracted prior to the revolution. In the same speech he also emphasized economic independence when he outlined how the country had returned to metal currency, stabilized its finances, and paid for arms and munitions without borrowing a cent from foreigners.[16]

The Carranza government was especially interested in asserting national control over the petroleum industry, since this industry was considered one of the basic factors in national economic development. The Mexicans believed that the foreign interests controlling the industry were not only taking large profits out of the country but were also pursuing oil exploration policies which

13. Zorrilla, 2:59, 139–42.
14. Glade and Anderson, *Political Economy of Mexico,* 116.
15. Alberto Pani, *On the Road to Democracy* (México, D.F., 1918), 40–42; Pani, who was then secretary of industry, commerce, and labor, stressed the same theme in other speeches.
16. Carranza, *Address Delivered by President Carranza . . . April 15, 1917,* 111.

did not take into consideration the long-range economic development of Mexico or even the most effective development of Mexican petroleum resources. Mexican officials pointed out a combination of wasteful practices (such as excessive flow and improper
storage in earthen basins) in some fields, and the complete lack
of development in others; possible exploitation of the latter was
based solely upon the future decisions of the companies involved,
and these would be shaped primarily by non-Mexican considerations. To remedy these problems and provide for balanced development, they wanted measures which would make the industry
"essentially and genuinely Mexican." Their stated goal was to
provide the "indispensable elements for the future development
and economic independence" of the country.[17]

The oil control issue also drew support from a broad cross
section of revolutionary groups and provided the national development group with the revolutionary credentials it needed in the
contest for influence in the revolutionary family. The support of
agrarians, laborites, and social reform intellectuals, some of whom
did want to eliminate any foreign presence, gave an aura of
radicalism to the issue which obscured the relative economic
orthodoxy of the national development group and provided them
with a protective political coloration.[18]

The revolution stimulated Mexican nationalism in many ways
and helped to spread national feeling throughout the country. The

17. José Vázquez Schiaffino, Joaquin Santaella, and Aquiles Elorduz,
Informes sobre la cuestión petrolera (México, D.F., 1919), 7–10, 12–13.
The Mexican view was valid; for substantiation of the combination of
wasteful practices and suppression of some development see testimony
of Dr. Van H. Manning, director of the Bureau of Mines, and E. L. Doheny, in U.S. Senate, *Leasing of Oil Lands: Hearings before the Committee on Public Lands,* 65th Cong., 1st sess., 1917, 26, 133; Henrietta M.
Larson and Kenneth W. Porter, *History of Humble Oil and Refining
Company* (New York, 1959), 299; U.S. Department of Commerce, Bureau of Foreign and Domestic Commerce, "The Petroleum Industry in
Mexico," *Commerce Reports,* 13 September 1920, 1218, 1221. Foreigners
controlled 97 percent of the Mexican oil industry: U.S., 73 percent; Britain, 21 percent; Holland, 4 percent; Spanish-Mexican, 2 percent; ibid.,
1217. On the problems of national control of resources and conservation
see Miguel S. Wionczek, *El nacionalismo mexicano y la inversión extranjera* (México, D.F., 1967), 187–89.

18. General Plutarco Elías Calles said that article 27 "is one of the
greatest conquests of our last revolution, sealed with the blood and lives
of those who struggled to secure social reforms of real importance for the
nation." Interview in *El Democrata,* 30 December 1919, SD 812.6363/619.

leaders of the revolutionary family hoped to institutionalize this nationalism so that Mexico would be better able to withstand foreign pressure—whether political, economic, or cultural. Most were very sensitive to any suggestion by the industrial powers that Mexico was an inferior nation which should humbly accept her assigned status and follow their guidance. This sensitiveness was revealed by an incident which occurred during a session of the American-Mexican Joint Commission in 1916. One of the U.S. commissioners delivered a lengthy preachment stressing the "necessity of Mexico's recognizing her obligations under international law" and threatening that if Mexico did not live up to her "international obligations she could never hope to have the respect of the other nations of the world." At that point Bonillas angrily erupted, "Then the other nations of the world can go to hell."[19]

Carranza personified this sensitive, stubborn nationalism, but he and other Mexican leaders did not envisage an isolationist policy for the country. As part of this reinvigorated nationalism they wanted Mexico to play an influential role in the international affairs of the hemisphere and to become a leader among the Latin American nations. In part, these ambitions reflected the developments of the latter part of the Díaz period. The assertion of a foreign policy independent of that of the United States, and as a counterweight to U.S. power in the hemisphere, was given additional stimulus by the impact of foreign pressures after 1911. Mexican leaders, however, came to realize the vulnerability of the country in the face of opposition from the industrial powers, especially if Mexico tried to assert control over the economy. Thus, the revitalized idea of Mexican leadership in the hemisphere was given a new twist—Mexico as the leader, or example for, the underdeveloped nations of Latin America in their drive for economic independence. If Mexico could encourage the spread of the principles of revolutionary nationalism, then she might gain supporters and even allies in her struggle to limit foreign involvement in her domestic affairs. Mexico would no longer stand alone as a proponent of nationalistic reforms and, in addition, would gain national prestige as a leader of the underdeveloped nations'

19. Franklin K. Lane to Lansing, 1 December 1919, SD 711.12/224½; an almost identical version in Thomas E. Gibbon, *Mexico under Carranza* (Garden City, N.Y., 1919), 78–79.

quest for development, economic independence, and equality of treatment in international relations.

Mexican leaders believed that the international power struggle between the developed nations could produce disastrous consequences for Mexico and other underdeveloped countries. They especially feared that U.S. involvement in the European war would lead to pressures for Latin American participation, thus further curbing their independence, and to major disruptions in foreign commerce. In an attempt to counter the pro-Allied drift of the United States, the Mexican government, in February 1917, tried to form a neutral bloc. Mexico sent a note to all neutral nations, including the United States, proposing an agreement over the absolute equality of treatment accorded the belligerent nations. This proposal also called for such a neutral bloc to offer "good offices" or "friendly mediation," and if these were refused then all the neutrals would take the necessary steps to limit the war to a "strict area" and would suspend commercial relations with the warring nations.[20] The Mexicans hoped that if such actions could not bring peace, they would at least keep the Western Hemisphere (south of Canada) out of the war. In order to succeed in the latter course, they would have to involve the United States in the "common accord." The U.S. government, however, rejected the Mexican proposal, and in a petulant tone chided Mexico for not cooperating with the anti-German "neutrality" policy of the United States.[21] To the State Department, the Mexicans were guilty not only of following an independent course of action but also of asserting a leadership role.

The Mexican government had stated in its note of 11 February that "peace is an imperative necessity for Mexico," and the country did remain neutral throughout the First World War. In adhering to this policy, Mexico was subjected to Allied diplomatic pressure, trade restrictions, and violations of her neutrality by military forces.[22] To try to counter these influences, Mexican officials gave limited encouragement to German activities in the country, and some hoped to develop closer relations with Japan.[23]

20. *Labor internacional,* 406–7.
21. Lansing to Ramón P. Denegri, 16 March 1917, ibid., 387–90.
22. Ibid., 413–25. For a discussion of these violations of neutrality see Zorrilla, *Historia de las relaciones,* 2:339–43.
23. Adolfo de la Huerta claimed that Carranza was ready to accept a German offer of arms after the United States entered the war. In return

Carranza and some of his colleagues became increasingly concerned that after the war the developed nations would concentrate their attention on policing the underdeveloped areas. Since Mexico was the prime candidate for such disciplinary operations, these men hoped to develop a foreign policy which would relate revolutionary nationalism to the aspirations of the other Latin American nations. In the process, they hoped to encourage unified hemispheric opposition to any U.S. intervention. The first indications of this development appeared in 1918. Ambassador Fletcher reported that the newspaper *El Pueblo* had called for a formal declaration of nonrecognition of the Monroe Doctrine, alliances with powerful nations in Europe and elsewhere, and the negotiation of treaties with Latin American nations to offset the influence of the United States.[24]

By mid-1919, the Mexican press was elaborating in more detail a set of propositions labeled the "Carranza Doctrine" derived from the president's speeches and writings. The major theme was: "Our work of saving the nation has more importance yet that Mexico may be the soul of the rest of the nations that suffer the same evils." As presented in the press, the new doctrine contained the following points:

1. Individuals who go to other nations must conform to the consequences and must not have more guarantees and rights than the nationals have. They must accept the law of the country just as it is. In the words of *El Pueblo*: "No more bayonets, no more cannon, no more dreadnaughts to follow a man who, through commercialism, goes in search of fortune and to exploit the richness of other countries."

2. Little by little all privileges and monopolies must end. Free and universal commerce should prevail, and in like fashion the equality of all peoples wherever they go.

3. The nonrecognition of the Monroe Doctrine in that Mexico does not consent that her foreign and domestic business be subject to the scrutiny and approbation of the United States.

4. The establishment of a real solidarity with other Latin American nations based upon the mutual respect of the independ-

---

Mexico was to participate in the war and recover her "lost territory." De la Huerta said that he, and others, persuaded Carranza to remain neutral; Roberto Guzmán Esparza, ed., *Memorias de Don Adolfo de la Huerta: Según su propio dictado* (México, D.F., 1957), 100–102.

24. Fletcher to Lansing, 30 June 1918, SD 711.12/109.

ence, the territory, the rights, and the interior organization of each country. Absolute nonintervention must be the basis for this solidarity, and these principles must be respected by all nations of the hemisphere.

5. Alliances should be negotiated with European or other countries, and a treaty system with Latin America. The promulgators of the Carranza Doctrine stated that this was a "brotherly" concept which embraced "all aspirations, all nations, and all races."[25]

The most official presentation of the Carranza Doctrine was written in 1919 by Hermila Galindo, in cooperation with Carranza. Entitled *The Carranza Doctrine and the Indo-Latin Rapprochement*, Miss Galindo's book emphasized nationalism, development, and the common aspirations of the underdeveloped world.[26] She described the principal policy of the stronger nations as one of holding dominion over the countries that produced raw materials. The underdeveloped nations had to assert control over their own resources and industrialize if they hoped to achieve "national liberation." Mexico had begun the work of Indo-Latin liberation and thus provided an example to other nations. Although Miss Galindo did not explicitly call for revolutions, she did indicate that liberation involved some internal change, since the ruling classes of many Latin American countries had joined with the imperialists.

The theme of Latin American unity echoed throughout the book, for the works of Manuel Ugarte, José Enrique Rodó, Vargas Vila, and Ruben Darío were cited continually as inspirations for the common task of liberation.[27] Yet Miss Galindo described the conflict between developed and underdeveloped

25. Fletcher, "Memorandum on the Carranza Doctrine," 2 October 1919, SD 711.12/219. The opponents of article 27 at the 1916–17 constitutional convention referred to the Carranza Doctrine; *Diario de los debates,* 792.

26. Hermila Galindo, *La Doctrina Carranza y el acercamiento indolatino* (México, D.F., 1919); filed as SD 812.00/23111c (I have followed the State Department's translation of the title). A translation of the book was sent to Wilson with two letters which Military Intelligence claimed were from Carranza to Miss Galindo; Fletcher to Wilson, 20 August 1919, SD 711.12/192½.

27. In varying degrees, all these writers were critical of the United States. In order they were from Argentina, Uruguay, Colombia, Nicaragua. For a detailed analysis of the ideas see Martin S. Stabb, *In Quest of Identity: Patterns in the Spanish American Essay of Ideas,* 1890–1960 (Chapel Hill, 1967).

nations as worldwide and included an entire chapter on "England in India" to illustrate exploitation outside the hemisphere. She called for a new international system based on nonintervention and internal self-determination. Such a system, however, could be effective only if each weak nation cultivated a strong love of country in its citizens and then presented a common front to the powerful. (Here she attacked socialists, syndicalists, and anarchists for breaking down national loyalties.) The common front was to be an internationalism of the underdeveloped countries based upon a vital nationalism which articulated common aspirations for development and independence.

The policies of the United States were criticized, but the book did not express a vehement anti-Yankeeism. Miss Galindo expressed a rather equivocal attitude toward the United States and even stated that the Latin American nations could commit themselves to some postulates of the Monroe Doctrine if the United States would "guarantee in a real and substantial fashion their independence and sovereignty." She also warned that a Republican victory in the United States would remove the "counterbalancing spirit" of Wilson, even though a few pages before she had stated that Wilson was powerless against the "dollar and trust men."

The book concludes with an exhortation for Latin American unity of purpose to preserve peace by preventing intervention. Common action was required to "constrain the United States to execute a genuine contract," guaranteeing the liberty and interests of these nations. It was hoped that the ideals of the Mexican Revolution would flower in other countries and produce this unity.

Statements of the Carranza Doctrine might vary in their treatment of some details (such as alliances) but all emphasized the question of foreign property and the importance of Mexico's actions for the international relations of the hemisphere. Antonio Manero, a prominent revolutionary publicist, argued in his *Mexico and American Solidarity: The Carranza Doctrine* that the U.S. interpretation of the Monroe Doctrine placed the economic development of Latin America under its control by limiting European capital.[28] Mexico had solved this problem through a formula of

28. Manero, *México y la solidaridad americana: La Doctrina Carranza* (Madrid, 1918).

international law which required the foreigner to assimilate into
the nation. This was the major function of article 27—to end
extraterritorial law. Manero declared that Mexico should cooperate with the United States as long as that country respected
the "absolute sovereignty of national institutions and laws." This
respect would bring a new era of frank cordiality between the
weak and the powerful nations.

The Carranza Doctrine presented a blend of the Calvo Doctrine,
the Drago Doctrine, and Mexican revolutionary nationalism. It
was not a chauvinistic outlook but one which stressed peace and
cooperation with a strong universalist flavor. The doctrine proclaimed the equality of all nations and races and called upon the
developed nations to respect the sovereignty of the underdeveloped
nations. Mexico's call for a new international system constituted
a direct challenge to the industrial-creditor nation concept of
world order. In addition, the United States was asked to give
more than lip service to the ideal of Pan-Americanism. The
leaders of the Mexican Revolution had asserted the principles of
national control over the economy in the constitution of 1917.
Now they proclaimed a doctrine which they believed would protect Mexican revolutionary nationalism by asserting it as a basis
of unity for Latin America and the foundation of a new pattern
of relations between the developed and underdeveloped nations.

The Wilson Administration Interprets
the Mexican Revolution

Early in his first administration President Wilson had declared
that one of the cornerstones of his Latin American policy was to
put an end to revolutions. The Mexican Revolution, however,
turned out to be a different kind of upheaval from the usual *golpe
de estado* which Wilson had in mind. The issues were much
deeper, the fires of national emotion more intense, and Wilson
came to a realization that intervention in such a conflict would
destroy the credibility of his administration's pronouncements
about self-determination. This realization did not stop him from
trying to shape the course of the revolution or the policies of the
revolutionary government, but it did help to create his dilemma
over the methods to be used and the intellectual justification for
such interference in Mexico's internal affairs. Wilson, as most

observers, could hardly deny that the people of Mexico had major grievances ranging from extreme poverty to illiteracy and that some changes were necessary. Díaz and the *científicos* could be faulted for not instituting some reforms, and thus for driving the people to revolution. But the lid had blown and the problem now was one of directing this upheaval into the paths of order, stability, and gradual reform, in order to prevent another revolution.

Wilson once described the philosophy of the French Revolution as "radically evil and corrupting." Such a revolution not only was disorderly but also produced rapid and violent changes in the socioeconomic system. To a man who criticized the "radicalism" of the Socialists and Populists in the United States, revolutionary change was compounded heresy. Firmly rooted in the inherent conservatism of mainstream Anglo-American liberalism, Wilson had no sympathy for fundamental socioeconomic change. Indeed, in his last effort at political writing, entitled "The Road Away from Revolution," he stressed the theme that revolutionary assaults against capitalism threatened civilization and democracy.[29]

The revolutionary leaders refused to accept Wilson's guidance, would not settle down after the elimination of Huerta and become Anglo-American style constitutionalists, and pursued policies which seemed to threaten "legitimate" foreign rights. Under these circumstances, how could the United States insure the proper behavior (play "Big Brother" as Wilson called it) of Mexico without being accused of opposition to the aspirations of the people? The resolution to this intellectual dilemma was provided by two arguments. The first professed sympathy for the downtrodden majority of the people but explained that the revolution had been promoted by demagogues who had no intention of helping them. The second acknowledged, reluctantly in some cases, the "original" ideals of the revolution but charged that the revolution had been betrayed by its leaders, especially Carranza. Secretary Lansing and Senator Fall espoused the first position, and Lansing explained: "It [the revolution] is a conflict between military oligarchies, the great body of the contestants being merely pawns in the game, who will be no better off after the struggle than they were before, no matter

29. For Wilson's political philosophy and views of Socialism and Populism see Henry W. Bragdon, *Woodrow Wilson: The Academic Years* (Cambridge, Mass., 1967), 260–61.

which party is victorious." Senator Fall varied the argument slightly by blaming outside agitators for the "infection" in Mexico.[30]

The "revolution betrayed" argument appealed to the more liberal North Americans, since it enabled them to support reform vocally while attacking the Mexican government. Secretary Houston, George Creel, Boaz Long, and President Wilson took this position and asserted that the Carranza government really did not speak for the people of Mexico.[31] Increasingly, Carranza himself became the focal point for this argument. By mid-1918, Ambassador Fletcher attributed all the problems in U.S.-Mexican relations to the "First Chief."[32] This argument in turn had a peculiar effect on the official perception of events in Mexico. By attributing so much power and influence to Carranza and his government, U.S. officials interpreted all anti-American pronouncements and acts against foreign interests by local and state officials as part of a uniform, centrally directed plot. Such interpretations vastly distorted the actual policies and pronouncements of the Carranza government.[33]

The official U.S. interpretation of the revolution combined both arguments, although the "betrayal" theme predominated. Lansing explained this position to the Five-Power Conference in August 1915 as "that we recognized the right of revolution against injustice and tyranny; that we recognized that the *principle* of the revolution, the *restoration of constitutional government*, had triumphed a year ago; . . . that personal ambition and personal greed were

30. Robert Lansing, "Memorandum: The Mexican Situation, May 4, 1914," SD 812.00/11984½; Fall to F. A. Sommerfeld, 8 July 1913, Fall MSS.

31. Wilson to Lansing, 19 April 1917, SD 711.12/36½; George Creel, *The People Next Door, An Interpretive History of Mexico and the Mexicans* (New York, 1926), 342–47; Houston, *Eight Years with Wilson's Cabinet* 1:118; Long, "Memorandum on the Mexican Situation," 10 August 1918, SD 711.12/130.

32. Fletcher to Polk, 26 June 1918, Polk MSS.

33. Carranza never succeeded in uniting all the states under his control and did not direct the affairs of all newspapers and various generals; E. J. Dillon, *President Obregón: A World Reformer* (Boston, 1923), 161–62. By a decree of 6 January 1915 generals were allowed to put villages into provisional possession of *ejidos,* but the villages often did not wait for this permission; Chester Lloyd Jones and George Wythe, "Economic Conditions in Mexico," report prepared in 1928, SD 812.50/161.

the causes of the factions."[34] The president supported this statement, which reflected his own political philosophy, and told Lansing that the Mexicans should be made to understand clearly what they could and could not do without the concurrence of the U.S. government.[35]

This raises the question of just what specific reforms U.S. officials had in mind when they expressed sympathy for the Mexican people. Most were quite vague, unless they were attacking the policies of Carranza. The few positive prescriptions, besides constitutional government and order, stressed gradualism above all. Secretary Houston wrote that it would take "generations" to bring the Mexican people "very far along the road to self-government and higher living." What they needed, he said, was "a good police force . . . , a system which would give the masses an interest in the land and in their products, an elementary vocational educational system, and an agricultural agency such as our Federal Department." But Houston felt that Villa's agrarian program could not be carried out without "grave trouble," and that if the people were given an interest in the land they would probably "make little use of their opportunities."[36] Lansing agreed with this argument, and cited the "general improvidence of the Mexican Indians," caused by "natural traits, environment and lack of education," as the reason why land reform was not expedient. Secretary Lane granted that Mexico needed a few reforms such as a land tax system and agricultural schools. Boaz Long doubted that anything could be accomplished by giving more income to the peons, since they were "naturally lazy" and inclined to dissipation. The peons did need a "certain amount of religious form or belief," however, to hold them "in check."[37] But these officials could be very specific about the policies they disliked; at the top of the list were those which asserted national control of the economy and an independent position in international relations.

34. *Lansing Papers* 2:543; italics added.
35. Ibid., 545.
36. Houston, *Eight Years with Wilson's Cabinet* 1:79, 117.
37. Lansing, "Memorandum: The Mexican Situation, May 4, 1914," SD 812.00/11984½; Lane, "The President's Mexican Policy," 16 July 1916, Lane MSS; Long, "Memorandum on the Mexican Situation," 10 August 1918, SD 711.12/130.

George Creel wrote that the culmination of Carranza's insolence and hatred came with the attempt (1918) to implement article 27 and confiscate U.S.-owned oil properties. In a long hymn of nostalgia for the good old days when Mexicans lived up to the motto "Respect for foreign rights constitutes peace," Boaz Long attacked the idea of "Mexico for the Mexicans." The "wildcat Constitution" of 1917, he argued, was part of a plot to destroy the economy of the United States. Ambassador Fletcher made a similar observation when he reported that the "radical anti-capitalistic" proclivities of the revolutionary party were synonymous with an anti-British and anti-American position.[38]

The official U.S. concern over confiscation had become almost paranoid by late 1916, and almost every action of the Mexican government dealing with taxation or regulation was denounced as such. For example, during the Joint Commission conference the American commissioners and State Department personnel were referring to the proposed new Mexican constitution as confiscatory. In point of fact, they were denouncing the constitution of 1857 (which U.S. officials later would praise in ritual fashion), since the famous revised article 27 was not even written until late in January 1917, and Carranza's draft constitution only slightly revised the 1857 document.[39] Of course, U.S. oil and mining interests were also denouncing the radical provisions of the "new constitution" and sending memorandums on the subject to the State Department and the American Commissioners.[40] One such

38. Long, "Memorandum on the Mexican Situation," 10 August 1918, SD 711.12/130; Fletcher to Secretary of State, 23 April 1917, SD 712.41/1; Creel, *People Next Door,* 345–47. In Juárez's original motto the word *ajeno* (other) was used instead of "foreign."

39. Morton, "Mexican Constitutional Congress of 1916–1917," 13, 16, 20–21. Long wrote that Carranza "abrogated a good Constitution and forced on Mexico a radical one." "Memorandum on the Mexican Situation," 10 August 1918, SD 711.12/130.

40. Frederic R. Kellogg, "Memorandum concerning the New Proposed Constitution of Mexico, December 26, 1916," SD 812.011/4; sent to members of the American-Mexican Joint Commission and based on a memorandum of 19 November 1916 written by Delbert J. Haff, Chandler P. Anderson, and Kellogg. The U.S. commissioners referred to information submitted through "official and other channels"; Lane, Gray, Mott to Wilson, 3 January 1917, SD 812.00/24325. Contacts between the interest groups and the American members of the Joint Commission are mentioned in Anderson Diary, 15 November and 29 December 1916, Chandler P. Anderson Papers, Library of Congress.

memorandum, drafted by Chandler P. Anderson, Frederic Kellogg, and Judge Delbert J. Haff, stated that the draft of the new constitution confirmed all their fears concerning radicalism and confiscation. They specifically cited articles 27, 28, and 33; the last two were derived almost word for word from the constitution of 1857. The Mexican regulatory efforts had been judged and convicted in advance.[41]

In a similar fashion, U.S. officials considered Mexico's neutrality during the war and the assertion of an independent diplomatic position in the hemisphere to be unfriendly acts. Ambassador Fletcher was quite candid about the criteria for "unfriendly" acts in Latin America:

In the fear of the gradual extension of this American influence in Mexico, I think, will be found the master-key of Mexico's present attitude in the great world war. . . .

I am convinced that President Carranza—and this means Mexico today—desires correct rather than cordial relations with the United States, and hopes to find in the victory or non-defeat of Germany in the great war, a defense or counterbalance of the moral and economic influence of the United States in Mexico.[42]

If resisting the growing U.S. influence in Mexico was considered unfriendly, the Carranza Doctrine was seen as a major threat to the United States. Fletcher described it as the "international program" of the Mexican government, although he did not think of the label "Carranzaism," and warned:

The so-called Carranza doctrine is to replace the Monroe Doctrine. The hegemony of the United States on this continent is to pass away, and our trade and influence must pass with it; presumably to be replaced by things German, or at any rate Latin

41. From 1913 the oilmen declared that almost every regulatory and tax measure of the Mexican government was confiscatory. In 1938 Mexico finally accommodated them by expropriating most of the foreign companies. See Mexican Petroleum Co., Ltd., to William Jennings Bryan, 18 December 1913, Moore MSS, and the numerous letters in the SD 812.6363 file during 1914 and 1915. Anderson was a prominent international lawyer, and served as State Department counselor from 1910 to 1913, and as legal adviser for American embassies and legations in Europe during 1914–15. Kellogg was an attorney for the Huasteca Petroleum Co.; Haff represented the Maritime Petroleum Co. and the Kansas City, Mexico, and Orient Railroad.

42. Fletcher to Secretary of State, 13 March 1918, Fletcher MSS.

America is to break away from Pan-Americanism and the United States.[43]

Fear of German "commercial, economic, and political exploitation after the war" was involved in official U.S. calculations. But fear that Mexico, and perhaps Latin America, would assert an independent position was just as important, perhaps even more so. Fletcher downgraded the role of German influence in Mexican policies, and frankly acknowledged the indigenous nature of these policies and ideas. "The least connection possible between Mexico and the United States is his [Carranza's] idea," the ambassador reported in June 1918, "and his official newspaper [*El Pueblo*] is preaching economic, financial, and diplomatic—every sort of independence of the United States."[44]

Mexican resistance to the influence and guidance of the "Big Brother" north of the Rio Bravo sometimes revealed the elitist, and even racist, side of big-power paternalism. Wilson labeled Carranza a "pedantic ass," because the "First Chief" would not accept his version of U.S.-Mexican relations. To Boaz Long, the Mexican leaders were "an improvident lot of politicians" who were incapable of running a government "according to our standard."[45] By 1919, the rhetoric of paternalism had become more edgy and Congressman Fiorello H. La Guardia declared: "Yes; I would go down with beans in one hand and offer help to the Mexican people, but I would be sure to have hand grenades in the other hand, and God help them in case they do not accept our well-intended and sincere friendship."[46] Franklin K. Lane complained to Lansing: "I wish that you could be given a free hand in this matter [Mexico]. I know it would be a stiff hand, an authoritative hand, and that is what these people need. They are naughty children who are exercising all the privileges and rights of grown ups." Indeed, Lane complained that the Mexicans be-

43. Fletcher to Polk, 26 June 1918, Polk MSS; Fletcher to Lansing, 3 July 1918, SD 711.12/116. Fletcher called article 27 the basic element in the doctrine and stated that it was the "international program of this government."

44. Fletcher to Polk, 26 June 1918, Polk MSS. See also Fletcher to Secretary of State, 30 March 1917, SD 711.12/36, and Wilson's approval of his analysis, Wilson to Lansing, 19 April 1917, SD 711.12/36½.

45. Wilson to Lansing, 19 April 1917, SD 711.12/36½; Long, "Memorandum on the Mexican Situation," 10 August 1918, SD 711.12/130.

46. *Congressional Record,* 66th Cong., 1st sess., 1919, 58, pt. 3:2421.

lieved in the words of Thomas Jefferson (equality of men), Karl Marx ("private property is robbery"), and Woodrow Wilson (self-determination).[47] In a sense Lane was correct; the underdeveloped countries were beginning to assert some of the principles which they found in the intellectual heritage of the developed nations. The industrial-creditor powers had had an impact which they did not expect.

A Note on American Property Losses

The severe property losses sustained by Americans in Mexico helped to shape the attitudes of U.S. officials in regard to the revolution in general and to the Carranza government in particular. Undoubtedly some of the losses produced hardships and suffering, and the emotional impact tended to carry over to almost all other property cases.

Property losses can be divided into two categories. One was the direct result of civil war. During the fighting, farms, ranches, mines, and businesses suffered physical destruction. The attacks on property by bandits and the unofficial taxes levied by some generals could also be attributed to the chaos of civil war. The second category was the result of actions of the Mexican government such as failure to pay interest on the foreign debt and the seizure of gold and silver from private banks.

It is impossible to make an accurate estimate of all these losses. An exaggerated index can be found in the claims submitted to the two U.S.-Mexican claims commissions. By 1931, these claims were listed as $759,852,662. This did not include the unpaid interest on the foreign debt, which was listed in 1922 as $200 million.[48]

The two governments took rather different approaches to the question of property losses. Officially the U.S. government did not differentiate between the types of loss and simply held the Carranza administration responsible for all. According to this view, all Americans in Mexico were there by "invitation" of the government and entitled to prompt and effective compensation.

47. Lane to Lansing, 1 December 1919, SD 711.12/224½.

48. Draft of the Agreement between the Mexican Minister of Finance and the International Committee, 16 June 1922, SD 812.51/775; see also A. H. Feller, *The Mexican Claims Commissions, 1923–1934* (New York, 1935), 60–68.

The Mexican government maintained that a state could incur no liability under international law for the acts of revolutionary forces other than the one which formed the new government. In addition, the government asserted that Americans caught in the turmoil of civil war were not entitled to special treatment. Carranza was willing to negotiate a settlement for property losses, but only after internal stability had been restored and Mexico's economy had revived. U.S. officials interpreted this position as an unwillingness on the part of the Mexican government to meet its "international obligations."[49]

49. In the Special Claims Convention of 1923 the Mexican government accepted responsibility for acts of all revolutionary forces; Feller, *Mexican Claims Commissions,* 21–23.

5 Keeping Mexico Quiet 1917-1918

During the war my job was to keep Mexico quiet, and it was done.
—Ambassador Fletcher, 1918

Policies and Interest Groups

Ambassador Henry P. Fletcher departed for Mexico in February 1917, after a discussion with Colonel House concerning the president's policy. House had stressed the theme that Fletcher must "do everything possible to avoid a break with Carranza."[1] Europe had first priority—especially after the United States entered the war in April—and the ambassador noted: "During the war my job was to keep Mexico quiet, and it was done." As he explained to Martin Egan of J. P. Morgan and Company, his job was to improve relations if possible, but to defer consideration of the "main question" until the war was over. The question referred to was the possible impact of article 27 on U.S. investments.[2] As part of the effort to improve relations the Wilson administration also tried to convince the Mexican government that it would be wise either to break relations with Germany or follow a pro-Allied type of neutrality. Colonel House informed the Mexicans that they could "not play safe except by playing with us."[3]

The general policy of "keeping Mexico quiet" was complicated by Mexico's neutrality and the problems this raised con-

---

1. House Diary, 4 February 1917, House MSS.
2. Fletcher to Polk, 3 December 1918, Polk MSS; Egan to Arthur Anderson, late July or early August 1917 (internal evidence and file location indicate this approximate date), Lamont MSS. Martin Egan, a partner in J. P. Morgan and Company, was in charge of Mexican affairs.
3. House Diary, 4 October 1917, House MSS.

cerning the stationing of Allied warships in Mexican ports. The Mexican government did object to such a breach of neutrality, and Secretary Lansing admitted that Mexico was "technically" correct. But he argued that the United States "from a practical point of view" could not withdraw protection from the oil wells even if this might result in war with Mexico. Wilson replied that the United States could not afford to be "too practical," since it was the champion of the "right of self-government and of political independence everywhere." He did not eliminate the possibility that the United States might have to take control of Tampico and the Tehuantepec railroad, but he believed that the oil fields could be protected without war. The president noted that all the larger U.S. ships "lie, of necessity, beyond the three mile limit," and that British influences controlled Tampico (and possibly Tehuantepec). He concluded: "There is absolutely no breach of the Monroe Doctrine in allowing the British to exercise an influence there which anti-American sentiment in Mexico for the time prevents our exercising."[4] The Mexican government continued to object but did not force the issue.

British diplomats, however, were urging a strong stand by their government to protest the seizure of British-owned railroads and other properties. Some even suggested a total break in relations with Mexico, and Fletcher asked Lansing to take steps to prevent such a rupture. The United States would then have to look after British interests and "become doubly unpopular."[5] The British did agree to cooperate with the policy of postponing property issues until after the war.

With the general policy guidelines set, Wilson and Lansing devoted their attention increasingly to the war. This meant that most of the problems stemming from Mexico's policies were handled by Frank Polk, Ambassador Fletcher, and Boaz Long.[6] These men were not in complete sympathy with the president's guidelines and sometimes became impatient with the restraints

4. Lansing to Wilson, 18 April 1917; Wilson to Lansing, 19 April 1917, SD 711.12/43a. For Mexican protests see *Labor internacional,* 413–20.
5. "Memorandum: From the British Embassy to Mr. Polk," 23 April 1917, SD 812.00/24735; Fletcher to Secretary of State, 23 April 1917, SD 712.41/1. Britain had not recognized the Carranza government but had maintained limited diplomatic contact with Mexico.
6. James R. Garfield noted, "Lansing pays no attention to Mexico. He leaves it entirely to Polk." Garfield Diary, 21 June 1918, Garfield MSS; see also Anderson Diary, 8 September 1917, Anderson MSS.

imposed by wartime strategy. They were not hardline interventionists, however, and for the most part they resisted pressures for measures which might lead to "forceful action" (the latter would have to receive the president's permission). Leon Canova was an interventionist and later in 1917 gave some encouragement to groups planning a counterrevolution. Lansing reacted angrily when he learned of Canova's contacts, and the latter's gamble at instant prestige failed.[7] The State Department did not want to see the renewal of warfare in Mexico, and even Senator Fall hastened to dissociate himself from the intrigues of some of his friends.[8]

Late in 1916 the representatives of various oil, mining, and landowning corporations formed a united front in order to present their position more efficiently to both the U.S. and Mexican governments. Frederic R. Kellogg, Frederic N. Watriss, Harold Walker, and Chandler P. Anderson handled most of the contact work for the combined groups.[9] These attorneys counted as personal friends several ranking State Department officials. Polk and Watriss had been law partners, and "Freddie" Watriss also dealt with Fletcher on a first-name basis. Anderson regularly visited his old friends Bert Lansing and Frank Polk and was allowed to see, and make extracts from, State Department communications. The briefs and memorandums prepared by these attorneys were regularly sent to Fletcher and sometimes were incorporated into the formal notes which the department sent to the Mexican government. In some cases, Polk and Lansing even requested these representatives to write the protest notes for the department. The rapport between the State Department officials and the attorneys for the interest groups was illustrated by Polk's letter to Fletcher introducing Judge Haff. Polk wrote: "He is a friend of Chandler Anderson's and a very responsible man in every way."[10]

7. Anderson Diary, 3 October, 6, 20 December 1917. Canova told Anderson about his involvement.

8. For details about one such intrigue see Charles F. Hunt to General Francisco Villa, 17 January 1917; Fall to Hunt, 21 February 1917; Fall to Lansing, 12 March 1917, Fall MSS.

9. Watriss to Polk, 21 November 1916, Polk MSS. Watriss was an attorney for the John Hays Hammond interests (land and mining companies); Walker represented the Doheny oil interests. John Bassett Moore did some legal work for these groups but did not actively participate in the lobby activities.

10. Polk to Fletcher, 8 October 1917, Polk MSS.

State Department officials and the corporate representatives agreed concerning the basic goals of protecting foreign property, but the interest groups wanted to adhere to a tough line in spite of the war. They focused their efforts on changing Mexico's policies and tried to cajole or pressure the State Department into a more forceful defense of their interests. Department officials generally sympathized with the fears of the interest groups, but they had to work within the administration's established guidelines.[11] Anderson considered these to be based on "timidity and feebleness" and argued, as did his colleagues, that if Carranza were confronted with a hardline demand to settle the question of guaranteeing foreign investments once and for all he would capitulate without a conflict.[12] Wilson and Lansing had decided in 1916 that the United States could not afford to take such a risk, and the Zimmermann telegram reinforced this decision. In the event of a conflict with the United States, Mexico could now count on some outside aid, and Germany, after the U.S. entry in the European war, would have nothing to lose from such involvement.[13] Thus the corporate representatives pushed a variety of tactics which they hoped might achieve the desired ends by less direct means.

11. For attitudes of officials see, Polk to Watriss, 26 December 1917, Polk MSS; Fletcher to Secretary of State, 23 April 1917, SD 712.41/1; Anderson Diary, 3 October 1917, Anderson MSS: Anderson noted that Polk said that he was inclined to take a "vigorous stand" against the destruction of private rights but that "forceful action" was not possible without instructions from the president.

12. Anderson Diary, 3 January, 8 March 1917, Anderson MSS; Anderson, "Draft Memorandum on the Mexican Situation sent to Mr. Frederic Kellogg and Mr. Loeb," 24 May 1917, ibid.; William Loeb represented the American Smelting and Refining Company.

13. Lansing to Edward N. Smith, 3 March 1917, Lansing MSS; Fletcher to Secretary of State, 30 March 1917, SD 711.12/36. The Zimmermann telegram was sent to the German ambassador to Mexico on 19 January 1917 (it was intercepted by the British, decoded, and sent to the U.S. government on 24 February). If the United States went to war with Germany, Foreign Secretary Zimmermann proposed an alliance between Germany and Mexico which would include the latter's recovery of Texas, New Mexico, and Arizona. The offer was renewed in May 1917, but Carranza stated that he would observe a policy of strict neutrality. See Arthur S. Link, *Wilson: Campaigns for Progressivism and Peace, 1916–1917* (Princeton, 1965), 342–43, and the appendix in which Link discusses Fredrich Katz's book *Deutschland, Diaz und die mexikanische Revolution, die deutsche Politik in Mexiko, 1870–1920* (Berlin, 1964).

They did not, however, completely abandon the hope that the administration could be pressured into a showdown with Carranza. When Wilson extended *de jure* recognition to the Mexican government in September 1917, several attorneys wanted to organize a publicity bureau to stir public opinion in an attempt to force a stiffer approach. Anderson finally convinced them that this was not a wise move. He noted in his diary that such a move would not have any effect on Wilson and that it would invite reprisals from the Mexican government. In addition, it would disrupt the interest groups' relations with the State Department and destroy Anderson's usefulness as a contact.[14] The issue came up again in December 1918, when the newly organized National Association for the Protection of American Rights in Mexico insinuated that the State Department had suppressed the facts about the oil situation. Polk chided his friends for trying to hamper the State Department's diplomatic efforts by fighting the issue in the press.[15]

In October 1917, Anderson thought that he had an indirect method of creating the desired pressure. He told Thomas W. Lamont that he wanted J. P. Morgan and Company to organize the bankers of the country and with "one voice" inform President Wilson that the bankers would refuse to cooperate in the Liberty Loan program until "he straightened out this Mexican situation."[16] Lamont refused to cooperate and the scheme died.

The war brought numerous businessmen into the executive branch of the government, and these dollar-a-year men tended to support the position of the interest groups. In some cases they even continued to wear both hats. Chandler Anderson became a counsel on international questions for the War Industries Board in November 1917 (serving until January 1919), and Frederick Proctor served as a legal adviser to the attorney general while retaining the same position with the Gulf Refining Company. This situation worried Colonel House. He had dinner one evening

14. Anderson Diary, 11, 20 September 1917, Anderson MSS. Polk and Lansing expressed their strong objections to such publicity activities.
15. Watriss to Polk, 31 December 1918; Polk to Watriss, 13 January 1919, Polk MSS.
16. Lamont to Egan, 17 October 1917. See also Egan to Lamont, 15 October 1917, Lamont MSS; Anderson Diary, 16 October 1917, Anderson MSS.

with Proctor and Attorney General Thomas W. Gregory, and after hearing the former lament for two hours about the fate of the oil companies in Mexico, House noted that, although Proctor had no "sinister purpose," it would be better for both Gregory and him "if the connection was severed."[17] In August 1918, when the oilmen thought they could gain administration support for a hard line, Judge Proctor was one of the representatives for the oil companies in their talks with Wilson's advisers. During the official consideration of the companies' proposals, Josephus Daniels noted that Mark Requa, general director of the Oil Division of the U.S. Fuel Administration, and Harry A. Garfield, U.S. Fuel Administrator, "seemed to lean toward the oil men." Both were dollar-a-year men, and Garfield was the brother of the other oil company representative, James R. Garfield. Daniels and Bernard Baruch opposed the proposals, which would have amounted to a declaration of war on Mexico.[18]

Baruch's opposition underlined a significant weakness in the position of the interest groups: leading businessmen did not uniformly support a hardline policy. The New York bankers refused to back this approach. Thomas Lamont expressed his agreement with Martin Egan's conclusions concerning the Anderson–Liberty Loan scheme: "If we are to have any part in such matters my judgment is that it should be 'with' the administration and in full understanding of what is being done all the time. The State Department has been both friendly and candid as to Mexico and I believe we are bound to keep out of any movements."[19]

State Department officials wanted to protect foreign property in Mexico and substantially modify the nationalistic impulses of the revolution. They wholeheartedly agreed with the principles of the interest-group attorneys, but the policy of keeping Mexico

17. House Diary, 23 May 1917, House MSS. Colonel House also feared that Ambassador Fletcher would push the oil companies' viewpoint because "Fletcher's affiliations have been largely with great wealth." House Diary, 18 July 1917, ibid.

18. E. David Cronon, *The Cabinet Diaries of Josephus Daniels, 1913–1921* (Lincoln, Neb., 1963), 328, 9 August 1918.

19. Lamont to Egan, 17 October 1917, Lamont MSS. Anderson noted in May 1917 that the movement for unity among the interest groups had been temporarily suspended because many "of our people were afraid that the Mexican government would penalize them in some way if they were thought to be organizing a protective association." Anderson Diary, 16 May 1917, Anderson MSS.

quiet meant that they would have to work with the Carranza government for the duration of the war. What would they do if the Mexican government tried to implement any policies which seemed, to U.S. officials and businessmen, to pose the threat of some degree of national concern over resources, that is, any apparent step in the direction of implementing article 27? Officially, U.S. policy was to meet these issues "when they arise" and not to "force an issue on these questions."[20] In actual practice U.S. officials did not pursue just a reactive kind of policy but tried in various ways to eliminate in advance any threat of national control. Both tactics, however, rejected the validity of important sections of the constitution of 1917, and implied some U.S. influence over Mexico's internal policies. This opposition to Mexican ambitions and policies complicated the job of keeping Mexico quiet and generally friendly. Indeed, the rather paranoid quality of suspicious sensitivity which produced an almost automatic adverse reaction to Mexican regulatory measures could be called the article 27 syndrome.

There were three possible approaches to obtaining some guarantee, commitment, or pledge from the Mexican government concerning the sanctity of foreign interests. One was the "forceful" method which would employ a firm demand, or ultimatum, backed by the implied threat of military action or severe economic reprisal. The interest-group attorneys and their clients favored this approach. Another stressed coaxing the Carranza government into the desired relationship by offering in advance some diplomatic and economic concessions. In practice most of these concessions turned out to be the relaxation of earlier restrictions, but friendship was publicly expressed and the factor of pressure was minimized. Ambassador Fletcher generally stressed this method until mid-1918. Wilson and Lansing supported him; Polk and Long had strong reservations; and the corporation attorneys considered it soft. The third approach was one of using the problems and needs of the Mexican government to maneuver it into the desired commitment as the price for U.S. assistance or concessions. It was not as blunt and demanding as the first, yet it was more direct and forceful than the second. And it provided the common ground for State Department–interest-group collaboration, since it stipu-

20. Lansing to Fletcher, 28 April 1917, *Lansing Papers*, 2:567.

lated a price, and a written agreement, for any relaxation of U.S. restrictions. Officials and lobbyists might argue about effective tactics, but the basic question of guarantees for foreign investments would be injected into almost every issue in U.S.-Mexican relations.

Arms, Oil, and General Pelaez

In 1917 the U.S. government still retained the embargo on shipments of arms and ammunition to Mexico and urged other governments to cooperate. In May the Mexicans tried to purchase arms from Japan, and the British, at the suggestion of the State Department, requested the Japanese to uphold the embargo. They agreed to "cooperate fully."[21] Just prior to the imposition of the embargo, the Mexican government had paid the Encinal Mercantile Company (Encinal, Tex.) for several million rounds of ammunition which had not been delivered. In June, General Pablo Gonzales told Ambassador Fletcher that he hoped the U.S. government might permit Mexico to receive this ammunition. During their discussion, the ambassador focused his attention on the acts and decrees of the government and certain provisions of the new constitution which had created "an unfortunate impression in financial, business, and religious circles in the United States." Gonzales made a strong appeal for good relations between the countries and stressed his own pro-U.S. views. Fletcher recommended the release of five million rounds of ammunition, since he was convinced that such action would enable the Mexican government to pacify the country, thus preventing conditions which could seriously interfere with the concentration of U.S. efforts in Europe.[22]

President Wilson approved the ammunition release but the State Department delayed the implementation. When, in response to letters from Congressman John N. Garner of Texas and the owners of the Encinal Mercantile Company, Wilson inquired about the delay, Polk replied that the department had been concerned with the problem of "how it was best to use this concession in order to gain the greatest advantage in our dealings with the Mexicans." Polk also stated that Fletcher originally recommended

21. British Embassy (Washington) to State Department, 19 May 1917, SD 712.94/24.
22. Fletcher to Lansing, 3 June 1917, SD 711.12/49; Fletcher to Lansing, 5 June 1917, Fletcher MSS.

the negotiation of an agreement ("covering questions now being discussed"), but now believed that the United States could gain more without making conditions than by trying to "drive a bargain for definite concessions."[23] Polk was trying to hide the debate within the department. In actual fact, the idea of a definite agreement was probably Polk's, with the concurrence of Lansing. Chandler Anderson suggested that conditions be imposed on Carranza, and, according to Anderson, both Polk and Lansing concurred. Counselor Polk told Anderson that Fletcher had recommended the release without conditions and several weeks later indicated that he had finally been persuaded to this view by the ambassador and Major Frank R. McCoy, the former Military Attaché in Mexico City. The date of this conversation coincided with the president's inquiry about the delay. Anderson, of course, became rather perturbed at Fletcher's attitude and told Polk that Carranza should be forced to conciliate the United States.[24]

Fletcher's actions concerning the export tax on oil reinforced Anderson's evaluation of the ambassador's "unsafe" advice. By a decree of 13 April 1917 the Mexican government levied an export tax (10 percent of value at port of shipment) on all petroleum products. The representatives of the oil companies informed the State Department that the tax was not only illegal—since all the foreign companies had obtained concessions prior to 1910 which exempted them from such taxes for differing periods—but "excessive beyond the point of being confiscatory."[25] Some in the State Department agreed with this evaluation, and Fletcher was instructed to discuss the tax issue with Carranza and urge the revocation of the decree.[26]

Fletcher, however, requested a reconsideration of these instructions, since "representations along these lines at this time will

23. Wilson to Polk, 9 July 1917; Polk to Wilson, 12 July 1917, Polk MSS.

24. Anderson Diary, 13 June, 9 July 1917, Anderson MSS. Fletcher's recommendation described the ammunition release as "a first step towards an understanding," Fletcher to Lansing, 3 June 1917, SD 711.12/49. A note from R. Hill, Office of the Counselor, to Polk urged that a *"quid pro quo"* be demanded; 6 June 1917, SD 711.12/50.

25. "Memorandum on Export Tax, May 5, 1917," enclosed in Harold Walker to Polk, 7 May 1917, SD 812.6363/286.

26. R. Hill to Gordon Auchincloss, 12 June 1917, SD 812.011/53; this evaluation of the illegality of the tax sent at the direction of Polk; Fletcher to Lansing, 7 June 1917, SD 812.011/49.

prove fruitless and possibly harmful." The ambassador further
noted that the Mexican government needed revenue and that
taxes on foreign oil and mining interests were "popular." Colonel
House supported Fletcher and observed: "The war had caused a
phenomenal advance in the price of oil, and yet they [British and
American oil companies] would have us go to war with Mexico
rather than allow that government to collect a reasonable tax.
The Mexican government has to live, and it cannot live without
taxes."[27]

Chandler Anderson prepared draft instructions protesting the
tax, and Polk said that these would be sent to Mexico if Fletcher
approved (the ambassador returned to Washington early in July).
Anderson then conferred with Fletcher and thought that they
agreed on the note with a few clarifications to be added. The
attorney soon began to suspect that the ambassador was "working
behind the scenes" to revise the note or prevent its delivery.[28] This
was indeed the case. The department did not send Anderson's
instructions but instead sent a note suggesting that the oil companies pay the taxes "under protest," while reserving the U.S.
government's right to protest in the future. When Harold Walker
notified Anderson about this change, the latter phoned Gordon
Auchincloss at the State Department and requested him to telegraph Mexico City in order to withdraw the instructions. Auchincloss said that he would comply if Polk approved.[29] The next day
Anderson held a private party at the Metropolitan Club so that
Ambassador Fletcher could meet the representatives of the "most
important American interests" in Mexico. They were not too
happy with the ambassador's policy discussion, and Anderson had
a "sharp exchange" with him about the tax instruction.[30] In spite
of their efforts, Anderson and his colleagues did not succeed in
forcing a showdown on the tax issue.

The State Department, however, did not object—it even gave
quiet support—to the private "diplomacy" of the oil companies.
This involved the payment of funds to General Manuel Pelaez,
an opponent of Carranza with property interests in the oil region.

27. House Diary, 18 July 1917, House MSS; Fletcher to Lansing, 7
June 1917, SD 812.011/49.
28. Anderson Diary, 7, 12 July 1917, Anderson MSS.
29. Ibid., 16 July 1917.
30. Ibid., 17 July 1917.

Pelaez had controlled the greater part of the oil fields around Tampico since May 1914, and in order to sustain his irregular forces he began, in February 1916, to demand cash payments from the foreign oil companies. The representatives of these companies would later claim that this payment was purely a forced "tribute," to prevent Pelaez from destroying the wells, and had nothing to do with positive support of a counterrevolutionary force. In reality, the companies were rather enthusiastic about the situation, and British embassy officials agreed with their evaluation.[31] Harold Walker, of the Doheny interests, informed the department in April 1917 that General Pelaez protected and assisted the American companies. When the tribute was increased later in the year, Walker reported that this did not worry the companies very much. He noted: "The whole field is now in the hands of an interested protector, who has diligently expelled anyone who 'habla en la garganta,' in other words, who is German, Austrian, or Swede. It is an anomalous situation, but in every way a situation which should be preserved."[32]

The State Department did not "officially" instruct the oil companies in regard to the Pelaez situation, but evidence exists of some indirect aid and encouragement. In August 1917 Walker wrote to Lansing: "The permission given to the Mexico City de facto government to import 2,700,000 cartridges has necessitated some jungle diplomacy to appease Pelaez, in which Mr. Auchincloss has kindly assisted us." The department did not discourage the financial support of Pelaez, and Boaz Long believed that the general blocked possible confiscation by Carranza. Walker told Polk that the State Department in February 1916 had advised the oil companies to pay the tribute, but he denied the charge that the Huasteca Petroleum Company supplied Pelaez with arms. Walker did mention that in February 1917 pressure was brought to bear on the company "from important sources" to ship rifles

31. Claude Dawson (consul in Tampico) to Secretary of State, 11 August 1916, SD 812.6363/245, reported that Pelaez would like to have an "understanding" with the U.S. government under which he would protect foreign oil properties in return for arms; Dawson recommended such a step. Extensive discussions of the Pelaez situation with Lansing and Thomas Hohler of the British embassy are reported in Anderson Diary, 11 March, 13, 30 April 1917, Anderson MSS.

32. Harold Walker to Gordon Auchincloss, 9 September 1917, SD 812.6363/312; Walker, "Memorandum: Fuel Oil Need and Supply for the War," 18 April 1917, SD 812.6363/296.

and cartridges to Pelaez. Huasteca opposed this action, he said, and would not engage in such activities without the request and consent of the State Department. Chandler Anderson, however, noted in his diary that Lansing told him the U.S. government would not prosecute anyone who supplied arms and ammunition to Pelaez.[33]

The commander of the U.S.S. *Annapolis* considered Pelaez to be a puppet of the oil companies and reported that his "army" consisted of oil field employees.[34] This evaluation oversimplified the situation, but a strong pattern of mutual dependency did exist. On one occasion an official of the Pelaez force objected to William Green's having contact with the Mexican army; Green, who was in charge of the Huasteca Petroleum Company facilities around Tampico reported: "I told my dear friend Pancho a few truths that were good for his soul, finishing up by pointing out that the very bread in his belly was being furnished by this company." The officer dropped his objections and gave Green a travel pass, with instructions that everyone in the auto was to be shot if more than the original number returned from the army camp.[35]

Such was the "anomalous situation" around Tampico which prevailed until 1920. And it provided another complicating factor in U.S.-Mexican relations, since Carranza considered such support for Pelaez to be a deliberate policy of encouraging counter-revolution. Although most State Department officials did not agree with this interpretation, Carranza did have some logic in his argument that financial support of antigovernment forces by U.S. interests constituted hostile action. (The double standard involved in the official U.S. view became quite apparent when U.S. officials angrily reacted to rumors of Mexican support for the IWW and

33. Walker to Lansing, 7 August 1917, SD 812.6363/303; Walker to Polk, 5 November 1917, SD 812.00/21457; Anderson Diary, 10 March 1917, Anderson MSS. Supplement no. 2 to Boaz Long Memorandum on Mexican Relations, 12 December 1919, SD 711.12/229½. Bonillas (Mexican ambassador to the United States) assured Polk that his government had no intention of conducting a campaign against Pelaez; Polk to Fletcher, 20 November 1917, Polk MSS. By September 1917, Pelaez was receiving about $50,000 per month. El Aguila and Penn-Mex (Doheny) paid $20,000 each, and the smaller companies paid lesser amounts; Walker to George Marvin, 9 September 1917, enclosed in Walker to Auchincloss, 9 September 1917, SD 812.6363/312.

34. U.S.S. *Annapolis* to Opnav, 12 November 1917, SD 812.6363/319.

35. William Green to George Paddleford, 12 February 1918, brought to the State Department by Harold Walker, SD 812.6363/389.

other "radical" groups in their own country.)[36] The Mexican government, during 1917–18, received numerous reports from private detectives in the United States—who had been employed to obtain intelligence about counterrevolutionary activities—showing the connections between Pelaez, the Felicistas movement (the Felix Díaz junta in New York), and various oil companies. Some of this evidence was circumstantial, but enough of it was either direct (signed agreements) or confirmed by other sources to justify support for the charges levied by Mexican officials.[37]

De Jure Recognition and Diplomatic Pressure

The representatives of U.S. corporate interests in Mexico and State Department officials objected to the provisions of the constitution of 1917 which affected foreigners and foreign property. They cooperated in several endeavors aimed at eliminating or substantially modifying these offensive articles.

During January 1917 the corporate groups tried direct pressure in Mexico. John Bassett Moore and Frederic R. Kellogg prepared an extensive legal brief concerning the treatment of foreign property, which was presented to Luis Cabrera. The attorneys bluntly stated that the Mexican government was not free "to change its economic or social ideals so far as the existing properties of foreigners are concerned without the repudiation of his [Carranza's] solemn promises." Such repudiation, they warned, would lead to the diplomatic and economic isolation of Mexico and, finally, to armed intervention. Any attempt to implement socialism "with explosive suddenness" would lead to the possible destruction of Mexico.[38] In addition, the corporations even tried to lobby at the constitutional convention in Querétaro. E. L. Doheny (Huasteca Petroleum) told his agent, R. E. Philippi, to work with Rafael Curiel (a delegate to the convention) and to cooperate

36. Draft letter, Lansing to Wilson, prepared by Boaz Long and enclosed in Long to Lansing, 7 December 1919, SD 711.12/228½.
37. Many of these reports were signed by Charles Jones. The detective agency employed Mexican-Americans to infiltrate the exile groups. See Copy of agreement between Herbert J. Carr (El Aguila Petroleum Co.) and Ignacio Pelaez; Juan Vegas (chief of the Consular Department) to Secretaría de Gobernación, 11 September 1918; all material in SREM, 837R, Leg. 12.
38. "Memorandum as to the Results of the Adoption by Mexico of an Anti-Foreign Policy," 18 January 1917, Moore MSS.

with the representatives of El Aguila (Lord Cowdrey's company) and ASARCO (American Smelting and Refining Company).[39] These efforts to modify the articles dealing with foreign property failed.

In cooperation with the corporation attorneys, the State Department also objected to the proposed articles. On 22 January 1917 (article 27 was submitted to the convention on 29 January) the department formally objected to articles 27, 28, and 33 (paragraphs 1, 2, and 3). The Mexican government was informed that these articles "seem to indicate a proposed policy toward foreigners which is fraught with possible grave consequences affecting the commercial and political relations of Mexico with other nations." In conclusion, the note stated that the U.S. government "can not . . . acquiesce in any direct or indirect confiscation of foreign owned properties in Mexico." This note was based upon the Kellogg-Anderson memorandum of 26 December 1916 and utilized the same arguments and terminology.[40]

Since the Mexican government ignored these official and unofficial protests and did not change the constitution, U.S. officials and businessmen pondered the question of how to have diplomatic representation without recognizing, or seeming to accept, the "objectionable features" of the document.[41] The corporation attorneys claimed credit for the piece of diplomatic scholasticism which accredited Ambassador Fletcher, "strictly to a *de facto* Government and not to a *de jure* government," thus avoiding "any semblance of recognition" of the new constitution.[42] But, as Polk explained to Martin Egan of the Morgan Bank (even after the

39. Frederic Kellogg to Leon Canova, 26 January 1917 (with message for Philippi), SD 812.011/19; Harold Walker to Philippi, 27 January 1917, SD 812.011/18; both messages were sent in code by the State Department.

40. Note enclosed in Alvey Adee to Charles Parker (representing the U.S. government prior to the arrival of the ambassador), 23 January 1917, SD 812.011/21. Relations between oilmen and State Department shown in Adee to D. J. Haff, 29 January 1917, SD 812.011/5; Secretary of State to Parker, 22 January 1917, SD 812.011/11a. The note of 23 January protested the new exchange rate for the peso as confiscatory.

41. William Loeb, Jr. (ASARCO), Chandler P. Anderson to S. C. Neale (American & Mexican Mining Co.), 2 February 1917, enclosed in Neale to Secretary of State, 3 February 1917, SD 812.011/23; Memorandum, Office of the Counselor to Polk, 27 March 1917, Arthur Bliss Lane Papers, Yale University Library, New Haven, Conn.

42. Kellogg to John Bassett Moore, 9 February 1917, Moore MSS.

extension of *de jure* recognition), the U.S. government accepted the Carranza government but had not "given approval to the new constitution"; "the question of the objectionable constitution was reserved for further discussion."[43]

The New York bankers learned about the nonrecognition of the constitution policy rather belatedly, and Egan asked Polk if the Mexicans clearly understood the distinction involved. Polk was not sure whether they grasped the legal subtleties of such a recognition policy, but he "did know that the Mexicans clearly understood that the government of the United States had not given approval to the new constitution."[44] In fact, this problem had bothered the State Department and the corporation attorneys since January. How could the Carranza government best be convinced that U.S. recognition was limited and that full recognition would require some changes in the constitution? Chandler Anderson and his associates decided that a treaty would accomplish these objectives. Such a treaty would eliminate the "practical confiscation" aspects of the constitution by prohibiting a retroactive application of the articles involved. If Carranza accepted this treaty, then he would be accorded full (*de jure*) recognition on 1 May 1917 when he was formally inaugurated as president. Anderson made the suggestion to Polk and was told to develop the plan in detail so that it could be submitted to the president.[45]

Anderson, however, began to have second thoughts about such a treaty. Since treaties were negotiated under provisions of the constitution, this kind of formal procedure could imply the recognition of the constitution even if Carranza were ousted. In addition, Lansing and Polk pointed out the complications involved in negotiating a treaty, and all three finally agreed that the desired results could be obtained through a less formal procedure. They decided that even limited recognition (*de facto*) would be conditioned by an official statement concerning the nonretroactive interpretation of the constitution.[46]

But, if Fletcher attended the inauguration of President Car-

43. Quoted in Egan to Lamont, 13 September 1917, Lamont MSS.
44. Ibid.
45. Proposed treaty discussed in Anderson to Polk, 8 March 1917, SD 812.011/57, and Anderson Diary, 8, 12, 20 March 1917, Anderson MSS. Harold Walker, William Loeb, and Walter Douglas (president, Phelps-Dodge) approved this move.
46. Anderson Diary, 29 March, 10 April 1917, Anderson MSS.

ranza, would the Mexicans assume that this act constituted full recognition? On the other hand, if he did not attend, the Mexican government would be insulted and new complications could arise. As Lansing informed Wilson: "The question arises whether Fletcher's presence at the ceremony will be a recognition of the *de jure* character of the Government and an acceptance of the Constitution."[47] Lansing and Polk decided that Fletcher should attend the ceremony, but that the State Department would send Carranza a formal notice emphasizing the reservations attached to this limited recognition. Anderson was requested to help the department prepare the proposed instructions.[48]

On 25 April 1917 Lansing sent Wilson the following proposed reservation:

Recognition is extended to General Carranza as the *de facto* President of Mexico on the understanding and with the reservation that he is recognized without prejudice to the position heretofore taken by the Government of the United States in regard to the decrees of the provisional government and the provisions of the new constitution, if interpreted and applied so as to impair vested rights of foreign owners of properties in Mexico, as to which the Government of the United States reserves full liberty of action, because, as already stated by the Government of the United States, (see instructions to Ambassador Fletcher of January 22, 1917) it cannot acquiesce in the confiscation of or discrimination against the rights and interests of American citizens acquired either under the constitution of 1857 and the laws emanating therefrom or otherwise.[49]

Wilson decided that such a formal statement might cause complications and that owing to the immediacy of other problems, such as the demands for withdrawal of U.S. warships from Mexican waters, the United States should not raise the property issue. When Lansing informed Anderson of the decision, he stressed the delicacy of the situation—"skating on thin ice" he called it. Fletcher, however, would not be given any new credentials and the *de facto* status of relations would be emphasized.[50] His instruc-

47. Lansing to Wilson, 25 April 1917, *Lansing Papers,* 2:565–66.
48. Anderson Diary, 17 April 1917, Anderson MSS.
49. *Lansing Papers,* 2:566.
50. Instructions in Lansing to Fletcher, 28 April 1917, ibid., 569; Anderson Diary, 28 April 1917, Anderson MSS.

tions stated: "In felicitating General Carranza, you will be careful to say or do nothing that would indicate a recognition of his government as *de jure* in character."[51]

In August 1917, Fletcher obtained from Carranza certain assurances concerning the nonconfiscatory nature of any actions implementing the constitutional provisions. In accord with his concept of concessions to Mexico, the ambassador then recommended the extension of *de jure* recognition without conditions. President Wilson agreed with this recommendation, and *de jure* recognition was extended on 31 August 1917.[52] Anderson and the other corporation representatives were angered and confused by this decision. According to Anderson's logic, the president was preparing the ground either for eventual intervention or for a postwar policy of socialism in the United States. The latter seemed more likely to Anderson, and he believed that he had persuaded Polk of the validity of this view. Polk, however, noted that he could not push the issue, and Anderson's efforts to create external pressures failed.[53]

Financial Needs and Diplomatic Pressure

Secretary Lansing consistently argued that the financial difficulties of the Mexican government would enable the United States to use the dollar as an instrument of diplomacy in influencing that government's policies and promoting stability. But dollar diplomacy also had to face the barrier of nationalism. As Lansing noted in October 1915:

The real problem Carranza will have to face is financial. . . . We can help him in this and I shall hint this to his representative. My fear is that Carranza is so obstinate, vain, and self-sufficient he will not wish to become in any way obligated to this country.[54]

51. Lansing to Fletcher, 28 April 1917, *Lansing Papers*, 2:567.
52. Fletcher to Lansing, 8 August 1917, Fletcher MSS; Anderson Diary, 8 September 1917, Anderson MSS. *De jure* recognition was extended by Wilson formally answering Carranza's letter of 1 May announcing his inauguration; Wilson to Carranza, 31 August 1917, *Papers Relating to the Foreign Relations of the United States, 1917* (Washington, D.C., 1926), 943.
53. Anderson Diary, 11, 12 September, 3 October 1917, Anderson MSS.
54. Lansing Private Notes 1915–16, 10 October 1915, Lansing MSS; see also Lansing to Wilson, 4 May 1916, SD 812.00/24920c.

Carranza did need money; his government approached foreign financial interests on several occasions during 1916 and 1917.[55] The fact that he did not want to become involved financially with the U.S. government complicated Lansing's use of dollar diplomacy.

The secretary, however, did not give up hope that eventually financial pressures would force Carranza to accept conditional assistance from the U.S. government or private bankers. Chandler Anderson agreed with this view but wanted to press the issue more intensely. He believed that a firm stand on the oil export tax of 1917 would hasten the process of forcing Carranza to "come to the United States for a loan." As a result, the United States could impose terms which would protect property and even force Mexico to abandon neutrality. Lansing did not want to force a showdown over the tax issue, and in any event, he told Anderson, Carranza would soon "reach the end of his resources."[56]

Such a prospect presented other problems. If the financial condition of the Mexican government became too chaotic, Carranza would be much less able to preserve internal order, and, if his government collapsed, a new civil war might result. The State Department would have failed to "keep Mexico quiet." Even if Carranza held power, financial exigencies might force him to make an accommodation with Germany which would vastly complicate the protection of petroleum supplies. In addition, some U.S. officials feared that British and French business interests might use Mexico's financial problems to force a unilateral settlement (which might be detrimental to U.S. interests) or even to help a counter-revolutionary movement overthrow Carranza before the end of the war.[57] All these factors added a cautionary note to the idea of demanding absolute guarantees for foreign property in return for any loan or relaxation of economic measures affecting Mexico's income.

The discreet manipulation of Mexican financial difficulties was further complicated by the touchy problem of the source for a loan. The U.S. government began to make foreign loans after its

55. Martin Egan to Thomas W. Lamont, 25 January 1916, Lamont MSS; Fletcher to Lansing, 8 August 1917, Fletcher MSS; Edgar Turlington, *Mexico and Her Foreign Creditors* (New York, 1930), 271, 274.

56. Anderson Diary, 11, 14 May 1917, Anderson MSS.

57. Ibid., 16, 29 May 1917.

entry into the war, and some European bankers and U.S. business representatives assumed that any Mexican loan would be made by the government. This assumption was based not only on the fact that private investment would have difficulty floating such a loan during wartime but also on the belief that only the government could, or would, force the Mexican government to make the requisite pledges.[58] But U.S. officials feared that even if Carranza did come to the government for money, such an act might stir enough anti-Yankee sentiment to eliminate him from office. As Secretary Lane told Martin Egan in May 1917, the government "would be glad to help, but it would have to be indirectly."[59] This meant that the New York investment bankers, especially J. P. Morgan and Company, would be brought into any serious loan negotiations.

J. P. Morgan and Company was definitely interested in the Mexican situation owing to its participation in the loans of 1899, 1910, and 1913 and its general interest in the U.S. stake in the Mexican economy. In January 1916, the bank expressed a willingness to cooperate with the administration in Washington if so requested.[60] In January 1917, Carranza's brother-in-law, General Zambrano, came to New York to request a loan of $10 million from the Morgan bank and to discuss possible U.S. investment in a "National Mexican Bank." Thomas Lamont informed the Mexican representatives that "it was impossible that anything could be done until the Mexicans had composed their own political differences and had manifested some disposition to protect foreigners in their persons and in their property and there could be devised a general plan of re-financing which would embrace all Mexican obligations and necessities." But Lamont assured the Mexicans that J. P. Morgan and Company was not hostile toward the Mexican government and hoped to be able to loan money to Mexico in the future.[61]

In May 1917, Agustín Legorreta, head of the Banco Nacional

58. Anderson Diary, 16 May, 17, 18 July 1917; Draft Memorandum on the Mexican Situation, 24 May 1917, Anderson MSS. Anderson noted the views of various representatives of U.S. and foreign interests.
59. Egan to Lamont, 28 May 1917, Lamont MSS.
60. Egan to Lamont, 25 January 1916, ibid.
61. Memorandum of interview between Mr. Lamont and Mr. Zambrano, brother-in-law of General Carranza and treasurer general of Mexico, 11 January 1917, ibid.

de México, a private firm, visited the Morgan bank, and Martin Egan gave him a letter of introduction to Secretary of the Interior Lane. The secretary gave Legorreta some encouragement concerning a plan "to have the Mexican government raise or mobilize a large quantity of food products for the United States and allied governments, the project to be financed by American bankers." The U.S. government would participate "indirectly." Egan believed that at least "the bare possibility" existed that something might be done for Mexico. Legorreta departed before his scheduled, private conference with Lansing, and these negotiations lapsed.[62]

During his visit to the United States in July 1917, Ambassador Fletcher also made inquiries about the possibility of a Mexican loan from private sources. Chandler Anderson and the representatives of other business groups became quite disturbed over Fletcher's attitude toward a Mexican loan. Anderson asked the president of the Guaranty Trust Company to urge Thomas Lamont to "make it entirely clear to Fletcher that it was impossible to borrow money from anyone in this country except the government."[63] Fletcher had already been in touch with J. P. Morgan and Company and it soon became apparent that while the bank officials had serious reservations about any sizable loan, they were not so dogmatic as the mining and agricultural corporations. Lamont suggested to Fletcher the possibility of a short-term loan guaranteed by the U.S. government. The intent of such a five- or ten-year loan would be to enable Mexico to "rehabilitate itself and make good the defaults on its outstanding obligations with the idea, prior to the maturity of this short-term loan, of consolidating its debt and refunding the present outstanding bonds with a new loan." To J. P. Morgan and Company, the first priority was the refunding of the defaulted bond issues, and, to achieve this, company officials preferred less dogmatic tactics than those proposed by other business groups. Morgan officials were also more willing to mesh their policies with those of the administration, and the diplomatic attitudes of their company would become increasingly important in U.S.-Mexican relations.[64]

---

62. Egan to Lamont, 28, 31 May 1917, ibid.
63. Anderson Diary, 17, 18 July 1917, Anderson MSS.
64. Lamont to Fletcher, 27 July 1917; Egan to Arthur Anderson (J. P. Morgan & Co.), late July or early August 1917 (based on internal evidence and file location), Lamont MSS.

Fletcher finally decided that only the U.S. government could really adjust the "financial snarl" in Mexico and returned to his post with the idea "that the situation locally should be nursed and built up wherever possible, and relations improved if possible."[65] The Carranza government, however, approached, and was approached by, several smaller banking groups during the latter half of 1917.[66] The U.S. government did not oppose the granting of a loan, but it did inform Carranza and the financial interests involved that guarantees concerning "valid vested interests" would have to be made by the Mexican government. Carranza refused to accept this condition, and the financiers were not willing to make a loan without the support of the government.[67]

In October 1917 the State Department sought to encourage the Mexican government to approach the U.S. government for a loan. This in turn would serve as the means of reaching a settlement on other issues. Fred I. Kent of the Federal Reserve Board wanted to go further and send an ultimatum demanding that Mexico either join the Allies and request a loan or submit to intervention; even Chandler Anderson felt that this was too aggressive.[68] Carranza, however, told one of his advisers—Thomas R. Lill—that he would not borrow from the U.S. government and that he held the latter responsible for Mexico's inability to obtain a loan from private sources. Carranza based this opinion on the fact that the State Department had opposed a loan proposal of $20 million which had been made in March 1917 by A. Iselin and Company.[69]

Carranza also resented the financial pressure produced by the rigid restrictions which the U.S. government had placed on the

65. Quoted in Egan to Anderson, July or August 1917, Lamont MSS.
66. Fletcher to Lansing, 8 August 1917, Fletcher MSS.
67. Fletcher to Lansing, 8 August 1917, Fletcher MSS; Lansing to J. C. O'Laughlin (American Export Banking Co.), 10 August 1917, Lansing MSS.
68. Memorandum by Leon J. Canova, 22 October 1917, SD 812.51/402; Anderson Diary, 20 September, 31 December 1917, Anderson MSS. Kent was deputy governor of the Federal Reserve Board of New York (1917–18) and director of the division of foreign exchange of the Federal Reserve Board until November 1918, also vice-president of the Bankers Trust Company (New York).
69. Lill to Auchincloss, 31 July 1918, SD 812.51/537. Chandler Anderson noted that the Treasury Department, according to his information, had refused in advance to coin any gold secured by Iselin unless Mexico agreed that it should be exchanged for American money at the normal rate; Anderson Diary, 18 June 1917, Anderson MSS.

exportation of gold, machinery, foodstuffs, and other goods. Mexico was selling products to the United States but could not touch the earnings or convert them into imports. Warnings reached the State Department during the fall of 1917 that food shortages and financial problems might lead to severe political disturbances in Mexico, but Fletcher and Polk decided to use the need for "gold and corn" as a lever for bargaining.[70] Formal negotiations for the relaxation of U.S. export restrictions began in November 1917. Secretary Lansing utilized delaying tactics and on 19 December, Luis Cabrera abruptly departed from Washington, D.C. Negotiations were resumed in January 1918, in Mexico.

Fletcher and Rafael Nieto, undersecretary of the Mexican Treasury, negotiated an agreement which made limited concessions to the Mexican objections. This proposal would permit the Mexicans to purchase several million bushels of corn and rice (no wheat or flour), and to withdraw immediately $15 million in gold. Mexico would then deposit the remainder of the reserves, and future accumulations up to a total of $20 million, in the Federal Reserve Bank. The Mexican government might issue paper money based upon these deposits, but at the fixed exchange rate of two pesos for one dollar, which would be a revaluation of the peso favorable to the United States. In addition, Mexico would be required to sell henequen at a low fixed price and forbidden to ship gold to any country except the United States, "unless some urgent government need required such export, and then only for limited amounts."[71]

Carranza rejected this agreement, and Secretary Lansing noted one U.S. reservation:

70. W. Blocker (vice-consul, Piedras Negras) to Secretary of State, 6 October 1917, SD 812.50/44; Fletcher to Polk, October 1917, Polk to Fletcher, 20 November 1917, Polk MSS. The U.S. trade policy contributed to severe price increases in Mexico; see the testimony of Thomas Lill, U.S. Senate, Committee on Foreign Relations, *Investigation of Mexican Affairs,* 66th Cong., 2d sess., 1919–20, 2 vols., Senate Doc. 285, 1:619.

71. Memorandum of an arrangement as a result of the conference attended by Ambassador Fletcher, Assistant Secretary Rowe, and Mr. Albert Strauss, representing the United States, and Ambassador Bonillas and Sub-Secretary Nieto representing Mexico, 7 February 1918, SD 812.51/535. A lower rate of exchange was often cited as an issue by U.S. officials; Fletcher to Secretary of State, 6 March 1918, U.S. Department of State, *Papers Relating to the Foreign Relations of the United States, 1918* (Washington, D.C., 1930), 605–6.

In particular, the Government of the United States would be unwilling to conclude with the Mexican Government any arrangement for mutual exchange of commodities which failed to recognize the just rights of Mexican owners of private property in the United States and by citizens of the United States in Mexico. In this connection, the Department is forwarding to you by telegraph its views concerning the legal features of the Mexican decree of February 19, 1918, taxing oil lands. This Government cannot acquiesce in any action taken by the Mexican Government whereby legitimate vested American interests are appropriated by Mexico.

Lansing also informed Fletcher that the Federal Reserve Board, the Treasury Department, and the Food Administration were not especially eager to authorize shipments of gold or food, but that they would cooperate with the State Department if negotiations were resumed. But, the secretary warned, "the Mexican people should not be permitted to labor under the delusion that a renewal of these negotiations is in any way vital to this Government."[72]

This "carrot and stick" approach underwent some changes in 1918 as a result of several factors. During the first half of the year, at least three American promoters had approached the Mexican government in regard to loan negotiations. None of these men was connected with the large investment banks in New York—although one group did propose to work with them—and each suggestion seemed to be related to attempts to obtain additional mineral concessions or preferential commercial ties. In each case, the State Department declared the necessity of obtaining guarantees from Carranza; and, in the case of the promoters associated with the Pierce Oil Company, the department warned that a loan could not be used as a lever either to obtain concessions or to commit the United States to armed intervention.[73] This competition between various "wildcat" promoters seemed to involve two difficulties: (1) the possibility that a promoter interested in speculative profit might arrange a loan without obtaining the

72. Lansing to Fletcher, 15 March 1918, *Foreign Relations, 1918,* 616–17.
73. Lansing to Fletcher, 25 April 1918, SD 812.51/535; Memorandum of a conversation between Boaz Long and W. H. Mealy (Pierce Oil Co.), 1 June 1918, SD 812.51/536.

guarantees demanded by the State Department—thus rendering this policy lever less effective; (2) the possibility that a scramble for preferential concessions would complicate the situation and make the protection of existing claims even more difficult.

Another problem was the pressure created by European interests in Mexico. Reports of German financial activity were continually received, and in March 1918 Ambassador Fletcher wrote that he had reliable information concerning a German loan of 800,000 pesos. And, said the ambassador:

As the Department is aware, there is good reason to believe that future, if not present, financial assistance has been offered by Germany to Mexico. It is the German aim to keep Mexico not only neutral in the war, but constantly irritated against the Allies and especially against the United States, in the hope of finding in Mexico a rich field for commercial, economic, and political exploitation after the war. This policy, under Carranza, is succeeding.[74]

Similar reports were received from one of Carranza's financial advisers, and all stressed the postwar goal of German economic penetration.[75]

Reports were also received which told of attempts by British interests to use Mexican financial problems as a lever to gain advantages. The specific issue involved the deal which Weetman Pearson made with the Mexican government. In exchange for his holdings in the Tehuantepec Railway and $10 million, Pearson was given the controlling interest in the Hawaiian-American Steamship Line. Leon Canova said that this was "probably a move on the part of the British oil interests to entrench themselves firmly with the Mexican Government as against the American oil interests."[76] The British Foreign Office replied to State Department inquiries with the veiled threat that American pressure to force cancellation of the deal would be reported to Carranza. The

74. Fletcher to Lansing, 10 March 1918, SD 812.51/420; Fletcher to Lansing, 13 March 1918, Fletcher MSS.

75. Lill to Auchincloss, 31 July 1918, SD 812.51/537.

76. Canova to Auchincloss, 4 January 1918, SD 812.51/409. The great distrust of British oil interests is brought out in a memorandum written by Leland Harrison, 23 January 1919, Leland Harrison Papers, Library of Congress; for the suspicion between U.S. and British companies see Garfield Diary, 15, 27 May 1918, Garfield MSS.

State Department was disturbed over the situation but settled for an "informal" statement that the United States could not agree that the move was a "desirable one."[77]

Oil Crisis of 1918

In other efforts to meet its financial needs and regulate the oil industry, the Mexican government tried to increase taxes on petroleum and implement the national control provisions of article 27. At the request of the oil companies, the State Department labeled as confiscatory the Mexican demand that foreign oil companies renounce their nationality and reorganize as Mexican companies. The Mexican government did not push this issue, but the oil tax decree of 19 February 1918 led to a prolonged controversy and almost produced a major crisis. The decree provided for taxes on oil lands, as well as on the rents, royalties, and production based upon contracts executed prior to 1 May 1917. These taxes were officially designated as national rentals and royalties. The decree also required the registration of petroleum lands and the opening of lands not registered to the filing of claims by third parties (denouncement). The registration of titles carried the legal implication of residual, national ownership of the subsurface deposits, and the oil companies refused to file on the grounds that such an act would constitute legal acceptance of article 27 and, *ipso facto*, confiscation. The issuance of the new titles would be the first step in their reorganization as Mexican companies. The oilmen were partially correct in their analysis. The Mexican government did want to establish the principles of national ownership of natural resources and the Calvo Doctrine. But this did not mean confiscation of properties. To most of the oilmen, however, there was no legal ground whatever between absolute ownership and confiscation, which meant in fact no area for legal maneuver and practicable compromise.[78] On 2 April

77. Memorandum from the British Embassy in Washington, 31 December 1917, SD 812.51/409; Auchincloss to Canova, 10 January 1918, ibid. The British also were suspicious of possible U.S. attempts to secure preferential treatment for trade and finance in Mexico; Foreign Office to the British Embassy in Washington, 16 March 1918, Sir William Wiseman Papers, Yale University Library.

78. Official opinion on confiscation in Polk to American Embassy (Mexico), 13 January 1918; oil company position stated in Harold Walker to

1918 the State Department sent a stern protest note to the Mexican government. After a lengthy sermon on confiscation and international law, Fletcher was ordered to say:

My Government is not in a position to state definitely that the operation of the aforementioned decree will, in effect, amount to confiscation of American interests. Nevertheless, it is deemed important that the Government of the United States should state at this time the real apprehension which it entertains as to the possible effect of this decree upon the vested rights of American citizens in oil properties in Mexico. The amount of taxes to be levied by this decree are in themselves a very great burden on the oil industry, and if they are not confiscatory in effect—and as to this my Government reserves opinion—they at least indicate a trend in that direction.

"Special attention" was directed "to the principle involved in the apparent attempt at separation of surface and sub-surface rights." On the basis of these theoretical possibilities, the State Department directly accused the Mexican government of confiscation and warned of "the necessity which may arise to impel it [the U.S. government] to protect the property of its citizens in Mexico divested or injuriously affected by the decree above cited."[79]

In January 1918, Mexican troops began to move into the Tampico oil fields in an attempt to wrest control from Pelaez. The latter increased his demands on the oil companies and harassed some of their facilities, usually by burning bridges and cutting water lines, to demonstrate his power. In the process, the oil companies lost some of their enthusiasm for Pelaez. But they made their peace with him and after the curtailment of the government campaign the status quo prevailed in the Tampico fields.[80] The British oil companies were reported to be supporting Carranza against Pelaez, but in the light of the February decree the foreign companies temporarily submerged their rivalry in order to present a united front. This cooperation was clearly evi-

Secretary of State, 18 January 1918, SD 812.6363/328. Mexican position is analyzed in Lorenzo Meyer, *Mexico y Estados Unidos en el conflicto petrolero, 1917–1942* (México, D.F., 1968), 88–93.

79. Fletcher to General Candido Aguilar, 2 April 1918, SD 711.12/104.

80. Doheny to Lansing, 17 February 1918, SD 812.6363/342; Dawson (consul) to Secretary of State, 19 February 1918, SD 812.6363/344; Walker to Auchincloss, 8 March 1918, SD 812.6363/372.

dent in El Aguila's asking Chandler Anderson to act as their legal adviser and to coordinate their interests with those of the U.S. companies, since the British company did not trust E. L. Doheny and wanted an influential representative in official and unofficial circles.[81]

Early in April 1918, Ambassador Fletcher sent a pessimistic résumé of U.S.-Mexican relations to Lansing:

There has been a gradual change for the worse in relations since the export embargo went into effect. . . . Our export and import restrictions, the enemy lists, and all our war measures, seem to have aroused the particular resentment of President Carranza and the men of his Government.

The ambassador linked the petroleum decree issue to this situation and, in a moment of insight, observed that the revolutionary party identified with Díaz those foreigners who had come to Mexico prior to the Carranza regime. In conclusion, Fletcher stated that he no longer felt confident that he could "keep the Mexican question from distracting our attention and efforts from the Great War." Instead, he now believed that Carranza intended to force the issue of foreign property rights.[82]

Lansing sent this letter to Wilson, and the president expressed his agreement with Fletcher's résumé. To Wilson, the gold export "difficulty" seemed to be one of the basic issues, and he suggested that Lansing confer with the Federal Reserve Board about "possible alterations or modifications of our present uncompromising position."[83]

Since past actions did not seem to be achieving the purpose of "keeping Mexico quiet," Wilson and the State Department gradually adopted a variety of tactics aimed at overcoming anti-U.S. sentiment and persuading Carranza to soft-pedal his nationalistic policies. During the remainder of 1918 the U.S. government utilized more extensive relaxation of economic restrictions, a new lending approach, and the connections between the AFL and the Mexican labor movements.

81. Anderson Diary, 4 February 1918, Anderson MSS; Wiseman to Lord Balfour, 27 March 1918, Wiseman MSS; T. B. Hohler (British embassy, Washington) to Auchincloss, 24 January 1918 (denies story that British oil companies were encouraging the campaign in the oil fields).
82. Fletcher to Lansing, 3 April 1918, SD 711.12/77½.
83. Wilson to Lansing, 18 April 1918, SD 711.12/78½.

The first demonstration of this diplomatic offensive came in May 1918 when the Federal Reserve Board approved General Obregón's application to import $4.3 million in gold, silver, and currency. Myron M. Parker of the War Trade Board had arranged for Obregón to have an interview with Frank Polk in April, and afterward Polk supported the general's application. Obregón also applied to the War Trade Board for the purchase of sugar, soap, corn, and jute twine; as a *quid pro quo* he would ship 30,000 tons of garbanzos (chick peas) to the United States. Parker enthusiastically supported these requests, since, as he informed Polk, "General Obregón . . . is one of the strong men in Mexico and his influence in preserving peace and cordial relations between the two countries will be almost invaluable."[84] Ironically, these moves may have had an adverse effect upon Carranza in the light of his deteriorating relations with Obregón.

On 7 June 1918, President Wilson delivered a speech to a group of Mexican editors. He stressed the need for good relations between the two countries and the idea that the only goal of U.S. policy was "disinterested service." In his concluding remarks, the president advised: "So soon as you can admit your own capital and the capital of the world to the *free use of the resources* of Mexico, it will be one of the most wonderfully rich and prosperous countries in the world."[85] Wilson and the State Department considered this speech an overture to Carranza which would lead to more friendly relations, and they were disturbed when the Mexican government released to the press the full text of the note of 2 April. Several Mexican newspapers promptly contrasted this note with Wilson's speech, and *El Pueblo* declared:

Each word of this kind has been followed by an aggression; so it was in regard to Vera Cruz and the punitive expedition. Fresh in the memory are the repeated assurances of non-intervention, of disinterestedness, of aid and assistance, and anyone can judge of their truthfulness seeing our ports blockaded, our frontiers closed, our communications interrupted, our correspondence censored, our subsistence in danger, our security in doubt and our com-

84. Myron M. Parker to Polk, 20 May 1918. See also Lansing to Governor William P. G. Harding (Federal Reserve Board), 20 May 1918, Polk MSS.

85. *Foreign Relations, 1918,* 577–80; italics added. Many Mexicans considered the speech to be hypocritical; see Zorrilla, *Historia de las relaciones,* 2:328.

merce fought without truce by an enemy more dangerous because more inconsequent.[86]

Fletcher and other observers believed that the publication of the note and the angry editorials represented the official reply to Wilson's speech. U.S. officials could not see any inconsistency between the speech and the note, and expressed shock over the Mexican charges of hypocrisy.[87] Yet, to the Mexicans, Wilson's idealistic phrases about U.S. disinterestedness could not be reconciled with what they regarded as a near ultimatum concerning a tax measure—or with past and present U.S. actions.

Some U.S. officials did have a vague understanding of these differences. Robert Murray, the Committee on Public Information representative in Mexico, declared that "intelligent and conservative" Mexicans responded favorably to Wilson's speech, while the entire Mexican government was guilty of "ignorance, folly, and Chauvinism." In a similar vein, the consul in Tabasco referred to the Mexicans' "absurd spirit of conceited independence."[88] Ambassador Fletcher noted that the angry editorials reflected the sentiments of "all simon pure revolutionists" and added that the Mexican government considered the note of 2 April to be "unjust, threatening and injurious to its pride and prestige and as interfering with the free enforcement of its fundamental law and the exercise of its sovereign rights." This was an accurate summation of the Mexican attitude, but to Fletcher it had little meaning, since the Mexicans "entirely overlooked" the "question of simple justice and national good faith."[89] What Fletcher, and other U.S. officials, considered simple justice and national good faith appeared to the leaders of the Mexican Revolution as legalisms to justify directing their country's internal affairs and preventing real economic change.[90]

86. Quoted in Fletcher to Lansing, 10 July 1918, SD 711.12/92.

87. Lansing to Wilson, 27 June 1918, SD 711.12/104; Fletcher to Lansing, 26 June 1918, SD 711.12/105; Robert Murray to George Creel, 14 June 1918, SD 711.12/95.

88. Murray to Creel, 14 June 1918, SD 711.12/95; Consul (Tabasco) to Secretary of State, 19 September 1918, SD 711.12/136. "The better class of business men have always been in our favor"; Consul (Yucatan) to Secretary of State, 20 September 1918, SD 711.12/140.

89. Fletcher to Lansing, 26 June 1918, SD 711.12/113.

90. At least a few people in the United States agreed; one letter to President Wilson accused him of worshipping property rights; Robert L. Hale (Washington, D.C.) to Wilson, 2 July 1918, SD 711.12/121.

In spite of this verbal exchange, the U.S. Food Administration continued its work on the relaxation of export controls. The agency reported a surplus of pork products, corn, and condensed milk, and the State Department now faced a dilemma. As Lansing reported: "It has occurred to the Department that if these facts become generally known, this Government's embargo policy towards Mexico would be generally considered as indefensible in view of the President's speech."[91] The secretary also was convinced that the president's speech had created a much better climate for negotiation, but this "good effect" would be lost if the United States did not act rapidly and with a more liberal attitude toward the question of export restrictions. The issues stemming from the oil tax decree threatened a possible crisis during the summer of 1918, since U.S. officials did not intend to make any modification in the position asserted in the note of 2 April. Lansing now decided that the United States should announce, without any preliminary negotiations, the adoption "of a most liberal embargo policy." He hoped that such action would produce negotiations "to settle once and for all the many commercial, financial and other questions now pending." Fletcher was also authorized to tell Carranza that the U.S. government would "be glad to facilitate a loan by private American interests . . . on terms mutually agreeable." No action would be taken by the department until Fletcher had conferred with Carranza.[92]

Fletcher reported that his interview with the Mexican president had been very cordial, and Carranza had stated that the friendly intentions of the United States could best be demonstrated by the reduction to a minimum of "present restrictions on commerce and intercourse." Carranza also agreed not to make a formal reply to the note of 2 April after the ambassador assured him that "protection" of interests involved many peaceful steps. Fletcher then recommended the immediate adoption of the trade liberalization plan. Within the next few weeks export licenses were issued for a wide variety of commodities, especially food products.[93] In

91. Lansing to Fletcher, 26 June 1918, SD 711.12/103.
92. Lansing to Fletcher, 24 June 1918, SD 711.12/102; Fletcher to Lansing, 25 June 1918, SD 711.12/103; Fletcher to Lansing, 3 July 1918, SD 711.12/112.
93. Fletcher to Lansing, 28 June 1918, SD 711.12/108; Lansing to Fletcher, 6 July 1918, *Foreign Relations, 1918,* 627–29.

the enthusiasm of wooing Mexico, Lansing conferred with the American Red Cross about sending hospital units to Mexico. The secretary considered announcing this plan without consulting the Mexican government (in a sense appealing directly to the Mexican people), but Fletcher warned against any activity or announcements without governmental permission.[94]

Early in July 1918 Fletcher warned that the "petroleum question" was now the major obstacle to good relations and that left unsettled it would frustrate all "attempts at friendship."[95] James R. Garfield, representing the U.S. oil companies, had been in Mexico since May trying to negotiate a change in the February decree. He was particularly interested in eliminating the requirement that the companies formally file their titles with the government. Alberto Pani told Garfield in all frankness that the "radical elements" were urging strict enforcement of article 27 and that the government had to take some steps to implement national control. Both Pani and Carranza argued that the registration of titles did not constitute confiscation.[96]

As a result of these negotiations, modifying decrees were issued in July, but Garfield and Fletcher considered these to be "purely technical and administrative." They believed that, if the decrees were accepted, the oil companies would be surrendering "all their previously acquired rights and titles."[97] Late in July, Carranza agreed to extend the registration period for fifteen days, after Garfield warned that the issue might lead to war.[98] Frank Polk was convinced that a "show-down" was imminent because "I do not see how it would be possible for us to compromise with them [the Mexican government] in any way."[99] Fletcher agreed with

94. Lansing to Fletcher, 11 July 1918, SD 711.12/103; Fletcher to Lansing, 12 July 1918, SD 711.12/118.

95. Fletcher to Lansing, 3 July 1918, SD 711.12/112; Polk to President Wilson, 31 July 1918, Polk MSS (Polk told Wilson that the oil nationalization question was one of the most difficult problems still facing U.S.-Mexican relations).

96. Garfield Diary, 22 May, 4 June 1918, Garfield MSS.

97. Fletcher to Polk, 30 July 1918, Polk MSS. The July decree also permitted third-party denouncements of oil fields which had not been exploited prior to 1 May 1917; this was an attempt to force the utilization of reserve fields held by the large companies.

98. Garfield Diary, 19, 20, 22, 25 July 1918, Garfield MSS.

99. Polk to Fletcher, 22 July 1918, Polk MSS; Garfield observed that "Lansing pays no attention to Mexico. He leaves it entirely to Polk." Garfield Diary, 21 June 1918, Garfield MSS.

Polk and wrote that "this petroleum question is so damnably important I have it on my mind all the time, and feel as you do that no compromise on the principle is possible." As Fletcher further explained, the "principle" was that cited in the note of 2 April.[100]

It should be noted that this conflict was not simply a case of oil needs for the war. Polk and other members of the administration were careful to keep separate the issue of possible nationalization (or confiscation) and the "practical question" of maintaining production and shipment of oil.[101] As Secretary of the Navy Josephus Daniels indicated to a Senate committee in 1917, any real threat to actual oil production would be met with military action. Units of the fleet were stationed at Tampico for that purpose.[102]

The oil companies now shifted their activities to Washington. Some oilmen, Doheny among them, believed that the U.S. government was prepared to use armed intervention and that further negotiations with Mexico were not needed.[103] James R. Garfield and Frederick Proctor discussed the oil companies' plan for forcing the Mexican government to modify its decree with Secretary of the Navy Daniels, Bernard Baruch, and State Department officials. All agreed that the president would have to be consulted, and Baruch and Harry A. Garfield met with Wilson on 9 August 1918. The proposal of the oil representatives was vetoed on the grounds that it would mean war with Mexico.[104] James Garfield, the principal attorney representing the Petroleum Producers Association, did feel that something had been gained. He wrote in his diary: "He [Wilson] now better understands our situation and

100. Fletcher to Polk, 30 July 1918, Polk MSS.

101. Polk to W. Wilson, 31 July 1918, ibid.; Polk, Confidential Diary, 25 July 1918, ibid.; Boaz Long, "Memorandum on Mexican Situation," 10 August 1918, SD 711.12/130; Polk to Lansing, 29 May 1918, Polk MSS. Cronon, *Cabinet Diaries of Josephus Daniels,* 328, 9 August 1918. Captain Louis C. Richardson (U.S. Navy, stationed in Tampico) reported that throughout the war Mexican officials always cooperated with him in preventing interference with the production and shipment of oil; Richardson to Chief of Naval Operations, 11 March 1919, Wilson MSS.

102. Cronon, *Cabinet Diaries of Josephus Daniels,* 233, 17 November 1917; Senate, *Leasing of Oil Lands,* 179–80; Daniels to Secretary of State, 14 June 1920, SD 812.00/24210.

103. Garfield Diary, 1, 2 August 1918, Garfield MSS.

104. Polk, Confidential Diary, 8, 9 August 1918, Polk MSS; Cronon, *Cabinet Diaries of Josephus Daniels,* 328, 9 August 1918.

believes in protecting our rights but is afraid the world would construe forcible intervention as example of action because of necessity—i.e. our need and that of the allies for oil."[105] Wilson also stated that he would not retreat from the principles asserted in the note of 2 April. After a conference with Colonel House later that month, Sir William Wiseman, the head of British Intelligence in the United States, also reported to his government that Wilson would insist on the Mexican government's handling the oil question in "accordance with recognized principles of international law and the rights of foreign nations."[106] James Garfield continued to work with Frank Polk on the oil decree issue and drafted the department's protest note of 12 August. He also tried to convince the oil executives that cooperation with the State Department's tactic of diplomatic pressure offered the best hope of success.[107] Carranza issued a new decree on 12 August 1918 which seemed to withdraw the requirement concerning filing of titles. Garfield noted that this "looks like a victory for us. At least we are safe for the present. This presents an entirely new situation."[108]

During the remainder of the year Garfield negotiated with Pani, who was drafting a comprehensive petroleum law. The executives and attorneys of the Petroleum Producers Association believed that Garfield was too compromising, since he accepted some regulatory provisions and did not support completely their demands for a statutory ceiling on taxes.[109] Garfield, however, was convinced that he had succeeded in eliminating the provisions of the 1918 decrees requiring registration of titles acquired prior to

105. Garfield Diary, 9 August 1918, Garfield MSS.
106. Wiseman to Sir Eric Drummond, 20 August 1918, Wiseman MSS; William Gibbs McAdoo to Joseph Tumulty, 21 November 1919, William Gibbs McAdoo Papers, Library of Congress. McAdoo said that the consistent policy of the administration had been to afford protection to the property of Americans in Mexico.
107. Garfield Diary, 12, 14 August 1918; Garfield to F. C. Proctor (Gulf Pipeline Co.), 21 November 1918, Garfield MSS.
108. Garfield Diary, 14 August 1918, ibid.
109. Garfield to Nelson O. Rhoades, 14 November 1918, and "Suggestions by Mr. Garfield referring to Memorandum relative to the proposed petroleum code of Mexico prepared by Mr. Kellogg, 4 December 1918," ibid. This proposed law contained the doctrine of "positive acts" which authorized validation of titles to oil lands only in those cases where some actual progress toward exploitation had been made; Zorrilla, *Historia de las relaciones*, 2: 330–31.

1 May 1917 and declaring that payment of taxes constituted full acceptance of article 27.[110] Garfield and Nelson Rhoades, a business associate, declared that they had had to "hurt" the Mexican officials and "wound their sensibilities" but they believed that the Mexicans would "yield every point."[111] Early in 1919—when the oil question seemed to be on the road to settlement—Garfield reported:

Our record with the Mexican government as representatives of the Association and the diplomatic record in the Department of State clearly and consistently sets forth the claims and the attitudes of the American companies.

As the net result therefore of our efforts the companies have thus far escaped the ills anticipated under the decrees of February 19, 1918 . . . and in addition have created a situation which can ultimately compel the recognition of their vested rights.[112]

The AFL and the Bankers, 1918

The most original tactic for influencing internal Mexican affairs developed as a result of Samuel Gompers's belief that the AFL could persuade the Mexican labor movement to adopt a pro-U.S. position. Gompers presented his plan for a Mexican-American conference to Felix Frankfurter of the War Industries Board, George Creel of the Committee on Public Information, and Secretary of Labor William Wilson. The conference was to be used as a platform for prowar propaganda. In addition, Gompers wanted government support for a prowar, Pan-American labor newspaper, to be distributed throughout Mexico. The three government officials decided that Gompers should go directly to the president and request the needed funds. Wilson approved the plan but insisted at first that the funds be given openly. Creel persuaded him that

110. Memorandum regarding the proposed petroleum law, 31 October 1918, Garfield MSS.
111. Rhoades to Garfield, 4 December 1918. Polk and Fletcher were optimistic about a favorable settlement for the oil companies; Garfield reported that the companies would not pay the taxes due in November so that the Mexican government's great need for revenue might reduce it to prompt action on the law; "Memorandum, Conference between Mr. Garfield . . . and Officials of the Department," 12 November 1918, SD 812.-6363/415; Fletcher to Polk, 1 November 1918, Polk MSS.
112. Garfield to Proctor, 4 February 1919, Garfield MSS. Fletcher reported that no attempt had been made to collect any of the taxes provided for in the 1918 decrees; Fletcher to Polk, 18 December 1918, Polk MSS.

a covert operation would be more successful.[113] Wilson authorized Creel's Committee on Public Information to underwrite the Mexican operation (the committee was already engaged in sending propaganda films to Mexico), and funds were channeled through a front organization entitled "American Alliance for Labor and Democracy."[114] Wilson gave Creel a secret appropriation of $50,000 from a special security and defense fund and later provided $10,000 for the November meeting of the Mexican-American Labor Conference. This meeting was to be used to foster support for the United States, but the war ended before the delegates assembled at Laredo. The Creel committee continued to subsidize the Alliance, and Gompers worked to assert a pro-U.S. influence in the Mexican labor movement.[115]

During the summer of 1918 the State Department also began to pursue a more vigorous course in regard to Mexican finances. The immediate background of this decision involved the reports of Thomas R. Lill and Henry Bruére. Both men had served for some thirteen months as financial advisers to Carranza, and in May 1918 they informed the State Department that they had laid the foundation for a new approach on the finance issue. Lill had been authorized by Carranza to approach President Wilson and the New York bankers in order to open loan negotiations, and his memorandum stressed the value of such a move in curbing German influence and putting the United States in a "dominant position" in regard to the "future economic development" of Mexico.[116]

113. Levenstein, "United States Labor Movement and Mexico," 91–99.

114. Ibid., 99–100. Wilson to Creel, 2 August 1918, George Creel Papers, Library of Congress. (Wilson asked, "Do you think it would be feasible to use the instrumentalities that he [Gompers] refers to just as we have been using the Y.M.C.A.?") Use of film mentioned in Consul (Acapulco) to Secretary of State, 24 October 1918, SD 711.12/152.

115. Creel to Wilson, 28 August 1918, Creel MSS; Levenstein, "United States Labor Movement and Mexico," 101–5.

116. Lill to Auchincloss, 31 July 1918, SD 812.51/537; Fletcher to Lansing, 30 May 1918, SD 812.51/434. Bruére and Lill had gone to Mexico at the invitation of Carranza, and with the full approval of Wilson and the State Department. They organized a commission for administrative and financial reorganization and brought in several North American professors to study various aspects of the Mexican government; Thomas R. Lill, "Memorandum Regarding the Organization and Work of the Commission," 31 July 1918, SD 812.51/538. Some Mexicans called it the "Punitiva Financiera," a play on words referring to "Punitive Expedition"; Rafael Trujillo, *Adolfo de la Huerta y los Tratados de Bucareli*, 2d ed. (México, D.F., 1966), 22.

The State Department sent this information to the president and requested authorization to try to induce the bankers to initiate loan negotiations. Wilson immediately approved the project and asked to see a more detailed plan. The latter request was conveyed to Lill and Bruére by Samuel Gompers.[117] The plan, sent to Wilson on 15 August 1918, called in essence for the refunding of the Mexican debt and the establishment of a joint commission to supervise the finances of Mexico. The granting of any loan, however, would be based upon the settlement of "all major questions of an economic and diplomatic character."[118]

Several conferences were then held between State Department officials and Thomas Lamont of J. P. Morgan and Company. At this point the problems of loans and guarantees merged with the specific interest of the investment bankers in the foreign bonds of Mexico. The Morgan Company had been under pressure from various European banks to take the lead in organizing a committee to represent the holders of Mexican bonds, and early in October the State Department approved the Morgan proposal to organize the International Committee of Bankers on Mexico.[119] Later, Lamont would reminisce about the informality of the proceedings: "The whole suggestion was sort of a spontaneous combustion arising from a lot of us fellows sitting around over there [at the State Department] one day and talking over the situation."[120] This committee, however, was to have the broad function of dealing with Mexican finances "as a whole." The specific instructions of the State Department spelled out the role of the committee in these words:

117. Anchincloss to President Wilson, 1 August 1918, SD 812.51/539, and Gordon Auchincloss Papers, Yale University Library; Wilson to Polk, 2 August 1918, SD 812.51/539; Bruére to Polk, 15 August 1918, SD 812.51/542. Auchincloss suggested that loan negotiations might divert Mexican attention from the oil issue.

118. "Memorandum for President Wilson in Reference to Mexico," by Thomas Lill and Henry Bruére, enclosed in Bruére to Polk, 15 August 1918, SD 812.51/542.

119. J. P. Morgan & Co. to Morgan, Grenfell & Co. (London) and Morgan, Harjes & Co. (Paris), 10 October 1918, SD 812.51/544; Lamont to Polk, 18 November 1918, SD 812.51/547.

120. Lamont to Norman H. Davis, 5 October 1920, SD 812.51/600; Memorandum for Mr. Vernon Munroe, 19 November 1929, Lamont MSS (the information in this memorandum supports the general accuracy of Lamont's memory).

. . . that any group formed shall be under the leadership of
American bankers and that the policy of the United States
Government regarding Mexico be the dominating influence in the
operations of this group. At the same time, the United States
Government believes that all negotiations respecting investments
under consideration should be carried on exclusively by the private bankers and not through the instrumentality of agencies of
this Government.[121]

The formation of such an "omnibus" committee, as Lamont
called it, had several advantages: (1) all questions involving
loans, bonds, reorganization of Mexican finances, and even the
National Railways of Mexico would be handled in an integrated
manner by one authoritative group; (2) the leading investment
banks of Europe and the United States would have to deal with
Mexico through an American-dominated committee which would
take its directions from the U.S. government; (3) Carranza would
be faced with a common bloc but not one involving official diplomatic representatives; and (4) a common front of the major
investment banks would render more difficult any attempts by
individual promoters to gain special advantages. In addition, the
U.S. government would be in a position to control the lending of
money to Mexico. Officials believed that a U.S.-controlled committee would counter pressure from European financial interests
which might force European governments to settle matters inde-
pendently and thus weaken the ability of the United States to
achieve guarantees from Mexico. As Leon Canova stated earlier
in the year: "We hold the whip handle at the present time. We
are the bankers of the world and have advanced large sums to
England."[122]

Working through the Morgan branches in London and Paris,
Lamont reached the major British and French financial interests.

121. J. P. Morgan & Co. to Morgan, Grenfell & Co. and Morgan,
Harjes & Co., 10 October 1918, SD 812.51/544.
122. Canova to Polk, 5 January 1918, SD 812.51/409. The points in
this paragraph are based on information in the following: Lamont to
Polk, 18 November 1918, SD 812.51/547; Lamont to Polk, 13 December
1918, SD 812.51/549; Lamont to Davis, 28 September 1920, SD 812.51/
619; Fletcher to McAdoo, 12 March 1919, Fletcher MSS; Fletcher to Polk,
18 December 1918, Polk MSS; Fletcher to Lamont, "Strictly Personal and
Confidential," 4 December 1918, Lamont MSS.

These interests saw some advantages in a common-front approach and raised very few objections to the Lamont plan. The British group inquired about the committee's plans for dealing with railroad, oil, and electrical interests, and Lamont replied that the committee would deal with all of these, probably in the form of subcommittees.[123] The French were concerned about the number of representatives they would have on the committee, but this was settled by a formula apportioning 50 percent of the committee seats to the United States and 25 percent each to Britain and France.[124] The American members represented the following companies: J. P. Morgan; Chase National Bank; Kuhn, Loeb; Ladenberg, Thalman; First National Bank, Kansas City, Missouri; Illinois Trust and Savings Bank; Guaranty Trust; National City Bank; Central-Union Trust; and Kidder, Peabody.[125] In August 1919, the Netherlands and Switzerland pressed for membership on the committee, and after some exchange of correspondence between Lamont and the State Department the decision was made to give each country one seat. The decision was based on the stated necessity for maintaining the unity of the creditor nations, provided that American control would be insured.[126]

During the latter months of 1918, Thomas Lill returned to Mexico and reopened negotiations with the Carranza government. Both Bruére and Lill were now working in conjunction with the Morgan Company and with the State Department. At least two conditional loan arrangements were proposed to Carranza during the latter part of 1918. In one instance Ambassador Fletcher utilized the services of Thomas P. Honey, a leading English banker about whom Fletcher wrote to Lamont, "He is perfectly willing to play along with us and under our leadership." Honey offered Carranza a loan of $150 million (to be floated through a syndicate which would probably have been organized by Morgan

123. Lamont to Auchincloss, 21 October 1918, SD 812.51/545. Three subcommittees were formed, representing public debt, railways, and industries.

124. Lamont to Auchincloss, 21 October 1918, SD 812.51/545.

125. Lamont to Davis, 28 September 1920, SD 812.51/619.

126. Lamont to Fletcher, 5 August 1919, and Fletcher to Lamont, 6 August 1919, SD 812.51/554; William Phillips to Lamont, 5 November 1919, SD 812.51/557. In spite of some misgivings the department decided not to ask for two additional American members; Belgium was given a seat in 1921.

and Company) if the Mexican government would accept seven conditions. These included the settlement of the petroleum question, the return of all foreign properties (especially railway and express companies and banks), the acceptance of all U.S. currency at a rate of two to one, recognition of the Huerta bonds, and an adjustment of foreign claims for damages. Carranza "flatly refused" to consider the proposition, and also turned down a loan proposal made by Lill which would have involved the conversion of the national debt.[127]

Rafael Nieto, the Mexican acting minister of finance, came to New York in February 1919 to begin detailed negotiations with the bankers. Bruére was quite optimistic that the settlement of all outstanding issues was now in sight, and a comprehensive financial plan was drafted for Nieto's consideration. The most important parts of the plan called for the refunding of the Mexican debt into a single comprehensive bond issue, the pledging of the customs revenues as security under some form of international supervision, the refunding of the indebtedness of the national railways, the organization of a new federal bank with an international directorate, and a treaty of amity and commerce which would provide "a satisfactory basis for the operation of business enterprises in Mexico by the nationals of other countries." The State Department, however, had come to the conclusion that a loan was now "out of the question" because of Carranza's repeated rejections of any conditions concerning foreign property.[128]

Nieto had not been authorized to conclude any arrangements, but when he left New York in March 1919 Lill was still optimistic in regard to the negotiations. He reported to Fletcher that "I think he [Nieto] leaves New York fully impressed with the fact that the American members of the International Committee are desirous of working out a solution of the Mexican problem and are disposed to do so in a very friendly spirit."[129] After Nieto presented the comprehensive plan to Carranza the negotiations were terminated. The archival record is not very clear at this

127. Fletcher to Lamont, "Strictly Personal and Confidential," 4 December 1918; Fletcher to Lansing, 21 November 1918, SD 812.51/471.

128. Bruére to Polk, 7 February 1919, SD 812.51/497; Polk to American Embassy (Mexico), 20 December 1918, Polk MSS.

129. Lill to Fletcher, 20 March 1919; see also Fletcher to McAdoo, 12 March 1919, Fletcher MSS.

point, but it seems that the Mexican president was opposed to the
proposals for international supervision and for a treaty.[130]

By the end of 1918, U.S.-Mexican relations seemed to be more
normal than they had been for years. None of the U.S. efforts to
change article 27 or persuade Carranza to settle accounts with
foreign investors had succeeded. But the Mexican government had
not tried to enforce the 1918 decrees. Some Mexican officials now
were convinced that Wilson was following a policy of "political
conciliation." The consul in New York reflected this attitude when
he cited the improvement in relations following Wilson's speech
to the Mexican editors and declared that the Wilson Doctrine and
the Carranza Doctrine actually were synonymous.[131] Ford Motor
Company officials were seriously considering a plan for the production of farm tractors in Mexico, and Lansing, in urging the
War Industries Board to give favorable consideration to the
firm's requests, noted that this action "may very well lead to a
solution of the entire Mexican problem."[132]

With the end of the war, however, some Americans hoped to
see, or force, a change in U.S. tactics. Ambassador Fletcher said
he could not stand two more years of "drift." Though he opposed
armed intervention at this point, he did advocate the formulation
of a "general and concrete" plan in conjunction with Britain and
France.[133] Senator Fall was preparing for a massive, propa-
gandistic Senate hearing on Mexican "depredations." And General
Leonard Wood pointed to Mexico when he expressed the hope
that the U.S. Army would not be demobilized too rapidly.[134]

---

130. Turlington, *Mexico and Her Foreign Creditors*, 275. Carranza
wanted a loan from the bankers as a preliminary part of any debt settlement, and believed that the bankers would comply; Carranza to Pani, 8
April 1919, A. J. Pani, *Cuestiones diversas contenidas en 44 cartas al
Presidente Carranza* (México, D.F., 1922), 50.

131. Emeterio de la Garza, Jr., "The Monroe Doctrine, the Wilson
Doctrine, and the Carranza Doctrine," October 1918; Consul (New York)
to Secretaria de Relaciones Exteriores, n.d. (in the file for material for
latter part of 1918), SREM, 802 R, Leg. 31 (13).

132. Lansing to Bernard Baruch, 10 September 1918, Lansing MSS.

133. Fletcher to Polk, 3 December 1918, Polk MSS.

134. Wood to Garfield, 1 December 1918, Garfield MSS.

6 The Specter of Mexican Revolutionary Nationalism: The Postwar Setting

When the war closes, the Mexican situation will soon again become one of our most important foreign problems, because it will involve not only Mexican conditions but those of the countries to the south of Mexico, Guatemala, Honduras, Nicaragua, Salvador, and Costa Rica. These Republics need development and will attract the cupidity of commercially ambitious nations.
—Boaz Long, 1918

Controlling the "Backward" Nations

As early as 1915, U.S. officials and businessmen began to talk about the "war after the war." This emotional term was used especially to describe the revival of economic rivalry between European nations and the United States, "a commercial war of the severest sort," according to Woodrow Wilson. By late 1918 this concern had produced a considerable body of literature, and the production increased during the postwar years. The problems of economic adjustment from war to peace and the recession of 1920–21 gave an added sharpness to discussions of tactics to advance or defend the economic-political hegemony of the United States in the Western Hemisphere. Many of these analyses linked control of markets and resources to foreign investments, and this led to renewed consideration of the problems of guaranteeing the proper behavior of the "backward" nations and controlling the economic rivalry of the industrial-creditor powers. Various tactics were proposed, many of them designed to promote such a high degree of U.S. economic and ideological predominance in Latin America that these nations would either become stable imitators

133

of their northern neighbor or at least be subject to external restraints on their activities. Such predominance would in turn
reduce the European economic and ideological presence to the
point where economic rivalry and the possibility of diplomatic
friction with these powers would be minimized.[1]

During the war the State Department devoted some attention to
the elimination of German direct investments in Honduras, Guatemala, and Haiti. Most were replaced by U.S. companies. Specific
actions to extend the hegemony of the United States in Latin
America were limited by the circumstances of war, but some
groups and individuals were deeply involved in planning for postwar policies. The Inquiry was one of the most significant of these.
An official group of experts formed in 1917 to develop plans and
background information for the American delegation to the pros-
pective peace conference, the Inquiry devoted considerable time
to the investigation of Latin America. According to Lawrence
Gelfand, Latin America received the benefit of more extensive
planning than any other area considered by this group. The Latin
American Division of the Inquiry worked very closely with the
State Department, and other government bureaus, such as the
Bureau of Foreign and Domestic Commerce. The State Department considered and approved all research plans, and Secretary
Lansing allocated funds for these projects directly to the Inquiry.
Based upon this close coordination with the State Department and
influenced by its objectives, the Inquiry produced almost three
hundred reports and documents dealing with Latin America. A
number of these were extensive investigations of trade, mineral
production, navigation, climate, agriculture, and industry (of
thirty-five reports on Argentina, for example, twenty dealt with
economic factors).[2] Latin America was obviously not going to be

1. For examples of such thought see Boaz Long, "Memorandum and
Arguments Relating to Constructive Steps Which Should Be Taken in
Central America before the Close of the European War," 15 February
1918, SD 711.13/55; Speech by Henry Cabot Lodge on 12 April 1921,
Congressional Record, 67th Cong., 1st sess., 1921, vol. 61, pt. 1, 160–61;
Julius Lay, "Interest of Department of State in Investment of American
Capital in Latin America," address delivered by the Acting Foreign Trade
Adviser of the Department of State at the Second Pan American Commer-
cial Conference, 5 June 1919, copy in Boaz Long Papers, Library of Con-
gress; Wallace Thompson, *Trading with Mexico* (New York, 1921),
132–39, 258–61.

2. Lawrence E. Gelfand, *The Inquiry: American Preparation for Peace,
1917–1919* (New Haven, 1963), 277, 281, 287, 316–17.

of major concern at a conference to end the European war. Thus, it seems clear that officials of the Departments of State and Commerce were demonstrating their deep interest in postwar economic expansion in Latin America by their utilization of the Inquiry as an investigative and intelligence service for the area. This attitude was well expressed in a State Department memorandum of April 1917 on the economic usefulness of the Trading with the Enemy Act. The author, Gordon Auchincloss, concluded that it "is submitted to you as a suggestion looking to the elimination of German controlled trade in South America and the substitution therefore of an American controlled trade."[3]

Almost all the analyses of the U.S. role in postwar Latin America stressed the relationship between U.S. prosperity and power, and economic predominance. In 1919, Julius Lay, acting foreign trade adviser of the State Department, said:

Our own industries will benefit by possessing an assured supply of raw materials, for many of the raw materials which are most necessary for our manufacturing plants are products of Latin-America, and are obtained by us chiefly from that part of the world at the present time. In view of the competition for many of these products between the great manufacturing nations, it is very important that companies controlled by American capital should be in a position to supply them to our factories.

Investments in Latin America will have a direct bearing on our export as well as our import trade. . . . Moreover, the new purchasing power of the country whose exports are increased by these investments and whose people receive wages from the foreign corporations, leads naturally to an increase in imports, and a large part of these imports will come from the United States.[4]

Secretary Lansing demonstrated the same ideas in his attempts to prevent British interests from securing a concession for the construction of steel and armament facilities in Brazil. He cabled the U.S. ambassador: "It is of the utmost importance to our interests in Brazil that no other than an American company should eventu-

---

3. Memorandum by Gordon Auchincloss for Mr. Harrison, 20 April 1917, Polk MSS. See also Harry N. Scheiber, "World War I as Entrepreneurial Opportunity: Willard Straight and the American International Corporation," *Political Science Quarterly* 84 (September 1969): 486–511.

4. "Interest of Department of State in Investment of American Capital in Latin America," Second Pan American Commercial Conference, 5 June 1919, Boaz Long MSS.

ally secure it [the concession] and the vast amount of trade it would control."[5] Thus, when President Epitacio da Silva Pessôa of Brazil visited the United States, Breckenridge Long, third assistant secretary, took him to see Charles A. Schwab of Bethlehem Steel and to inspect the Hog Island shipyard. Schwab was anxious to cooperate with the department, since he believed that those who controlled the iron mines of Brazil would "control the world in 75 to 100 years."[6]

In some of the discussions of the U.S. role in the underdeveloped area to the south, economic predominance was linked not only to specific economic objectives but also to broader considerations of stability and hegemony. U.S. officials believed that the expansion of trade and investments would help to stabilize the countries of Latin America, because such expansion would automatically promote their economic development along orthodox (i.e., private enterprise) lines. The corresponding reduction of the role of European capital would also contribute to stability since economic rivalries and diverse attempts to protect investments were believed to be disruptive factors.[7] Economic predominance would also promote U.S. hegemony in Latin America and this in turn would make it easier for the United States to enforce order and stability. In the process the expanded definition of U.S. security interests would also be protected. In a letter advocating the expansion of steamship operations for the Panama Railroad Company, Newton D. Baker summarized these views:

The Caribbean Sea has been called the American Meditteranean [*sic*]. . . . The Panama Canal is a great possession which it is our duty to maintain and protect. Its protection requires not merely adequate military foresight but commercial facilities which will be created and nursed in the interest of solidarity of commercial interests between the countries and islands surrounding the Caribbean and the United States.[8]

5. Secretary to Ambassador (Morgan), 24 June 1918, *Papers Relating to the Foreign Relations of the United States, 1919*, 2 vols. (Washington, D.C., 1934), 1: 205.

6. Breckinridge Long Diary, 25 June 1919, Breckinridge Long Papers, Library of Congress.

7. See James Weinstein, *The Corporate Ideal in the Liberal State* (Boston, 1968), 249–50, for discussion of activities of Lamont and the State Department aimed at taking control of certain Latin American financial holdings of Britain and France.

8. Baker to Woodrow Wilson, 26 July 1919, Baker MSS; see also Wilson to Baker, 1 August 1919, ibid.

The theme of protecting investments in underdeveloped areas emerged as one of the basic points in arguments concerning trade extension, acquisition of raw materials, stability, and U.S. hegemony. Boaz Long noted: "So long as the major portion of the oil production in Mexico is controlled by Americans, American commerce with foreign countries after the war is safeguarded by that fact."[9] The specific fear of an oil famine during the immediate postwar years was an important element which officials, businessmen, and policy-popularizers stressed in their analyses of the Mexican problem.[10] But many of these men were equally concerned over the challenge which revolutionary nationalism in Mexico, and in other underdeveloped countries, presented to the entire spectrum of U.S. international economic interests. A Department of Commerce circular of October 1918 stated:

In its bearing upon our future commercial relations with Latin America, the status of our investments in Mexico involves far-reaching possibilities. If all our foreign investments were to be transferred from the state of property duly acquired, with guaranties of permanence . . . to the state of temporary concessions requiring renewal from time to time by contracts . . . , we should face an unprecedented situation. Our commercial relations, not only with Mexico, but with all of Latin America, depend upon mutual confidence.[11]

Secretary of the Interior Lane was quite blunt in his analysis of the attempts of underdeveloped nations to assert control over their

9. Boaz Long, "Memorandum on Mexican Situation," 10 August 1918, SD 711.12/130.

10. See John A. De Novo, "The Movement for an Aggressive American Oil Policy Abroad, 1918–1920," *American Historical Review* 61 (July 1956): 854–76. E. L. Doheny (Huasteca Petroleum Co.) did not agree with this pessimistic evaluation and in late 1918 stated, "Demand will not outstrip supply for generations"; *Wall Street Journal,* 25 December 1918, 7. The years 1919 and 1920 were marked by scarce oil and high prices, but abundant production started a price decline during the fall of 1920; Larson and Porter, *History of Humble Oil,* 173–76. Thus, the fear of an oil famine for the United States was declining in some official circles by late 1920; see Bureau of Foreign and Domestic Commerce, "The Petroleum Industry in Mexico," *Commerce Reports,* 13 September 1920, 1216–30.

11. This was a mimeographed circular and parts of it are reproduced in *Congressional Record,* 65th Cong., 3d sess., 1919, 57, pt. 5 and appendix: 380–81; and Confidential Memorandum (Army Intelligence) to Lt. Hill for Transmission to State Department, 9 October 1918, SD 812.6363/414. For related views see William S. Culbertson, *Commercial Policy in War Time and After* (New York, 1919), 322–26, 333–36; Chester Lloyd Jones, *Mexico and Its Reconstruction* (New York, 1921), 5–7, 304–9.

resources and the status of these countries in the world order of capitalist powers:

When I say that Russia may go her own way, and Mexico hers, I say so with a sense that I have a right in Russia and in Mexico, and also a right to see that they do not go their own way to the extent of blocking my way to what of good they hold.

"The world is mine," is not the mere dramatic utterance of an escaped convict or of an overmastering leader of men. . . . What a people hold, they hold as trustees for the world. . . . It is good American practice. The Monroe Doctrine is an expression of it. . . . That is why we are talking of backward peoples and recognizing for them another law than that of self-determination, a limited law of self-determination, a leading-string law.[12]

As Lane pointed out, protecting investments, both actual and potential, raised the issue of controlling the "backward" nations and the problems which this in turn created for the principle of the "Open Door."[13] President Wilson was quite concerned with the resolution of these interrelated problems, and General Tasker Bliss wrote that the president had been "very much impressed" by the South African Jan Smuts's paper which stressed "putting a considerable part of the world under tutelage of one or another of the great powers."[14] Wilson, Colonel House, William S. Culbertson of the Tariff Commission, David Hunter Miller of the State Department, and Bernard Baruch were generally agreed that the old methods of "tutelage" had led to war between the industrialized nations. These men advocated an internationalized control of the "backward" nations, and some aspects of this new system became part of the plans for the League of Nations. They hoped that this method of controlling the underdeveloped world would

12. Lecture prepared for delivery at Princeton University, March 1922. See also Interview of Franklin K. Lane by the editor of the *Oil Trade Journal*, 10 June 1919, Lane MSS; William S. Culbertson, Memorandum of 31 January 1918 on Foreign Enterprise in Underdeveloped Regions, William S. Culbertson Papers, Library of Congress.
13. Earlier, Lane had expressed concern over possible rivalry between the United States and various European powers in respect to policing Mexico; Lane to Lansing, 1 December 1919, SD 711.12/224½.
14. Bliss to Newton D. Baker, 21 January 1919, Baker MSS. See also George Curry, "Woodrow Wilson, Jan Smuts, and the Versailles Settlement," *American Historical Review* 66 (July 1961): 970–76; N. Gordon Levin, Jr., *Woodrow Wilson and World Politics: America's Response to War and Revolution* (New York, 1968), 245–51.

not only prevent wars between the industrial-creditor nations but would also protect capitalism from socialist revolutions. In this context capitalism was identified with democracy, civilization, and freedom.[15]

Influential and articulate Americans, however, heatedly disagreed over the internationalization of the policing function, and some of the opposition to the League of Nations stemmed from the idea that the United States (under the Monroe Doctrine) must be the only policeman in the Western Hemisphere. Opponents of the League, such as Congressman Norman J. Gould (New York), used Mexico as a case in point when they argued that the United States could not effectively protect or advance its investments in Latin America if the police function was internationalized.[16]

Various officials, businessmen, and academics were searching for other methods of controlling and influencing the "backward" nations of Latin America, and Mexico was one of the prime targets. Direct rule and military intervention were losing popularity, and a relatively limited number of persons in responsible positions would publicly support either course as a primary tactic. Even the advocates of a military solution often veiled these sentiments in cloudy rhetoric in their public statements. Armed intervention was not discarded as a tactic, but it was increasingly defended as a last, and temporary, alternative. The attempt to develop nonmilitary tactics and indirect methods of control characterize the postwar period.[17]

15. Woodrow Wilson, "The Road Away from Revolution," *Atlantic Monthly* 132 (August 1923): 145–46.
16. *Congressional Record,* 65th Cong., 3d sess., 1919, 57, pt. 5 and appendix: 378–80; Speech of Henry Cabot Lodge, ibid., 67th Cong., 1st sess., 1921, 61, pt. 1: 160–63. President Wilson hedged on the application of international police functions to the Western Hemisphere.
17. U.S. Senate, Committee on Foreign Relations, *Investigation of Mexican Affairs,* 2 vols., 66 Cong., 2d sess., 1919–20, Senate Document 285, 3368–73; the committee called for sending a "police force" into Mexico as a last measure in a proposed series of steps. See also Boaz Long, "Memorandum on Mexico," 10 August 1918, SD 711.12/130; F. C. Proctor to T. W. Gregory (Department of Justice), 14 September 1918, Garfield MSS (Long and Proctor called for a limited occupation of the Tampico region). William Jennings Bryan also suggested temporary occupation of the oil fields, and the taking of Lower California, with Magdalena Bay, as compensation for losses by American citizens; Josephus Daniels Diary, 17 December 1919, Josephus Daniels Papers, Library of Congress.

Many policy proposals stressed a combination of economic and ideological tactics. In part these were to tie the economies of Latin American countries to the economic system of the United States, but these tactics were also given a distinct educational mission. The latter function reflected the growing idea that one of the most effective and lasting ways of controlling Latin America was by changing the social value structure of the elite groups first and then of the rest of the population. This was not a new concept, but it became increasingly important in tactical formulations which were seeking to avoid military solutions. The process of changing values was still called "Americanization." This was no longer regarded as an automatic development engendered simply by contact, and there was growing doubt that it could be imposed through "free elections" or U.S.-imposed constitutions. Education by various methods became one of the key concepts in analyses of tactics.

The theorists of U.S. influence in the "backward" regions believed that "educating" the Latin Americans in the North American value structure would gradually create stability and willing acceptance of U.S. hegemony. The reasoning involved proceeded as follows: if these "backward" people accepted North American values they would become staunch advocates of development through private enterprise, the necessity of attracting foreign capital, the creation of a favorable climate for business, and, especially on the part of labor, the need for patience and hard work. The result would be respect for contracts, payment of valid debts, protection of private property, and a free field for foreign (preferably U.S.) enterprise. The United States would then not really need to do much of anything to promote or protect order, stability, and investments; and the countries involved would gladly accept U.S. predominance as the basis for their protection and prosperity.

In 1918, Boaz Long prepared an extensive memorandum in which he developed various tactics for control and "education."

I submit that the proper infusion of American influences be the developing of these countries educationally and agriculturally which will produce a condition analogous to our advantage better than that contemplated by either Senator [unnamed senators who advocated conquest]. To me, annexation from the Rio Grande to Panama seems unnecessary to the extension of our influence over that section. . . . The business of these countries and the friendship of their people will almost certainly be obtained and conserved through the adoption of practical and humanitarian measures of notable advantage, and American prestige be injured by advancing thoughts of ultimate intervention or domination. Intervene when necessary, but do not threaten or talk of it in advance.[18]

Among the practical measures cited were U.S. control of banking, investments in natural resources, control of communications facilities such as wireless stations, and the development of education.

Several years later, Leland Harrison, another State Department official, stated his belief that experience in the southwestern states of the United States proved that Latins "when educated can develop a community of interests with the American citizens of Saxon origin." This was to constitute a basic tool for the spread of "our beneficent influence" over the Caribbean countries. The extension of the "commercial power" of the United States was one way to accomplish this objective. But Harrison stressed that the economic must be combined with the ideological:

It seems to me, therefore, that, if in making alliances or treaties with the Caribbean countries, we can incline them to adopt certain standards of education which will enable those desiring to matriculate in American schools to do so easily, we have laid the foundation of the *system* which will do much during the next century to establish *common interests* and *aspirations* throughout the countries of this hemisphere.[19]

The author also noted that financing and business followed old school ties. Will A. Peairs of the Chamberlain Medicine Company expounded similar views in 1921 when he reported to the National Foreign Trade Convention on the progress of the Mexican-American Scholarship Foundation.[20]

Thomas Lamont stressed the educative function of American bankers in their dealings with Mexican officials. De la Huerta and Obregón were not lacking in ability or brains he noted, but they

18. "Memorandum and Arguments Relating to Constructive Steps . . . ," 15 February 1918, SD 711.13/55.

19. "The Pros and Cons Regarding the Establishment of a School in Central America," n.d. (probably 1924 or 1925), Leland Harrison Papers, Library of Congress; italics added.

20. "Our Trade and Relations with Mexico," *Official Report of the Eighth National Foreign Trade Convention* (New York, 1921), 352.

were "untutored" and had "no ideals to live up to."[21] Other analysts concentrated on the need to change the values of the masses. Chester Lloyd Jones, political scientist and State Department official, wrote about the need to create "the economic impulse," which was composed of "the property sense," "emulation of the economic success of others," "the desire for influence," and the development of wants. Even the *mestizo* had not developed enough new wants to "make him in fact as well as in appearance, a person of Western European civilization."[22] Arguing against armed intervention, James Carson, an official of the American Chamber of Commerce of Mexico, praised the "uplifting influence" of American business. He believed that the Spanish heritage constituted the "deep-seated disease" of Mexico.[23]

Various schemes were proposed for direct "educational" action in Mexico. Ellsworth Huntington, the geographer, proposed bringing about changes by attacking sickness, since health played an important role "in molding the Mexican character." He suggested that the young people of North America be encouraged to do voluntary work in Mexico under the auspices of the International Red Cross.[24]

In 1922, the Right Reverend Francis Canon Kelley, protonotary apostolic to the pope, visited the State Department and told Leland Harrison that the U.S. government "could make use of the potentialities of the Catholic Church for what might be called propaganda purposes in Latin America in order to dispel the fear and hatred of the Latins of the Colossus of the North." Kelley reported that he had proposed to Andrew Carnegie that he provide the funds to educate Latin American priests in the United States so that they might disseminate the "truth" about the United States.[25]

21. "Remarks of Thomas Lamont before the Dutch Treat Club, Lincoln, Nebraska, March 14, 1922," Lamont MSS.

22. Jones, *Mexico and Its Reconstruction*, 112–13, 159–60.

23. "Upon the Indian Depends Mexico's Future," in George H. Blakeslee, ed., *Mexico and the Caribbean: Clark University Addresses* (New York, 1920), 35–43. See also Roger W. Babson (president of the Babson Statistical Organization and a member of the Federal Central American Commission of 1916), "A Constructive Policy for Mexico," ibid., 156–59.

24. "The Factor of Health in Mexican Character," ibid., 44–53.

25. Memorandum of Conversation with the Right Reverend Francis Canon Kelley, 3 May 1922, Harrison MSS.

Most of the ideas concerning the building of educational facilities did not even reach the stage of specific proposals. In late 1923 a former president of the University of Texas sent to prominent businessmen a proposal to establish in Mexico City "an American educational institution akin to Roberts College in Turkey." Thomas Lamont thought that the project might have a positive effect on U.S.-Mexican relations, but nothing developed.[26]

One of the more peculiar proposals, however, did reach at least temporary fruition. In 1929 a group of "Old Blue" Yale alumni decided that the University of Mexico needed a U.S.-style football team, coached by a Yaleman. The primary function was to teach the "high ideals" of American sportsmanship to Mexican youth. The originator stressed the "uncalculable benefits" for these youth in the development of intercollegiate football. Ten Yale alumni, including Arthur Bliss Lane, first secretary of the U.S. embassy, contributed $500 each, and Reginald Root (Yale '26) went to carry the spirit of Eli to the land of the matador and the fighting cock.[27] The venture did not last long, and in 1933 Lane tried to persuade Yale to subsidize a coach in Mexico. He explained: "I may say that not only should [the] presence of a Yale man here redound to the credit of Yale in Mexico, but at the same time the offer of a Yale man to further the teaching of football in Mexico should have a substantially good effect on the relations between the two countries."[28]

In actual practice, of all the ideas about "educating" Mexicans, the one concerning the role of business proved to be the most useful, and the one most used. Boaz Long had grasped the reasons for this in 1918: "Possibly it would be well for those of us who distrust Carranza to consider that he probably has corresponding sentiments towards our national motives. It would seem easier to let individuals, or bankers, or even oil men accomplish unofficially what we might prefer to do officially."[29] Highly personalized diplomacy, both official and unofficial, did become increasingly

26. Memorandum for Vernon Munroe from Thomas Lamont, 30 November 1923, Lamont MSS.
27. Arthur Constantine to Arthur Bliss Lane (1929), 30 July 1929, Lane MSS.
28. Lane to George P. Day (Yale University Press), 4 April 1933, ibid.
29. "Memorandum on the Mexican Situation," 10 August 1918, SD 711.12/130.

important after the war. The activities of George Creel, the Committee of Oil Executives (composed of presidents of the major
companies), Thomas Lamont, General J. A. Ryan, and Dwight
W. Morrow provide excellent examples of this significant development in U.S.-Mexican relations. All these individuals and groups
tried to "educate" Mexican officials in orthodox economic values
and to encourage them to modify or eliminate those policies which
affected foreign interests. The leaders of the revolutionary family,
it was hoped, would realize the difficulties and risks involved in
any lasting defiance of the industrial-creditor world order and
return Mexico to the fold of well-behaved "backward" nations.
In pursuit of this goal, most Americans involved in negotiations
with the Mexicans were constantly on the lookout for the new
Porfirio Díaz.

U.S. Role in the Mexican Economy

As minister to France during the latter part of the Carranza era,
Alberto Pani tried to promote the flow of European capital to
Mexico—especially into the petroleum industry. He also conferred
with members of the British section of the International Committee of Bankers on Mexico and reported that these financiers were
applying pressure on the government for a restoration of diplomatic relations. In his discussions with British bankers and the
French government, Pani stressed the point that unconditional
recognition would provide the basic element for a satisfactory
solution of the issues involving British and French investors and
would open the way to new investments. Pani and Carranza believed that closer economic and political relations with European
nations would counter the preponderant influence of the U.S.
government and the economic power of the large U.S. oil companies.[30]

30. Pani to Carranza, 26 February, 5 March, 16 July, 3 September 1919,
17 March 1920, and Carranza to Pani, 8 April 1919, Pani, *Cuestiones
diversas,* 47–49, 51–59, 268–72, 278–80, 355–61, 50. The sensitivity of
U.S. government and business officials to these efforts is revealed in "Memorandum from the Division of Mexican Affairs," by Boaz Long, 25 January 1919, Polk MSS; Summerlin to Secretary of State, 16 December 1919,
SD 712.41/4. Some congressmen and State Department officials expressed
concern over the possibility of increased British penetration of the oil
industry, but the oil executives were just as upset over the encouragement
the Mexican government gave to the small U.S. companies (especially

These efforts produced rather limited results, and the economic role of the United States in Mexico increased after World War I. Cleona Lewis has made the following evaluation of U.S. investment trends: 1914—$853.5 million; 1919—$908.9 million; 1924—$1,005.1 million; and 1929—$975.2 million.[31] The number of British mining companies, on the other hand, declined from fifty in 1913 to nineteen in 1929.[32] Mexican import percentages provide another indicator of economic trends:[33]

	1910–11	1924
U.S.	55.2	72.6
Britain	11.6	7.0
Germany	12.5	7.2
France	8.7	5.0
Others	12.0	8.2

In 1929 G. Butler Sherwell made a detailed study of the state of the Mexican economy in 1926. A summary of his evaluation of several industries is as follows:[34]

Mining—98 percent owned by foreign interests. Mexican holdings had declined after 1910 as a number of small Mexican properties were absorbed owing to financial difficulties.

Henequen—increased foreign ownership of plantations (12 percent of total output).

Coffee—almost equally divided in 1910 among Mexicans, Spaniards, and others. By 1926 North Americans and Germans were predominant; the former on the east coast and the latter on the west.

Cotton—86 percent foreign owned (North Americans, Germans, and British).

AGWI); Harold Walker to Capt. Paul Foley (U.S. Shipping Board), 30 December 1919, SD 812.6363/618; Walker to Lansing, 13 December 1919, SD 812.6363/608; M. L. Requa to R. S. Morris (ambassador to Japan), 14 December 1920, SD 812.6363/773.

31. Cleona Lewis, *America's Stake in International Investments,* 606.

32. J. Fred Rippy, *British Investments in Latin America: A Case Study in the Operation of Private Enterprise in Retarded Regions* (Minneapolis, Minn., 1959), 55–56.

33. Ministerio de Relaciones Exteriores, *Memoria de Labores Realizados por la Secretaría de Relaciones Exteriores de Agosto de 1925 a Julio de 1926* (México, D.F., 1926), 33.

34. Sherwell, *Mexico's Capacity to Pay,* 40–49.

Chicle, rubber, guayule, bananas, and other fruits—almost 100 percent foreign owned, principally by U.S. interests.

Refined sugar—95 percent controlled by North Americans and Germans.

In the petroleum industry the Mexicans improved their position. Using Mexican government figures, Chester Lloyd Jones and George Wythe, commercial attachés in Mexico, made the following estimates of the percentage of investments in the industry to June 1926.[35]

	1924	1925	June 1926
U.S.	57.46	47.24	53.84
English	26.16	32.88	28.54
Dutch	11.37	2.15	8.10
Mexican	3.29	11.49	6.02
Other	1.99	6.24	3.49

The increase in Mexican investment in the oil industry and the taxation of foreign companies helps to account for the increase in the national income retained in the country. In 1926, 53 percent of the total export earnings of Mexico returned to the creditor nations. This marked a 12 percent improvement over 1910. On the whole the Mexican economy was stronger in 1929 than in 1910. Noticeable progress had taken place in the development of highways, irrigation projects, telephone systems, and the production of electric power. The latter increased from 52 million kwh (1922) to 156 million kwh in 1927. The country still faced major economic problems and was certainly not wallowing in affluence. Oil production declined after 1921, and the large U.S. companies argued that article 27 was destroying the Mexican economy by frightening away new capital during the 1920s. This argument had a kind of validity for these companies. But this must be interpreted in the light of the oil executives' rather exaggerated view of security and profitability, and their belief that they could force Mexico to restore the Porfirian economic-legal system.

Foreign investments in Mexican petroleum continued, and even increased, after the enactment of article 27. Of the total capital invested in the industry in July 1926, 78 percent came in after

35. Jones and Wythe, "Economic Conditions in Mexico, 1927," SD 812.50/161, 174.

1916.[36] But the major U.S. companies did begin to cut back on investment after 1921. Transcontinental officials (Standard of New Jersey) decided in 1921 to curtail investment substantially, and in 1925 began to transfer machinery and pipelines to Colombia and Venezuela. This decision was not based upon unprofitable operations. Standard had recovered its advance to Transcontinental by 1924 and received $36,500,000 in dividends from the subsidiary from 1925 to 1928. By the end of 1928 a substantial part of the assets of Transcontinental had been liquidated.[37]

Enforcing Article 27

In facing the issue of petroleum development, Mexican leaders had three options: (1) to expropriate and develop petroleum under national auspices; (2) to accept the companies' position and hope for the best; or (3) to attempt to establish a policy which would leave production basically in private hands but give the government leverage to shape the course of development and the allocation of some of the profits. From 1917 to the oil expropriation of 1938 Mexican leaders tried to follow the third course. The basic problem involved in any implementation of policy was the fact that the largest companies controlled much of the land believed to be the richest in oil potential. In 1919 one company attorney estimated that U.S. companies had purchased or leased about ·80 percent of the most promising oil lands.[38] And these companies based their exploitation policies solely on their own concept of company interests, arguing that they had this right by virtue of fee simple ownership, or through leases from persons holding such ownership. Article 27 of the constitution established a legal basis for contesting this highly monopolized control of

36. Ibid., 125, 167, 180. Peak petroleum production was reached in January 1922; 1921 was the year of highest production for the period. Mexico ranked second in world production from 1918 until 1927; John W. F. Dulles, *Yesterday in Mexico: A Chronicle of the Revolution, 1919–1936* (Austin, Tex., 1961), 290–95.

37. George S. Gibb and Evelyn H. Knowlton, *The Resurgent Years, 1911–1927* (New York, 1956), 364–65. Lewis, *America's Stake in International Investments,* 588, shows a drop in total oil investment after 1924.

38. Harold Walker to Capt. Paul Foley, 30 December 1919, SD 812.6363/618. For an official Mexican statement see Speech of R. V. Pesqueira to the Petroleum Institute of America, 19 November 1920, SD 812.6363/739½.

exploitation. Theoretically the Mexican government could grant concessions for oil production in proven fields to smaller companies. Such actions would promote oil development, weaken the control of the large companies, and reinforce the basic principle of national ownership of subsoil resources (the concessions would be granted to companies which accepted article 27 and became Mexican corporations).

Because of the extensive holdings of the large companies, any concession program would entail some encroachment on these and would require the retroactive application of article 27. This became the crux of the diplomatic-legal argument over the article. The State Department claimed that the Mexicans could not apply the article to rights "legally acquired" prior to the ratification of the constitution of 1917. Companies such as Jersey Standard argued against any application of article 27, since all its holdings were acquired after May 1917. Without retroactivity, the effect of national control would have been severely limited.

Mexican leaders retreated under pressure from the U.S. government and the oil companies and tried to effect limited retroactivity through the granting of concessions in the designated federal zones and the doctrine of positive acts. Various smaller U.S. companies, such as Atlantic, Gulf, and West Indies (AGWI), and even British interests were encouraged to file denouncement claims on lands in the federal zones. Several such concessions were granted during the latter part of 1920.[39] In addition, the Mexican government tried to separate the unexploited holdings of the large companies from their working fields through the doctrine of positive acts. As originally stated, this doctrine asserted that companies could claim a kind of ownership of the subsurface oil on those properties which they had begun to work prior to May 1917. For the unexploited holdings the companies would have to apply for confirmatory concessions which would carry the obligation to accept article 27. If they were unwilling to do this, then the properties would be open for the granting of concessions to other companies.

39. One oil executive stated in December 1920 that denouncement titles had been granted on eight tracts of land owned or leased by U.S. companies and that out of 1,100 denouncement petitions filed, over 200 involved lands of U.S. companies; Chester O. Swain to Norman Davis, 31 December 1920, SD 812.6363/778.

After 1920 the doctrine of positive acts became the major legal tool which the Mexican government used to effect a limited application of article 27. For the most part the U.S.-Mexican oil controversy of the 1920s would center on the meaning of positive acts and the extent to which the doctrine would be applied to the properties of the oil companies.[40] Yet the doctrine was only the visible, legal symbol of the ongoing conflict between revolutionary nationalism and the legal-economic order of the industrial-creditor nations.

The postwar fears that the U.S. predominance in the Mexican economy would be eliminated by either European competition or Mexican radicalism proved to be wrong. In most areas the United States expanded its presence. The economic situation in Europe and the actual policies of the Mexican leaders played important roles in this regard. In addition, whatever success U.S. economic interests enjoyed in Mexico was based more on the activities of certain less ideological business groups than on "skillful" diplomacy or official meddling.

40. Person, *Mexican Oil*, 43–45; Antonio Gómez Robledo, *The Bucareli Agreements and International Law* (México, D.F., 1940), 31–32, 96–101.

7 Confrontation Diplomacy and the Article 27 Syndrome, 1919–1921

Says one William Randolph Hearst:
"Mexico is quite accurst
by a dreadful kind of soil
that is full of gold and oil,
That we gentlemen of leisure
think was put there for our seizure,
It's absurd for any Greaser
to object when we would seize 'er."
—Gale's Magazine, 1919

Crisis of 1919

Early in 1919 George Agnew Chamberlain, U.S. consul general in Mexico, declared: "The Mexican situation is an abscess which cries for a lancet." Within a year the consul would retire in angry frustration to write a petulant novel about the evil Mexicans, but in 1919 he believed that the time of confrontation and accountability had arrived.[1] This view was also held by officials such as Lansing, Polk, and Fletcher and by numerous congressmen, border state politicians, and businessmen with Mexican holdings. On 1 March 1919 Frank Polk, as acting secretary of state, sent Chamberlain's dispatch and a memorandum by Fletcher to President Wilson. The covering letter complained:

I look for very serious and increasing foreign and domestic pressure upon the Administration for some action in regard to Mexico.

1. Chamberlain to Fletcher, 1 March 1919, SD 711.12/187. The novel was entitled *Not All the King's Horses* (1919). His racist, militant views are articulated clearly in a tract for the times, *Is Mexico Worth Saving?* (Indianapolis, Ind., 1920).

150

The Mexican question is being agitated in Congress and out, and the Department is in constant receipt of complaints on account of the exactions of the Carranza Government; its failure to protect the lives and property of foreigners; its seizure and retention of foreign banks and public utilities; its absolute neglect of its obligations and debt, and its general incompetence and unfriendly and unfair attitude to legitimate foreign interests.[2]

Fletcher elaborated on these charges, and stated that two courses of action were open: (1) to let matters drift and "confront the clamor at home and abroad"; or (2) to demand that the Mexican government either "perform its duties" or accept the assistance of an American or international commission to restore "order and credit."[3]

Wilson was devoting all his attention to the Peace Conference and did not read these documents until he returned from Paris in July. In the interim an intensive campaign for a hardline policy against Mexico had been launched by the National Association for the Protection of American Rights in Mexico, and Republican congressmen such as Albert B. Fall, Norman J. Gould, and Frank Brandegee.[4] Party politics and economic interests formed the basis of this hardline alliance, and the Congress became one of the main forums for its arguments. Congressional strategy was designed to stir up the American public and to exert pressure on the executive branch. Speeches, resolutions, and hearings on the Mexican question were much in evidence by midsummer.[5]

2. Polk to Wilson, 1 March 1919, SD 711.12/187.

3. Fletcher to President Wilson, 1 March 1919, SD 812.00/23111a.

4. The association in 1919 included a cross section of U.S. business interests, but the oil interests, especially Doheny's Huasteca Company, provided most of the funds, and the active leadership. The bankers played a minor role at first, and most dropped out by 1921; see various reports in the Fall and Lamont MSS. Information about activities in "Memorandum: The National Association for the Protection of American Rights in Mexico," by Leland Harrison, and sent to Frank Polk, 23 January 1919, Harrison MSS; Harold Walker to Fall, 5 June 1919, Fall MSS; W. F. Buckley to Fall, 10 February 1921, ibid. The account sheets of the association for 31 May 1921 show that the Huasteca Petroleum Company had provided $188,393.95, to $55,081 by all other groups; Lamont MSS.

5. The House Rules Committee conducted an investigation of the Mexican situation since 1910, and the Senate Foreign Relations Committee also began an investigation of U.S. policy. Congress and oil interest activities in Fletcher to Frank Polk, 23 July 1919, Fletcher MSS; Robert H. Murray to Fletcher, 17 July 1919, ibid.; Harold Walker to Senator Duncan U. Fletcher (Florida), 29 May 1919, enclosed in Walker to Polk, 31 May

Early in 1919 the representatives of the major oil companies had decided to concentrate their efforts on obtaining government support for a total defeat of Mexican regulations. As a result, the efforts of James R. Garfield and Nelson Rhoades to obtain a *modus vivendi* with Mexico in regard to the 1918 decrees were rapidly de-emphasized. Garfield knew that many of the oilmen were reluctant to compromise and that the end of the war in Europe might encourage them to drop such efforts. He compared these executives to the dog in the fable who, with a bone in his mouth, saw his reflection in a pond, tried to seize the bone's reflection, and thus lost the bone he had.[6] In March 1919 Garfield noted: "I am utterly disgusted with them and am glad to be rid of this employment under conditions existing."[7]

The actions of the oil companies and the protective association had an impact on the Mexican government. In May, Rhoades reported: "The oil companies and their protective association are undoubtedly making a very serious mistake . . . and they are suffering the ills of their propaganda through their protective association." He also noted that the attorney for the association had been expelled from Mexico and that all the concessions of the Yaqui Delta Land and Water Company had been canceled.[8] More serious problems arose when the Carranza government renewed its efforts to implement article 27. The government now concentrated on lands which either were unexploited or were being explored prior to drilling new wells. The secretary of industry announced that companies wanting to drill new wells had to obtain permits. These would be granted after the applicant registered his title and promised to accept the Organic Law on Petroleum when passed by the Mexican Congress. The Mexican government also began to grant a few denouncement titles to unexploited lands which had not been registered. Both foreign

---

1919, SD 812.6363/464. Speeches and resolutions in *Congressional Record*, 66th Cong., 1st sess., 1919, 58, pt. 2: 1173–78, 1192–93, 1391–93, 1901–2; pt. 3: 2416–26, 2926–27, 3196–3200; pt. 9: 8886–87.

6. Garfield to F. C. Proctor (Gulf Pipeline Co.), 21 November 1918, Garfield MSS; see also Garfield to Rhoades, 17 January 1919, ibid. Garfield Diary, 15 January 1919, ibid.: "Polk gave me last notes of Fletcher's to Carranza—they are exactly what we have desired—admirably worded."

7. Garfield Diary, 15 March 1919, ibid.

8. Rhoades to Garfield, 3 May 1919, ibid. The concessions involved water rights.

and mixed companies received these titles; and at least one U.S. company (AGWI) was included.[9]

The major U.S. oil companies would not request permits with the attached conditions. Some stopped drilling new wells, while others continued operations in defiance of Mexican policy.[10] Ambassador Fletcher—now in Washington to stay—urged the Mexican officials to grant "provisional permits" and threatened to block shipments of arms and ammunition if such permits were not issued.

Mexican stability still had some priority, and State Department officials did not want to crack down too harshly on Mexican efforts to crush armed opposition. Frank Polk congratulated General Jacinto Treviño for the killing of Emiliano Zapata and General A. Blanquet and expressed the hope that Villa would be next. Even in late May 1919 the department asked the governors of Texas, Arizona, and New Mexico to permit the Mexican army to cross their states in pursuit of Villistas (Governor W. F. Hobby of Texas refused).[11] Testifying before the Senate Foreign Relations Committee in June, Polk stated that the United States had a choice between Carranza and intervention, since one opposition leader was "dissolute" (Díaz) and another was a "ruffian" (Villa). "They were tempted to invade Mexico," Polk noted, "but thought

9. Mexican regulations in Secretaría de Industria, Comercio, y Trabajo, *Legislación petrolera* (México, D.F., 1922), 154. Titles discussed in Watriss to Polk, 10 April 1919, SD 812.6363/439; Harold Walker to Capt. Paul Foley (U.S. Shipping Board), 30 December 1919, SD 812.6363/618.

10. Frederic R. Kellogg, "The Mexican Oil Situation," in Blakeslee, *Mexico and the Caribbean*, 54–72; Watriss to Polk, 27 June 1919, Polk MSS. The term "major" U.S. oil companies designates the eleven groups which were active in the Association for the Protection of American Rights in Mexico. The most important of these were the Doheny interests (Pan-American Petroleum and Transport Company), the Texas Company, Standard Oil of New Jersey, and the John Hays Hammond interests (Continental Mexican Petroleum). A 1916 report by a group of independent operators divided the some four hundred companies in Mexico into three classes: the four dominating companies, twenty-five lesser companies which usually supported the first group, and the small independent producers "with small holdings and limited means"; E. Dean Fuller, "The Oil Situation in Mexico in Relation to American Investments: An Argument on Behalf of Various Independent Interests," 19 December 1916, SD 812.6363/255.

11. Frank Polk, Confidential Diary, 21 April 1919, Polk MSS. For border crossing see Fletcher to Summerlin, 11 April 1919, SD 812.6363/444; Breckinridge Long Diary, 31 May 1919, Long MSS.

it would be a mistake to stay there too long as American property would be destroyed."[12]

In June 1919 the Mexican government began to send military forces into the oil fields in order to stop drilling operations by companies which had not secured permits. The representatives of the large oil companies deluged their friends in the State Department with demands for action. Frederic N. Watriss—representing the Petroleum Producers Association—wrote to Polk: "You have given me repeated assurances that you would not permit confiscation and that when an overt act amounting to confiscation was committed, it would be up to the United States to act. I submit that the time for some action has arrived. . . . Please go to the bat."[13] Several oil representatives admitted that they wanted armed intervention.[14]

Polk and Fletcher opposed intervention at this point, but both were fearful that pressure from Congress and the interest groups might force the administration into such a course of action. Mexican officials were informed by Fletcher that no more permissions for the exportation of ammunition would be issued until the Mexican government "indicated a more compromising spirit with reference to provisional permits to drill for American oil companies." Polk informed Ignacio Bonillas, Mexican ambassador to the United States, that the oil situation might force the president to withdraw recognition.[15]

Carranza did authorize the issuance of provisional drilling permits. But in order to receive these the companies would have to promise formally that they would be subject to legislative regulations that might be enacted in the future and would have to produce proof of possession of the lands involved. The companies refused to accept these conditions. As Watriss explained, "We acquired lands in Mexico in full conformity with its laws, and we demand the privilege of exercising fully and unconditionally the rights incident to ownership."[16]

12. Frank Polk, Confidential Diary, 21 June 1919, Polk MSS.
13. Watriss to Polk, 27 June 1919, ibid.
14. Frank Polk, Confidential Diary, 9 July 1919, ibid. Claude Dawson (consul, Tampico) to Secretary of State, 10 June 1919, SD 812.6363/476. The official name for the oil association was Association of American Producers of Petroleum in Mexico.
15. Memo, Fletcher to Polk, 7 July 1919, Fletcher MSS; Polk to Fletcher, 17 July 1919, Polk MSS.
16. Watriss to Secretary of State, 12 August 1919, SD 812.6363/513. The companies argued that filing manifestations of title would constitute

From this point until late January 1920 U.S.-Mexican relations deteriorated rapidly. Demands for armed intervention increased. American Legion posts, the Patriotic Order Sons of America, the governor of Texas, oil company representatives, and some consuls in Mexico joined in the clamor stimulated by the National Association for the Protection of American Rights in Mexico and congressional interventionists.[17] Senator Fall and Harold Walker collaborated in the campaign. For example, when the American Legion asked Fall to submit a resolution on Mexico for their 1919 convention, the senator confidentially requested Walker to prepare the draft. The oil representative made extensive use of the Democratic platform of 1912 which, he stated, had been "forgotten as completely as the seventh commandment at a catshow." Presumably Walker was referring to the biblical injunction. But his theology generally swam in oil, as when he referred to publicity concerning the oil situation in Mexico as being "for the greater glorification of God."[18]

All this publicity convinced many in both countries that intervention was coming. Chandler Anderson was so sure of intervention that he told Bernard Baruch the administration would select Baruch or Vance McCormick as governor general of Mexico— Baruch was not interested in the job. Acting Secretary of the Navy Franklin D. Roosevelt must have felt that he was being ignored in the rush of events, for he sent two letters to the State

recognition that the Mexican government owned the subsurface; Summerlin to Secretary of State, 21 July 1919, SD 812.6363/486; Watriss to Fletcher, 24 July 1919, Fletcher MSS. Fletcher felt that Carranza could be pressured into eliminating the "string"; Fletcher to Polk, 23 July 1919, ibid.

17. W. F. Hobby to Lansing, 25 August 1919, SD 711.12/210 (the Texas governor stressed the open door for Mexico); Consul, Mazatlan, to Secretary of State, 22 August 1919, SD 711.12/215; National Camp, Patriotic Order Sons of America to President Wilson, 7 December 1919, SD 711.12/233; Fourth New Jersey Post of the American Legion, to Secretary of State, 19 December 1919, SD 711.12/243; E. L. Doheny, "The Mexican Question: Its Relation to Our Industries, Our Merchant Marine, and Our Foreign Trade," enclosed in Harold Walker to Secretary of State, 19 December 1919, SD 812.6363/609; Speech by J. Will Taylor (Tenn.), *Congressional Record*, 66th Cong., 1st sess., 1919, 58, pt. 9: 9098–99. Note from Fletcher to A. A. Adee, 30 September 1919, SD 812.00/23273a, concerned weekly dispatch of summaries of the Mexican situation to counter both Mexican propaganda and the "campaign" of the National Association.

18. Walker to Fall, 5 June 1919, Fall MSS; Dan Jackson (secretary of the Senate Subcommittee on Mexican Relations) to Walker, 6 October 1919, ibid.; Walker to Jackson, 7 October 1919, ibid.

Department requesting advance notice in case of armed intervention. Wilson returned these with the penciled note, "See Roosevelt
and read riot act."[19] Warnings about the menace of "kaiserism"
no longer aroused much interest, but "bolshevism" provided a
suitable replacement for intervention propagandists. E. L. Doheny,
self-appointed "expert" on the subject, warned that prominent
Mexicans were trying to stir up revolution and bolshevism in the
United States. He also was convinced that Bolsheviks controlled
the major U.S. universities, and that bankers such as Thomas
Lamont and Frank Vanderlip were being converted to the doctrine. All this agitation tied in with the growing red scare in the
United States. But it is interesting to note that the use of such
rhetorical tactics against Mexico generally predated the overall
scare. Leading Mexicans were verbally converted by U.S. propagandists from kaiserism to bolshevism.[20]

The militant voices were loud, but they hardly constituted a
major public movement. The number one foreign policy issue was
the peace treaty, and there were determined voices opposing
intervention. The Board of Foreign Missions of the Methodist
Church, the Federal Council of the Churches of Christ in America,
the League of Free Nations Association, John Farwell Moors (a
Boston banker), and Secretary of the Navy Daniels were among
those in the opposition. Magazines such as the *Nation* and the
New Republic were also campaigning against intervention.[21]

19. Chandler P. Anderson Diary, 27 August 1919, Anderson MSS;
Roosevelt (acting secretary of the Navy) to Lansing, 7 August 1919, SD
711.12/194½; Lansing to President Wilson, 19 August 1919 (penciled
note at bottom), SD 711.12/195½; Lansing to Roosevelt, 22 August 1919,
Lansing MSS (the secretary did not read the riot act).

20. Speech by Norman J. Gould (N.Y.), 3 March 1919, *Congressional
Record*, 65th Cong., 3d sess., 1919, 57, pt. 5: 379. Doheny's comment in
Arthur Pound and Samuel T. Moore, *They Told Barron: The Notes of
Clarence W. Barron* (New York, 1930), 14; see also Senator Fall to Secre-
tary of State, 13 November 1919, SD 711.12/227; For the actual role of
Communists see Harry Bernstein, "Marxismo en México, 1917–1925,"
Historia mexicana 7 (April–June 1958), 497–516.

21. Board of Foreign Missions of the Methodist Episcopal Church to
Secretary Lansing, 10 December 1919, SD 711.12/236; Federal Council
of the Churches of Christ in America to Secretary Lansing, 15 December
1919, SD 711.12/242; James G. McDonald (chairman, League of Free
Nations Association) to Lansing, 15 August 1919, SD 812.6363/508. John
Farwell Moors, *Shall We Intervene in Mexico?* (New York, 1919), published by the League (this Boston banker argued that at least one million
men would be needed for an intervention); Committee on Cooperation

Although most State Department officials did not completely agree with the hardline interventionists, they were seeking ways "to impress upon the Mexican Government that it would be absolutely necessary for them to extend a more efficient and adequate protection to American lives and property in Mexico."[22] In late July Counselor Polk and Ambassador Fletcher drafted and dispatched a telegram which stated that the United States "may be forced to adopt a radical change in policy with regard to Mexico." They hoped that this threat would prompt the Mexican government to change its policies and would indicate to American citizens the department's concern over the Mexican situation.[23]

President Wilson approved the general contents of the note, but department officials faced the problem of obtaining his consent for the specifications of such radical change. Early in August 1919 Wilson finally read Fletcher's memorandum of 1 March 1919 and inquired whether Fletcher still agreed with the "suggested courses of action" and, if so, what would he suggest in the event Mexico did not respond to "our call" to do her duty internationally.[24] Fletcher replied that he still believed a stern warning to the Mexican government offered the only hope for shocking that government into performing its duties and thus averting intervention. Fletcher also recommended that "upon the next serious occasion" the department send a note reviewing in detail the history of U.S.-Mexican relations since the "failure of the Atlantic City Conference [1916]" in a "last effort to avert intervention." "Should this last effort prove unavailing," he wrote, "I would propose that this Government then take, alone or in conjunction with other governments, steps to restore orderly conditions in Mexico."[25] In an additional effort to win the president's support, Fletcher and Lansing sent articles and memorandums dealing with the Carranza Doctrine. Fletcher wrote that the Mexican govern-

---

in Latin America (Samuel Guy Inman) to Secretary of State, 3 September 1919, SD 711.12/211; Daniels to Wilson, 17 July 1919, and Wilson to Daniels, 19 July 1919, Daniels MSS (Wilson called the information "cheering").

22. Acting Secretary of State to Summerlin, 21 July 1919, SD 412.11-Carton, Hiram/Orig.

23. Fletcher wanted to release the note to the press; Fletcher to Secretary of State, 30 July 1919, SD 711.12/216.

24. Wilson to Secretary of State, 4 August 1919, SD 711.12/187.

25. Fletcher to Wilson, 18 August 1919, SD 711.12/187.

ment was "preparing to launch an active, perhaps secret, anti-American campaign throughout Latin America." And Lansing informed the president that Carranza had set out to destroy the Monroe Doctrine and to replace Pan-Americanism with Indo-Latinism.[26] Wilson agreed that the situation was "exceedingly serious," but his only specific proposal was for Fletcher to return to Mexico in order to "exercise a restraining influence on Carranza." On 26 August, Lansing noted that the president "does not think it wise to act now."[27]

By mid-August 1919 Lansing and Fletcher were prepared to accept intervention, but both still hoped that some kind of diplomatic shock treatment might jar Carranza into cooperating. Both were honestly convinced that a tough diplomatic stance would avoid the need to take the last step.[28] Wilson, however, was not prepared to initiate the process which could possibly cause a major crisis. The fight over the treaty was headache enough.

The president suffered a severe stroke in early October 1919, and during the next four months Lansing and Fletcher, with assistance from Boaz Long, who was primarily concerned with Cuba, took the United States very close to the brink of war with Mexico, as close as the country had been at any time since 1916. Two issues provided the setting for Lansing's subtle, and sometimes ambivalent, maneuvers. These were the Jenkins case (involving the arrest of a U.S. consul) and the controversy over issuing oil-drilling permits. Both issues had their specific and symbolic dimensions. Obtaining Jenkins's release from jail and the permission to drill oil wells were important concerns. But the fundamental issue was the protection of foreign citizens and businesses from the impact of revolutionary nationalism. To the secretary and his colleagues these developments were intimately related to the Mexican government's hostility to the United States as a country, the "American way of life," and U.S. hemispheric hegemony. They believed that Mexican officials were trying to

26. Fletcher to Wilson, 20 August 1919, and Lansing to Wilson, 21 August 1919, SD 711.12/192½.
27. Wilson to Lansing, 22 August 1919, SD 711.12/193½; Note by Lansing, 26 August 1919, SD 812.00/23111b.
28. Fletcher to Secretary of State, 16 August 1919, Fletcher MSS. Sixty thousand troops had been massed on the border with airplanes and tanks; *New York Times,* 21 August 1919.

foment social disorder and even revolution within the United States. Lansing became concerned over reports that the black former heavyweight boxing champion, Jack Johnson, had "been spreading social equality propaganda among negroes in Mexico and . . . endeavoring to incite the colored element in this country."[29] He also accepted at face value the reports assiduously collected by Senator Fall's subcommittee on U.S.-Mexican relations that Mexican officials were collaborating with the IWW and the Bolsheviks, and that the Mexican government was discussing a defensive alliance with Japan.[30] Lansing was convinced, however, that if the Mexican government could be forced to accept the U.S. definition of effective protection for foreign lives and property the other irritants would be automatically eliminated.

The secretary hoped that the Mexican government could be pressured by methods short of war. This required careful balancing and meant that he had to establish a working relationship with the Republicans of the Senate Foreign Relations Committee, who threatened to force precipitate action, and deal with an incapacitated president who held the key to any ultimate action such as breaking relations.[31] The entire situation was further complicated by the growing debate over the peace treaty and the revelations concerning Lansing's behind-the-scenes dissent with some of Wilson's policies during the peace negotiations. The documentary record is not entirely clear in regard to some aspects of the secretary's maneuvers in the Jenkins case, but it is quite precise concerning the oil controversy.

In October 1919 U.S. Consul William O. Jenkins was kidnaped by an antigovernment band led by Federico Córdoba, a subordinate of Manuel Pelaez. The kidnapers announced that their action was designed to prove that the Carranza government could not protect foreign nationals, and after Jenkins's ransom was paid by private sources he was arrested by the government on

29. Lansing to Summerlin, 27 October 1919, SD 812.4016/a.
30. Josephus Daniels Diary, 4 December 1919, Daniels MSS; Lansing to Embassy, Tokyo, 16 November 1919, SD 712.94/27a. The Japanese ambassador stated that his country wanted to keep out of the difficulties between the United States and Mexico; Memorandum by Breckinridge Long, 10 December 1919, SD 711.12/239.
31. Senator Fall to Secretary of State, 13 November 1919, and Note by Boaz Long, 14 November 1919, SD 711.12/227; Long reported that he and Fletcher had called on Fall.

charges of collusion with the rebels.[32] Some proponents of a get-tough-with-Mexico policy now made the treatment of Consul Jenkins a focal point for agitation.

Secretary Lansing displayed some tactical ambivalence in handling the Jenkins case. He knew that Jenkins had a record of bad relations with the Carranzistas dating back to 1914 and was considered to be antigovernment.[33] Lansing probably knew that Jenkins was something of an operator and had been speculating in Mexican real estate with depreciated currency. Senator Fall knew this and perhaps Jenkins's reputation provided a degree of moderation to the reactions of Fall and some of his colleagues.[34] After all, intervention on behalf of a land speculator might have adverse political effects.

Would the Jenkins case be suitable for the "next serious occasion" which Fletcher had discussed in his August memorandum? The ambassador thought so and was ready to move decisively. Lansing agreed but had to move carefully in his assumed role of "prime minister." He convened the cabinet on 18 November 1919 and a vigorous debate took place. Secretaries Lane and Albert Burleson, the postmaster general, spoke for "drastic measures," while Secretaries Wilson, Baker, and Daniels opposed such action. Lansing and A. Mitchell Palmer, the attorney general, did not think that conditions justified "going in."[35] The cabinet decided to postpone the issue for a week, and during this time Lansing considered various ways in which the episode might be used to shock the Carranza government.

On 20 November, the State Department formally demanded the release of Jenkins. The note warned that the harassment of the consul "cannot but have a very serious effect on relations between the two countries." The next day Fletcher drafted a forty-eight hour ultimatum which threatened the severing of diplomatic relations to be followed by "steps to protect the rights of its [U.S.] citizens in Mexico." Lansing told him "to can it" and

32. Charles C. Cumberland, "The Jenkins Case and Mexican-American Relations," *HAHR* 31 (November 1951): 586–603.

33. Ibid., 586–87.

34. EJK (Kearful) to Fall, 13 December 1919, Fall MSS.

35. Lansing, Desk Diary, 18 November 1919, Lansing MSS; Josephus Daniels Diary, 18 November 1919, Daniels MSS.

the ultimatum was not dispatched.[36] Fletcher then began work on a more limited plan to withdraw recognition from Mexico. Such a course would require presidential consent, and Fletcher attempted to secure authorization from President Wilson for the plan. He was unable to obtain any action by the president, and as liaison man between the State Department and the Senate Republicans, the ambassador reported these activities to Senators Fall and Brandegee. He suggested to them that some form of congressional action might reinforce the department's position. The ambassador wanted the president to lay the Mexican situation before the Congress in order to receive support for "effective measures," including force. As he told Lansing, "our policy of patience and forebearance has utterly failed, and . . . we are at the parting of the ways."[37]

Cabinet meetings on 25 and 26 November failed to produce a consensus in regard to conditions in Mexico and the best course of action in securing Jenkins's release from prison.[38] At this juncture Lansing was beginning to feel somewhat frustrated in his twin efforts to lead the administration and provide cooperative guidance to the Senate. The U.S. policy of diplomatic protest and patient negotiation did not seem to be effective in forcing a change in Mexican policy, and the idea of drastic action leading to war appeared to be gaining influential supporters in Congress. Lansing believed that it was his duty to maneuver the administration into a new tactical position. The majority of the cabinet and the ailing president presented definite obstacles to this course. The secretary was not eager for conflict, and he did not want to be pushed hastily into a military situation, but by late November he seemed to be losing his campaign for a third approach and began to give some consideration to the militant alternative.[39]

36. Lansing to American Embassy, Mexico, 20 November 1919, SD 125.61383/182; Fletcher to Secretary of State, 21 November 1919, Fletcher MSS; Lansing, Desk Diary, 22 November 1919, Lansing MSS.
37. Fletcher to Lansing, 25 November 1919, SD 312.11/8839½. See also Lansing, Desk Diary, 24 November 1919; C. V. Safford to Fall, 24 November 1919 (2 letters); Memorandum of Conversation with Fletcher, by C. V. Safford, 24 November 1919, Fall MSS.
38. Safford to Fall, 26 November 1919, Fall MSS.
39. "Interview with the Mexican Ambassador *in re* the Jenkins Case," 28 November 1919, Private Notes, Lansing MSS. In a memorandum the solicitor noted that severance of relations presaged hostilities, and that the

On 27 November 1919 the Mexican government answered the U.S. note by declaring that the U.S. demand had no legal basis. To Lansing this was the height of insolence.[40] The next day Ambassador Ignacio Bonillas visited the State Department, where the secretary informed him bluntly that unless the Mexican government "made a radical change in its attitude toward the United States," the American people would soon force a break in relations. This would "almost inevitably mean war," Lansing declared, pointing to Germany as an example of what Mexico might expect. Bonillas, according to Lansing, displayed astonishment, rage, and consternation, and turned pale. When he left there was no hand-shaking. Lansing confided in his private notes:

If my interview with Bonillas does not bring Carranza and his advisors to their senses, nothing will. It seemed to be a last resort to get the Mexicans to change their policy and prevent an explosion in Congress and the adoption of drastic demands for action. Bellicose as was my manner and language during the interview, it was really intended to prevent war.

To Lansing, this diplomatic tongue-lashing was the last peaceful effort to change the policy of Carranza. He wanted to secure Jenkins's release but he also wanted to push Carranza into a resolution of the "basic" issues. He had noted earlier in the private notes for the day:

A satisfactory settlement of the Jenkins case might check this agitation [in Congress and the press] for a time but the numerous and flagrant violations of American rights, both of persons and property, are really at the bottom of the present excitement. The unjust treatment of Jenkins is only an incident. I am not at all sure that the issue between this country and Mexico might as well come now as at some later time. I have sought to avoid coming to an open repture [sic] in every way possible, hoping against hope that sense and decency would finally penetrate the thick skull of President Carranza. It is apparently useless.[41]

United States should be prepared for an expeditionary force or blockade; Memorandum by Woolsey, 25 November 1919, SD 711.12/223¾.

40. Memorandum, Conversation between Lansing and the Mexican Ambassador, 28 November 1919, SD 711.12/229¾.

41. Interview with the Mexican Ambassador *in re* the Jenkins Case. 28 November 1919, Private Notes, Lansing MSS.

The secretary was not only mentally preparing himself for a military resolution of the situation, but he was also spreading the word among his colleagues. In the cabinet meeting the same day (28 November) Lansing stated: "If we go into Mexico it will settle our difficulties and unite us here." He also discussed the Mexican situation with Third Secretary Breckinridge Long, who noted: "He thinks a war might be a good remedy for the local internal situation."[42] The secretary was referring to the wave of strikes with accompanying violence, growing unemployment, fear of Bolshevik inroads among the idle workers, bomb reports, IWW agitation, and race riots which swept the United States in 1919. And he speculated that war might once again provide national unity. He was also voicing his agreement with the argument, propounded by Fall and the oilmen, that the Mexican government was partly responsible for "red agitation" in the United States.[43] Secretary Daniels disagreed with this line of reasoning and urged Lansing to move with caution. Breckinridge Long indicated his belief that a war with Mexico might be "very unpopular."[44]

Lansing did move with care during the next few weeks, but not in the way Daniels envisaged. The secretary of state realized that he would have very little support among his colleagues for any attempt to use the Jenkins case as "the incident" needed to launch a more militant policy. Joseph Tumulty, Wilson's secretary, informed him that Wilson would not go to war with Mexico and that the issue should not be pushed.[45] Lansing realized that the Jenkins case had become too charged with domestic political controversy. The president regarded the agitation as a "Republican political trick," and a majority of congressional Democrats seemed very reluctant to follow a militant course.[46] Lansing confided to Chandler Anderson that he had not consulted the president or reported to him about the Jenkins case because he feared that

42. Josephus Daniels Diary, 28 November 1919, Daniels MSS; Breckinridge Long Diary, 28 November 1919, Long MSS.
43. Josephus Daniels Diary, 4 December 1919, Daniels MSS. An unidentified Washington source released so-called documentary information concerning a 1915 Mexican plot to invade the United States with Negro troops; *New York Times*, 28 November 1919.
44. Josephus Daniels Diary, 28 November 1919, Daniels MSS; Breckinridge Long Diary, 28 November 1919, Long MSS.
45. Josephus Daniels Diary, 4 December 1919, Daniels MSS.
46. Memorandum of conversation with Fletcher, by C. V. Safford, 24 November 1919, Fall MSS.

Wilson would tie the hands of the department and prevent any action. But the last stage had come, and the secretary stated that "he had almost reached the limit of his authority without the President's approval, because the next step was the severing of diplomatic relations." Lansing did not think that he could take that step "on his own responsibility."[47]

The secretary of state had been working other angles, however, to prepare the way for an eventual showdown with Carranza on a less politicized issue. This involved close cooperation with congressional leaders and secret conferences with Senator Fall. On 1 December 1919 the senator arrived in Washington and went directly to Lansing's house. The secretary noted that the meeting was "very satisfactory." Fall approved the "present policy" and agreed to "keep waters quiet as to Mexico" and to prevent an immediate report of his subcommittee. Lansing wrote in his diary: "Am in some doubt whether Pres. [president] will like it when he learns of it. I am right, so I don't care."[48] The new angle was to separate the politically tainted Jenkins controversy from other issues and from the push for more militant tactics. Jenkins contributed to the necessity for such a separation when he told a *New York Times* reporter that he had made much money since the revolution started and that he wanted to cause trouble for the governor of Puebla by remaining in jail (he had refused to post bail).[49]

Lansing was maneuvering the administration toward a situation in which Carranza actually could be confronted with the severing of diplomatic relations under circumstances where the executive and legislative branches could be unified in support of this drastic step. Senator Fall knew what Lansing was trying to do and thought that he was providing an effective tool for the secretary's policy when he included a request for the president to break relations with Mexico in his concurrent resolution endorsing the State Department's position. Lansing, realizing the adverse effect such a "request" would have on Wilson, sent Fletcher to tell Senator

47. Chandler P. Anderson Diary, 4 December 1919, Anderson MSS.
48. Lansing, Desk Diary, 1 and 2 December 1919, Lansing MSS. For supporting information by former Consul General Chamberlain see *Is Mexico Worth Saving?* 191–95.
49. *New York Times*, 4 December 1919. The Mexican government had charged Jenkins with perjury, and this caught the State Department by surprise; ibid., 29 November 1919.

Henry Cabot Lodge that he would "prefer that action upon it be deferred as it might embarrass him in handling the Jenkins case."[50] The secretary knew that he had to have Wilson's support for further action and that this entailed the moderation of public pressure from congressional Republicans to calm presidential hostility to possible escalation of the diplomatic crisis.

As part of this maneuver Lansing now decided to use the Jenkins case to regain Wilson's confidence by trying to convince the president that his secretary of state had been working all along to avoid a confrontation with Mexico and to hamstring the congressional Republicans. The opportunity to implement this grandstand play came on 5 December when members of the Senate Foreign Relations Committee went to see Wilson in his bedroom. The day before, Lansing telephoned Tumulty to deny the press reports that the State Department had anything to do with the Fall resolution and explained his cooperation with the Foreign Relations Committee as giving the "Republicans all the rope they wanted about going to war with Mexico."[51] The same day Lansing also requested Secretary Daniels to send ships to Mexico; such action had been recommended by William Randolph Hearst.[52] The secretary of state informed the president that he had not communicated with him about the Jenkins case because of its complexity and "because there was *no possibility* of that case developing a situation which could possibly warrant intervention in Mexico." The danger, Lansing continued, was that the forthcoming report of Senator Fall's subcommittee would cause Congress to "demand drastic action." He continued: "I have seen this coming for some time . . . and it was with that purpose [to avert such congressional demands] that I sought to divert attention to the Jenkins case which I knew *could not possibly result in a rupture between the two Governments.*" Then the secretary dropped the first hint of a new confrontation:

50. Memorandum by Henry P. Fletcher, 9 December 1919, SD 812. 00/23263½; Lansing, Desk Diary, 1, 2, and 4 December 1919, Lansing MSS. Lodge was chairman of the Senate Foreign Relations Committee.

51. Lansing, Desk Diary, 4 December 1919. The committee vote to visit the president was 6 to 5.

52. Josephus Daniels Diary, 4 December 1919, Daniels MSS. Lane confided to Lansing that the Republicans would win in 1920 on the issue of eliminating the Mexican "trouble"; Lane to Lansing, 1 December 1919, SD 711.12/224½.

The real Mexican situation is the whole series of outrages and wrongs which Americans in Mexico have suffered during the Carranza administration. There is no doubt that the complaints are numerous and justified and that the indictment which can be drawn against Carranza will appeal very strongly to the people and arouse a very general indignation.

Lansing then assured Wilson that he could confront the senators secure in the knowledge that the State Department could handle the Jenkins case "without endangering our relations with Mexico."[53] The picture which the secretary tried to convey was that of a very loyal supporter of the president working to control a potentially rampaging Congress in the interests of peace. In a sense this was partially true, but Lansing did give Wilson distorted information and only hinted at the course of action he was preparing.[54]

The "smelling committee," as Wilson called the senatorial group, visited the White House on 5 December. Fall informed the president that he was praying for him. Wilson later described his reaction:

If I could have got out of bed, I would have hit the man. Why did he want to put me in bad with the Almighty? He must have known that God would take the opposite view from him on any subject.[55]

Shortly before the visit Lansing had called the White House to convey the information that Jenkins had been released, "a bombshell thrown in at the psychological moment," he noted.[56] How could Wilson possibly distrust him after this?

The "crisis" that Lansing now planned to use for the showdown with Carranza was the question of oil supplies. This issue was tied to the controversy over drilling permits. Early in the fall the oilmen thought that they could resolve the entire question of article 27 by working with various Mexican officials to shape the petroleum law which was being prepared by the Mexican Senate.

53. Lansing to Wilson, 5 December 1919, SD 711.12/225½A.
54. Chandler P. Anderson Diary, 4 December 1919, Anderson MSS; Lane to Lansing, 1 December 1919, SD 711.12/224½; Lansing, Desk Diary, 2 December 1919; all of these indicate the nature of Lansing's distortions.
55. Houston, *Eight Years with Wilson's Cabinet*, 2: 140–41.
56. Lansing, Desk Diary, 5 December 1919, Lansing MSS.

In its final form this law would have recognized all rights "heretofore legally acquired in petroleum lands," declared article 27 nonretroactive and abrogated all of the 1918 decrees. Carranza opposed the bill, and it was defeated by a 26-to-17 vote early in October 1919. The Senate then began consideration of the bill prepared by the executive branch, which Fletcher called "thoroughly unsatisfactory."[57]

Oil company representatives held additional conferences with Mexican officials and attempted to push a very mild regulatory law developed by Candido Aguilar, governor of the state of Veracruz. At first these officials seemed to be quite receptive. But the situation changed rapidly in mid-November when the Mexican army once more began forcibly to close down the drilling operations of U.S. companies which had not obtained permits.[58] The State Department did very little at this point, since Lansing and Fletcher still believed that the Jenkins case offered the best lever to force a change in Mexican policy and did not think it expedient to connect the two issues explicitly.[59]

By late November the oil companies were crying total disaster. The Texas Company and Transcontinental (subsidiary of Standard Oil of New Jersey) reported that the appearance of salt water in the older wells meant that they were becoming increasingly dependent upon oil from wells drilled, or in the process of being drilled, without permission.[60] Since the companies refused to accept the provisions of the permit decree, to comply with the national petroleum code when adopted, the crisis was one of their

57. Harold Walker to Burton Wilson, 25 September 1919, SD 812.6363/546; Fletcher to Lansing, 8 October 1919, SD 812.6363/646. See for details, Meyer, *México y Estados Unidos*, 93–94.

58. Burton Wilson to Chester Swain and Harold Walker, 14 October 1919, SD 812.6363/563; Amos Beaty (Texas Co.) to Lansing, 16 November 1919, Lansing MSS; Union Oil Company of California to Secretary of State, 17 November 1919, ibid.

59. "Memorandum of Conversation between F. J. Kearful and E. H. Talbot of Mt. Rainer, Maryland, November 17, 1919," Fall MSS; a penciled note "For Fall" stated, "Fletcher is anxious not to make the Mexican issue an oil issue, and I fully agree." Walker noted that the oil question was not included in current public discussions so that the "public mind" would focus on "American life and liberty" and not property; Harold Walker to Fall, 1 December 1919, ibid.

60. Fletcher to Secretary of State, 26 November 1919, Fletcher MSS; Fletcher to Lansing, 3 December 1919, SD 812.6363/647; Association of Oil Producers in Mexico to Secretary of State, 3 December 1919, SD 812.6363/591.

own creation. According to "oil logic," accepting the decree meant accepting the "confiscatory" article 27; therefore they refused to obey the law. If the Mexican government prevented unauthorized drilling (i.e., enforced the law), then Mexico would be responsible for any oil shortage in the United States. The issue was not confiscation. It was whether the oil companies would accept the *principle* of national control of natural resources and obey the laws or whether they could force the Mexican government either to ignore or to repudiate the principle. To achieve the latter goal the companies needed the active and militant support of the U.S. government, and they launched a massive campaign, complete with a "red scare," picturing a nation of idle factories, stalled railroads, and stranded fleets.[61]

Lansing, Fletcher, and Boaz Long were already true believers in "oil logic" and agreed that this was one of the basic issues of international relations. Others, such as Josephus Daniels, were not convinced by the oil companies' shouts of alarm; but some were converted by the campaign. John Barton Payne, chairman, U.S. Shipping Board, later head of the Red Cross, underwent such a process between 4 and 10 December.[62]

Lansing and Fletcher told the oilmen that the oil question should still remain separated from the Jenkins crisis, but the secretary was preparing the way for action.[63] A hint of this came after Lansing's secret testimony before the House Foreign Affairs Committee when Chairman Stephen G. Porter informed the press that the department means business "this time." In elaboration the congressman discussed the basic issues. Mexico could not be allowed to be anti-U.S., he declared, since this created the theoretical possibility that the Monroe Doctrine might be violated in the event Mexico sought allies in her dispute with the United States. He then stated:

61. The Producers Association combined all these charges in its letter of 8 December, which was sent to numerous congressmen, President Wilson, and the State Department; SD 812.6363/597–601; Chester O. Swain (Standard Oil of N.J.) to Fletcher, 3 December 1919, SD 812.6363/603.

62. Payne to Secretary of State, 4 December 1919, SD 812.6363/592; Payne to President Wilson, 10 December 1919, SD 812.6363/605.

63. Fletcher to Lansing, 3 December 1919, SD 812.6363/647; Lansing to President Wilson, 5 December 1919, SD 711.12/225½A. In a conversation with Bonillas on 2 December, Fletcher switched the discussion to the oil problem; Fletcher to Secretary, 2 December 1919, SD 125.61383/170½.

Property rights have been violated, and the Mexican Courts have declared constitutional the confiscatory provisions of the Mexican fundamental law. . . . If we permit the property rights of our nationals in Mexico to be thus violated, where can we stop? Suppose Brazil and Argentina and Germany and other nations adopt such a confiscatory law; our interests abroad would be wiped out.[64]

The last shred of hope for a voluntary retreat by the Mexican government seemed to be gone when the Mexican Senate passed the executive petroleum bill on 8 December.

State Department wheels were already turning to produce the arguments which officials hoped would convince the president that a "serious crisis" was at hand. On 7 December 1919 Boaz Long prepared a cover letter summarizing the confiscatory policies and anti-American actions of the Mexican government and suggested that it be sent to the president with a memorandum which he was drafting. Carranza was the villain throughout this letter, the principal reason being that "Carranza's mind has proved a fertile field for the seeds of radical socialism, which, when planted there, seem quickly to have taken root, and later to have flowered in the Bolshevistic constitution of May 1, 1917." Long also cited the reputed link between Mexican officials and Bolshevik activity in the United States. He concluded with the strong recommendation that the United States break relations with Mexico "as the most effective way, short of armed intervention, of conveying to the Mexicans the conviction that we mean what we have said with respect to the protection of American life and the non-confiscation of American property." According to Long, such action would "probably" produce a more congenial Mexican leader, but if not then the "certain remedy of intervention by our armed forces might be ultimately tried."[65]

Long's memorandum was even more militant in tone and conclusions. About two-thirds of it concerned the oil question and various other economic problems. An appendix listed 198 Americans killed by Mexicans since 1911; this included some skeletons which were "presumed" to be the remains of U.S. citizens. Lansing requested Fletcher to make an immediate review of the docu-

64. *New York Times,* 2 December 1919.
65. Long to Secretary of State, 7 December 1919; draft letter, Long to President Wilson, SD 711.12/228½.

ment, and the ambassador recommended that exhibit three be sent to the president as soon as possible because of the "urgency of some decision as to our policy in the oil controversy."[66]

Prior to receiving the Long memorandum Fletcher had again stressed the urgency of a policy decision by the president. He stated that a number of oil companies could hold out "only for a few weeks longer," and then they would be forced either to suspend operations or to accept the Mexican "contention." If the latter occurred, "everything which the Department has done in its efforts to secure justice for the American companies will be thereby swept aside."[67] Lansing was now ready for another attempt at maneuvering the president into a hardline position in regard to Mexico. On 19 December 1919 Lansing sent a note, prepared by Fletcher, to Wilson announcing, "A serious crisis has arisen with respect to oil supplies from Mexico." This was a most carefully worded communication. It was moderate in tone and designed to lead Wilson to a logical conclusion. The president was informed that oil production had been stopped by the Mexican government because the companies would not accept "nationalization"; and "the limit of diplomatic pressure in this whole matter seems to have been reached." Lansing pointed out that he had "carefully refrained" from making any demands or threats, but the U.S. note of 2 April 1918 did warn that the government would protect the property of its citizens if necessary. The president was then asked what further steps he wished to take. This was followed by a rather direct nudge in the direction of the anticipated decision. Lansing noted that Carranza would go up to the point of a "definite break" with the United States before abandoning his oil policy. If the United States did nothing, "then Carranza will undoubtedly gain his point, which entirely aside from all questions of loss of prestige, may seriously affect the supplies of oil to the United States."[68]

There is no evidence of a response to this note. Fletcher then prepared a memorandum specifically detailing a step-by-step plan

66. Memorandum by Boaz Long (Division of Mexican Affairs), 12 December 1919; Fletcher to Secretary of State, 13 December 1919, SD 711.12/229½.
67. Fletcher to Secretary of State, 11 December 1919, Fletcher MSS.
68. Lansing to Wilson, 19 December 1919, SD 812.6363/620. Fletcher also noted that Gregory and McAdoo had prepared a memorandum for the president.

which would lead either to the Mexican government's acceptance of the U.S. position or to the termination of diplomatic relations. The ambassador called it his "Xmas gift."[69] Lansing incorporated most of the proposals in the document as well as the wording of Fletcher's "Observations on Attached Memorandum" in a letter to President Wilson. According to the proposed plan, the ambassador would return to Mexico and make the following proposals: (1) that the Mexican government formally agree to take more effective means for the protection of the lives, rights, and property of Americans; (2) that the Mexican government agree by treaty to constitute a joint American-Mexican commission, or a mixed commission with a third party as umpire, to adjudicate all claims of citizens of both countries; and (3) that the Mexican government agree by treaty to submit to the Hague tribunal the question of the effect of the constitution of 1917, and all decrees and regulations issued thereunder, upon all property rights of American citizens acquired prior to its promulgation, and that, pending the final decision, the Mexican government immediately suspend the enforcement of all laws, decrees, and proceedings affecting these American rights. The third provision would allow the Mexican government to collect production and export taxes which were not "prohibitive in nature" and were levied without regard to nationality.

If the Mexicans asked about the arms embargo, they would be informed that it would be lifted as soon as they accepted the proposals. The ambassador would wait for four weeks for the "acceptance in principle" of the proposals. He would then declare that if they had not been accepted by the end of another week, the United States would terminate diplomatic relations.

After outlining the plan, Lansing stressed that intervention was not a "necessary consequence" of breaking relations. It was a "possibility," but the probable result would be the checking of the hostile attitude of the Mexican government. And the termination of relations might well lead to the elimination of Carranza by "patriotic" Mexicans. Even if these results were not forthcoming, the United States would be in a position to use recognition as a bargaining lever with the victor of the 1920 presidential election.

69. Fletcher to Polk, 22 December 1919, Polk MSS; Fletcher to Secretary of State, 22 December 1919, ibid.; Fletcher, "Observations on Attached Memorandum," 22 December 1919, ibid.

The secretary concluded with what he must have considered a clever manipulation of Wilson's well-publicized dislike of the major oil companies: "I may add however that I have reason to believe that the proposed plan will not meet with cordial approval of the oil companies whose rights are affected by the nationalization policy of the Carranza Government."[70]

This remark may have been true for some oil representatives, but for the most part Lansing and the oil companies were in almost complete agreement. This was not because Lansing was pressured into taking this position; if anything he remained rather aloof during this period. Lansing, Fletcher, and the oilmen shared basic assumptions about the sanctity of property and the need to protect foreign investments. At a State Department conference of Lansing, Polk, and representatives of the Association of American Producers of Petroleum in Mexico (8 January 1920), Ira Jewell Williams, president of the Panuco Boston Oil Company, and Chester O. Swain, attorney for Transcontinental Petroleum, suggested withdrawal of recognition. Swain also recommended that naval vessels be sent to Mexican waters; Lansing had made this request on 4 December. Williams suggested that a public announcement be made "to clear up all doubt of the cooperation between the oil companies and the State Department." Lansing did not want such publicity, since he still hoped that the president would accept the proposed plan.[71]

It became increasingly evident, however, that Woodrow Wilson did not intend to act on the recommendations in the letter of 3 January. On 15 January 1920 the Petroleum Producers Association made a direct appeal to President Carranza. The group stated that the companies were willing to accept provisional permits, valid until the Mexican Congress passed an organic law for petroleum, provided that acceptance of such permits would not "destroy

70. Lansing to Wilson, 3 January 1920, SD 711.12/263a. Lansing changed the deadline proposed by Fletcher from three to five weeks and dropped Fletcher's statement that article 27 practically closed the door to foreign capital.

71. Memorandum of Conference between Secretary Lansing and Representatives of the Association of American Producers of Petroleum in Mexico, 8 January 1920, SD 812.6363/641. Lansing publicly denied that he was cooperating with Senator Fall; one oilman thought that publicizing the connection would aid their cause in the United States and Mexico; W. F. Buckley to F. J. Kearful, 30 December 1919, Fall MSS.

or prejudice such rights as they may have." In return the association agreed that by issuing the permits the Mexican government was not surrendering any right or principle "which it may desire to sustain." On 20 January Carranza accepted this proposal.[72]

This temporary truce allowed both sides to save face, without specifically settling any of the outstanding issues. According to the *Wall Street Journal* the companies believed that these arrangements would become permanent because they were convinced that a "friendly government" would be elected in 1920. With a visible lack of enthusiasm, Ambassador Fletcher noted: "This practically settles the present acute phase of the oil controversy." R. C. Tanis, of the Division of Mexican Affairs, was more optimistic in his observation that the recent "concessions" had produced a "more or less satisfactory status of the oil situation."[73]

Fletcher, disgruntled over the failure to push for a final settlement of the basic issues, resigned his position in late January. He wanted to publish his letter of resignation and a memorandum attacking the policy of the Wilson administration. Lansing suggested the elimination of only one paragraph. John Bassett Moore, however, persuaded Fletcher to "make a quiet exit."[74]

The secretary's actions from November through January proved to be the final blow in his increasingly tense relations with the president. As early as September 1917 Wilson had asked Colonel House about the advisability of requesting Lansing's resignation. The president thought that Lansing led "too strenuous a social life," consumed an infinite number of cigarettes and quantities of black coffee, and associated with "society folk and reactionaries."[75] The secretary's rather devious maneuvers during the controversies of late 1919 added to the reservoir of Wilson's suspicions. The Washington, D.C., and New York press commented in detail

72. Association of Producers of Petroleum in Mexico to Venustiano Carranza, 13 January 1920, enclosed in Harold Walker and Burton Wilson to Secretary of State, 15 January 1920, SD 812.6363/624; Secretary of State to Embassy in Mexico, 22 January 1920, SD 812.6363/628a.

73. *Wall Street Journal,* 23 January 1920; Fletcher to Polk, 22 January 1920, Polk MSS; Memorandum by R. C. Tanis, 11 February 1920, SD 812.6363/619.

74. Fletcher to Lansing, 20 January 1920, Lansing MSS; Memorandum of Conversation with Henry P. Fletcher, by John Bassett Moore, 21 January 1920, Moore MSS.

75. Edward M. House Diary, 9 September 1917, House MSS.

about Lansing's cooperation with Senator Fall and the reputed
State Department hints about a new, tough policy.[76] Wilson's
feelings were vividly revealed when he later warned Secretary of
State Bainbridge Colby to beware of Lansing because he "is by
nature and practice a snake in the grass."[77]

Resolution of the Crisis

The rhetoric and events of 1919 represented an attempt by a
relatively small group of politicians, diplomats, investors, and
newspapers to create a crisis. It was really a psychological campaign which foundered because in fact Mexico did not seriously
threaten U.S. interests, and a significant collection of officials and
businessmen realized this. Various factors irritated U.S.-Mexican
relations and prevented completely harmonious relations. None
of these was of sufficient magnitude to create a unified war movement in the echelons of power.

Some people may have believed the dire threats of national
disaster mouthed by the major oil companies and their allies, but
the impact of this propaganda was significantly reduced by contradictory evidence. In late November 1919 an official of the
American Smelting and Refining Company reported that conditions were "greatly improved," and all of the company's smelters
and most of its mines were working. In December El Aguila Oil
Company, now controlled by Royal Dutch Shell, announced plans
to double its production in 1920. A *Wall Street Journal* writer
noted that the troubles in Mexico over oil production had been a
world benefit, since the oil fields might otherwise have been ruined
by overdrilling and the surplus production would have been
wasted.[78] Joseph P. Guffey, president of Atlantic Gulf Oil Corporation, ranking official in the Democratic party, and friend of
Woodrow Wilson, sent to the White House a letter from his resident manager in Mexico. This oilman reported that companies

76. *Washington Post,* 5 December 1919; *New York Tribune,* 12 December 1919; *New York Times,* 2, 4, 12 December 1919.
77. Wilson to Colby, 5 November 1920, SD 812.00/26464; see also
Josephus Daniels Diary, 29 February 1920, Daniels MSS.
78. *Wall Street Journal,* 8 September, 21 November, 13 December 1919.

which obeyed the law were well treated and statements about confiscation were "absolutely false." He concluded:

I am enclosing herein small clipping from the San Antonio Express
of December 20th, that is supposed to show that the arbitrary
action of the Mexican Government is endangering the supply of
oil for the American Shipping Board, when the truth of the matter
is that these companies, by carrying out the policies they observed
in the years 1915–16–17 and 18, could have drilled all the wells
they want to. I hope you can see your way clear to help some way
counteract these evil influences.

Guffey added his own support to this evaluation.[79]

To a great extent the atmosphere of crisis disappeared rapidly
because Mexican actions did not threaten the U.S. oil supply.
Lansing, Fletcher, Boaz Long, and the Association for the Protection of American Rights in Mexico failed in their attempt to
generate a diplomatic showdown through manipulation of a non-
existent threat.

The Navy Department and the Shipping Board did believe that
the U.S. oil companies were overcharging the government and
several proposals were made for direct governmental acquisition
of fuel oil in Mexico. None of these materialized, but they indicated that the major problem for government shipping was not
Mexican restrictions on oil production.[80] During 1920 Standard
of New Jersey, Texaco, Gulf, and Sinclair doubled their Mexican
production. Doheny's Pan-American Petroleum and Transport
Company, and its subsidiaries, reported a 40 percent net increase
in earnings for the same period.[81]

79. Mordelo L. Vincent to Joseph P. Guffey, 24 December 1919, enclosed in Guffey to Tumulty, 31 December 1919; see also Tumulty to
Polk, 2 January 1920, Polk MSS.

80. Josephus Daniels Diary, 1 March, 3, 10, 20 April 1920, Daniels
MSS; Van Manning (U.S. Geological Survey) to Franklin K. Lane, 19
January 1920, SD 812.6363/684, criticizes the secretary for relying on oil
company representatives for information. The Shipping Board, the Emergency Fleet Corporation, and various private investors wanted to obtain
oil directly from Mexico and bypass the established companies; Josephus
Daniels Diary, 1 March, 3, 20 April 1920, Daniels MSS; Memorandum,
Office of the Foreign Trade Adviser, 27 December 1920, SD 812.6363/
771.

81. *Wall Street Journal,* 6 August 1921; *Annual Report of Pan American
Petroleum & Transport Company and Subsidiaries: 1920* (New York,
1921).

Recognition, Oil, and Bonds, 1920

By early February 1920, U.S.-Mexican relations appeared to be on a much more friendly basis than at any time since the fall of Madero. The Mexican Foreign Office initiated conversations leading to negotiations for a mixed claims commission treaty. At the suggestion of Joseph Guffey, Henry Morgenthau volunteered his services as ambassador to Mexico in order to improve "the relations between the two countries." The former ambassador to Turkey expressed his complete agreement with a nonintervention policy. Wilson accepted the offer and nominated Morgenthau for the post.[82] Senators Lodge and Fall successfully blocked action by the Foreign Relations Committee. A number of committee members believed that the lack of ambassadorial representation would be a blow to the prestige of Carranza and would constitute a form of nonrecognition.[83]

Senator Fall's subcommittee on Mexican relations had been holding hearings off and on since the latter part of 1919 in an attempt to build a case for severing relations and possibly intervention. Most of the testimony was anti-Mexican, since Fall's investigators had scoured the country searching for anyone willing to tell about an atrocity. Almost 69 percent of the incidents related to the committee took place during the period 1911–16. If anything, the committee proved that stability had improved under Carranza. The final report listed 550 American citizens killed in Mexico between 1911 and 1920. Fall eagerly publicized these "foul crimes" of the Mexican revolutionaries, and some subse-

82. Lansing to Henry Morgenthau, 23 February 1920, and Morgenthau to Admiral T. Grayson, 28 February 1920, Henry Morgenthau Papers, Library of Congress. See also Memorandum for Albert B. Fall, 26 February 1921, SD 711.12/317; E. J. Dillon, *Mexico on the Verge* (New York, 1921), 35–36, reporting an interview with Carranza in March 1920, in which the latter said that relations with the United States had never been so cordial.

83. Polk to Morgenthau, 3 May 1920, Senator Gilbert M. Hitchcock to Morgenthau, 6 May 1920, Morgenthau MSS; Henry Cabot Lodge to Albert B. Fall, 2 April 1920, Fall MSS. Fall believed that a "cabal" existed between Morgenthau, Joseph Guffey, and the Guggenheim mining interests; Fall to Senator Frank Brandegee, 12 April 1920, ibid. This was the beginning of the persistent story that Guffey was the stalking horse for the international English-Jewish conspiracy to control Mexican oil; R. S. Sharp (special agent in charge of New York office of the Intelligence Service) to R. C. Brannerman (chief special agent, State Department), 12 August 1921, SD 812.6363/940½.

quent writers have done likewise. Fall, and others, conveniently overlooked another set of figures. During the Veracruz occupation and the period 1916–19 the armed forces of the United States killed at least 541 Mexicans *on Mexican soil*.[84] But this fact had no relevance for the objectives of the Fall committee.

Since the Carranza government had been overthrown in May 1920, the final report of the Fall committee demanded that the U.S. government seize this opportunity to impose by treaty a specific set of conditions prior to the recognition of the new Mexican administration. The heart of the stipulated treaty would be the complete exemption of U.S. citizens from the requirements or limitations of articles 3, 27, 33, and 130 of the constitution of 1917. If the Mexican government signed such a document, then the committee would be willing to make a government loan for rehabilitation. If the treaty was refused, then the Mexicans were to be told that failure to restore order and peace would lead to a police action. Using the words of William McKinley in April 1898, the committee stated that such an occupation would restore peace and order; restore American citizens to their properties; open the mines, fields, and factories; and establish self-determination for the Mexican people.[85]

The "opportunity" mentioned by the Fall committee came when the revolt led by General Obregón ousted Carranza in late May 1920.[86] Carranza had lost support for a variety of reasons. Among these was the fact that while he had not been able to assert control effectively over natural resources, he was still re-

84. I am indebted to Edward Rice for compiling the above statistics from the two-volume report of the Senate, *Investigation of Mexican Affairs* (1920). Correspondence between Wallace Thompson and Fall (Fall MSS) gives some details of the search for favorable witnesses carried out by the "Murray Hill Group" (directed by William F. Buckley and named for their headquarters in the Murray Hill Hotel). Mexican casualties from 1916 to 1919 are listed in "Supplement Number 2: Addenda to Memorandum on Mexican Relations," by Boaz Long, 12 December 1919, SD 711.12/229½. For Veracruz figures see Quirk, *Affair of Honor*, 103, and Jack Sweetman, *The Landing at Veracruz: 1914* (Annapolis, Md., 1968), 123.

85. U.S. Senate, *Investigation of Mexican Affairs*, 2:3368–73; Hitchcock to Morgenthau, 6 May 1920, Morgenthau MSS.

86. In May 1920 the State and Navy Departments prepared for possible intervention in Mexico. Additional ships were sent to Veracruz, and a Marine Emergency Expeditionary Force of 1,200 men was assembled at Pensacola, Florida; Josephus Daniels to Secretary of State, 14 June 1920, SD 812.00/24210; Josephus Daniels Diary, 2, 3, 9 May 1920, Daniels MSS.

garded by foreign governments as an enemy and an advocate of nationalization. The statements and actions of the leaders of the revolt and of the provisional government clearly indicated that the new leaders hoped to assert national control but that they also wanted to explain carefully to the United States that this would not mean the elimination of U.S. economic interests or the encouragement of an anti-U.S. position in the hemisphere. In this context the elimination of Carranza, and the Carranza Doctrine, would, it was hoped, clear the air and allow the new government to proceed with national control, not expropriation, while establishing cordial relations with the United States.[87]

George T. Summerlin reported that Obregón had told him that Carranza's anti-U.S. policy had been "a great mistake." The chargé concluded with the statement, "He [Obregón] seemed to appreciate the necessity of clearing up all misunderstandings with us and intimated that he wished 'to play the game.' "[88] In June 1920, Provisional President Adolfo de la Huerta sent Félix F. Palavicini to visit several governments in western Europe in order to spread the word that Mexico wanted to build good relations with the United States. And private negotiations with the major oil companies were resumed.

In late June 1920 the Mexican government sent Iglesias Calderón to the United States as high commissioner to negotiate recognition. His visit was preceded by glowing reports about orderly conditions prevailing and the exceptional "deportment" of the new leaders: "Foreigners have been treated with exquisite consideration. Their rights and privileges have not been restricted; their property has been untouched."[89] Wilson asked the State Department for advice concerning recognition. Undersecretary Norman H. Davis recommended unofficial discussions with Calderón. If these proved to be satisfactory, a note should be sent to the Mexican government showing gratification and en-

87. For reasons behind the overthrow of Carranza see Dulles, *Yesterday in Mexico,* 89–90, 96; Meyer, *México y Estados Unidos,* 104.

88. George T. Summerlin to Charles M. Johnson (Division of Mexican affairs), 9 June 1920, Morgenthau MSS. For attitudes of new leaders see Adolfo de la Huerta to Francis J. Dyer (consul, Nogales), 10 May 1920, SD 812.00/24017; "Memorandum of Conversation with Colonel Myron Parker by G. Howland Shaw," 12 May 1920, SD 812.00/24892 (Parker represented General Obregón).

89. "Report on the Political Situation in Mexico by CMJ [Charles M. Johnston]," 15 June 1920, Norman H. Davis Papers, Library of Congress.

couraging it to "meet our requirements." Wilson accepted this advice to deter recognition until "further evidence" of Mexican intentions had been provided.[90]

Davis held several conversations with Calderón and stressed the protection of foreign lives and property, the nonretroactive interpretation of article 27, and the foreign debt issue. The under-secretary strongly urged the Mexican government to perform a variety of specific acts. These included the elimination of all bureaus established in Latin America to spread anti-U.S. propaganda, the dismissal of the Mexican ambassador to Argentina, the return of the Wells Fargo Express Company to its private owners, the modification of article X of the 1879 contract between the Mexican government and the Mexican Telegraph Company (which gave the government franking privileges over the Central and South American lines of the company), and the settlement of the claims of the Tlahualilo Plantation Company and the Richardson Construction Company, both engaged in agricultural development in the Yaqui Valley. The Mexicans had not realized that recognition would entail such a variety of conditions, and such meddling in the internal affairs of their country. Calderón was not authorized to make binding agreements and the talks proved to be most inconclusive.[91]

The new government also moved ahead with limited measures to promote national control and development of petroleum resources. Circular no. 10 of 10 July 1920 set the general conditions under which concessions would be granted in the federal zones. The most controversial of these zones were the strips of land adjoining all navigable streams—twenty meters in width to the high tide mark, and ten meters in width from there as far as the stream could be navigated by rafts. The Mexican leadership did not see any contradiction between the limited national control asserted by the establishment of federal zones and a policy of friendship with the United States.[92]

90. Davis to Wilson, 25 June 1920, Davis MSS; Wilson to Davis, 26 June 1920, Wilson MSS.

91. "Memorandum of Interview with Señor Iglesias Calderón," 30 June and 9 July 1920, Davis MSS; Calderón to Davis, 11 July 1920, SD 711.12/466.

92. "Memorandum: Division of Mexican Affairs to Norman Davis," 9 August 1920, SD 812.6363/716; "Summary of Interview with Adolfo de la Huerta, by George Summerlin," 14 September 1920, SD 812.6363/732½.

The oil companies claimed absolute control over all land adjacent to streams which they had purchased or leased, and denied the right of the government to create such zones. The companies terminated negotiations and appealed to the State Department. On 13 August 1920 Chargé Summerlin was instructed to protest the implementation of Circular no. 10 because it appeared to threaten confiscation.[93] Once again the oil question had become the most visible symbol of the broader conflict of interest between U.S. investors and the Mexican revolutionary nationalists.

As the negotiations between the Mexican government and the United States unfolded, the Mexicans found that the State Department was very evasive. In the course of negotiations over the next few months they discovered that the basic elements of the Fall committee's plan had become official policy. In late May, Senator Fall told Harold Walker that he was "in close touch with Mr. Colby" and that they were in agreement over a policy of "no recognition" until Mexico had shown by its acts that "it will treat all Americans justly." Fall also noted that Colby was "in sympathy" with his plan for a treaty guaranteeing U.S. interests as a condition of recognition.[94]

In September 1920 Mexican officials informed the State Department that they would like to settle the oil controversy by direct negotiation with the companies. In a conversation with Roberto Pesqueira, finance representative of Mexico, Undersecretary of State Davis replied that the settlement of this one issue would not "automatically result in recognition." Davis then said: "It would be impossible now to state just what would remove all of the obstacles to recognition." The Mexican government would have to show that it not only desired to protect life and property, and respect valid rights, but that it had taken "definite and effective measures" to repair the damages committed and given "proper assurances against a repetition of past inability or reluctance to comply with the ordinary international obligations incumbent upon a member of the Society of Nations."[95] This was a most

93. Chester O. Swain to Secretary of State, 3 August 1920, SD 812.6363/707; Alvey Adee to Summerlin, 13 August 1920, ibid.
94. Walker to Doheny, 27 May 1920, Fall MSS. Earlier, Fall had worried that Colby might reverse the policy of Lansing and Polk; Fall to Senator Frank Brandegee, 12 April 1920, ibid.
95. "Memorandum of Conversation between Mr. Pesqueira and Norman Davis," 23 September 1920, SD 711.12/530.

imprecise statement, but behind the lack of clarity lay a hardline recognition policy which included the extensive modification of article 27. Davis was too skilled in diplomacy to set forth in exact terms the U.S. price for recognition. This was being done on a piecemeal basis and would culminate in the demand that a treaty filled with guarantees be concluded prior to recognition. As Secretary Colby wrote to Wilson, "Mexico should give convincing proof of her ability . . . to sustain her international obligations, such as the protection of life, and property acquired in good faith, and in conformity with Mexican law."[96]

How to get beyond these "rather skittish overtures," as Colby termed them, was the perplexing question. At this juncture George Creel volunteered to go to Mexico to try to work out some type of settlement with the Mexican government.[97] Wilson offered to designate Creel as a "personal representative" but the former head of the Committee on Public Information wanted to go as a free agent. The writer guise fooled few people, and one of Senator Fall's secret agents picked up his trail at the border.[98] In his conversation with Creel, President Wilson had insisted upon two aspects of any settlement: (1) Mexico's recognition of her obligations under international law (protection of life and property, and payment of just claims); and (2) that article 27 should not be given retroactive effect in the sense of confiscating duly acquired rights. Creel viewed these as points for a general understanding and not as the prelude to a treaty prior to recognition. In this spirit he discussed the issues with General Obregón, Minister of War Plutarco Elías Calles, and Provisional President de la Huerta: "At every point there was agreement, and when I returned to Washington Roberto Pesqueira came with me, duly empowered to enter into the formal understandings upon which recognition was to be based.[99]

After participating in talks between Pesqueira, Colby, and

96. Colby to Wilson, 25 September 1920, Wilson MSS.

97. Colby to Wilson, 25 September 1920, Wilson MSS; Creel to Morgenthau, 13 May 1921, Morgenthau MSS; Wilson to Colby, 27 September 1920, Wilson MSS.

98. George Creel, *The People Next Door*, 357–58. For secret agents see A. Mitchell Palmer to Wilson, 8 November 1920, Creel MSS.

99. Creel to Morgenthau, 13 May 1921, Morgenthau MSS. General Obregón said he knew Pesqueira had been given full powers; Summerlin to Secretary of State, 12 November 1920, SD 812.00/24770.

Davis, Creel drafted an "informal agreement to serve as the basis for a protocol." It provided for the formation of a claims commission, an arbitration commission, and a pledge that Mexico would not give retroactive effect to article 27. Creel believed that recognition would quickly follow Wilson's approval of the informal agreement. Late in October 1920, however, Pesqueira called him to complain about the difficulties he was encountering trying to see Colby.[100] Returning to Washington, Creel helped to arrange for the publication of the agreement in the form of a letter from Pesqueira to Colby. The secretary's reply stated that this letter was "a very significant and a very gratifying and reassuring statement of the attitude and purposes of the new government of Mexico."[101]

Creel and the Mexican officials now believed that recognition was assured. But they failed to see a basic contradiction between the positions outlined in the two letters. Pesqueira had stated that he was prepared to sign a protocol embodying the terms of the informal agreement *after* recognition had been extended. Colby concluded his letter with the statement that Pesqueira's letter "offers a basis on which the preliminaries of recognition can proceed."[102] The Mexican government did not intend to accept ironclad conditions prior to recognition and Colby, with Wilson's support, wanted more than an informal agreement. When recognition was not forthcoming President de la Huerta raised some reservations about the nature of Pesqueira's mission, and Creel angrily attacked Colby for his intransigence and delaying tactics.[103]

Creel then made a personal appeal to President Wilson. After

100. Creel to Secretary of State, 23 October 1920, SD 812.00/24746½; Creel to Morgenthau, 13 May 1921, Morgenthau MSS. Creel arranged an unsuccessful meeting between Doheny and Pesqueira; U.S. Senate, *Leases upon Naval Oil Reserves: Hearings before the Committee on Public Lands and Surveys,* 68th Cong., 1st sess., 1924, pt. 8, 2124.

101. "Proposed draft of a letter from Roberto Pesqueira to Secretary Colby, to be dated October 28, 1920," and "Proposed press release, by Secretary of State Colby, October 29, 1920," both enclosed in Colby to Wilson, 28 October 1920, SD 812.00/24757a.

102. Ibid.; Wilson penciled his approval on the bottom.

103. Creel to Colby, 12 November 1920, SD 812.00/24774½; Colby to Creel, 17 November 1920, ibid.; Creel to Colby, n.d., SD 812.00/24764½; on 9 November, Johnston (Division of Mexican Affairs) recommended suspension of all talks because of reports that de la Huerta would reject conditional recognition; SD 812.00/24765½.

criticizing the dogmatism and "mumbo jumbo" of the State Department, he concluded:

At every point the Mexicans have stood foursquare with you. At every point we have bilked them.

If Pesqueira goes away, and makes his statement before he goes, you turn Mexico over to Harding and the oil people.[104]

Wilson met with Creel, Colby, and Davis. The State Department position prevailed, and Creel wrote: "The whole attitude of Colby and Davis was based upon the theory that the Mexican people were acting in ill-faith, and that we could not do business with them except through hard and fast, and formal agreements." Prior to Pesqueira's departure in late November, Colby presented him with a verbal pat on the head combined with a notice that recognition would only follow the negotiation of a treaty embodying the informal agreements. The Mexicans dropped recognition efforts for the remainder of Wilson's lame-duck term.

Mexican officials had tried to reach an understanding with the United States, but they did not intend to surrender all hopes of recovering some control of petroleum resources or to do public penance for recognition. George Creel probably summarized their attitude quite accurately when he wrote:

I found a very distinct bitterness, bred by many unfortunate experiences with foreign investors, also of the abnormal sensitiveness that invariably marks the attitude of a proud people in dealing with a stronger nation, but under all I saw a very real patriotism, a profound belief in the idealism of the United States and an intense desire for peace and friendship between the two Republics.[105]

In pushing for recognition of the Mexican government, Creel was joined by Secretaries Daniels and Albert S. Burleson, and by Henry Morgenthau. The latter predicted that the Republicans would go to war with Mexico.[106] In the light of such promptings and predictions, why did Wilson refuse to recognize the Mexican

---

104. Creel to Wilson, 19 November 1920, SD 812.00/24782½.

105. Creel to Morgenthau, 13 May 1921, Morgenthau MSS; Colby to Wilson, 25 November 1920, SD 812.00/24701½.

106. Josephus Daniels Diary, 20 November 1920, Daniels MSS; Morgenthau to Wilson, 23 September 1920, Bainbridge Colby Papers, Library of Congress.

government? Creel believed that a combination of Wilson's illness and incapacity and oil company pressure on a pliable State Department provided the answers. He later wrote that "from the first I encountered a spirit of mysterious opposition in the State Department."[107] He was partially correct in his evaluation. But oil company pressure per se was not a major factor (oil representatives often took opposite sides on the recognition issue).

Colby and Davis wanted a broad settlement of all economic issues along the lines proposed by the Fall committee; and they wanted concrete actions by the Mexican government to repudiate any retroactive interpretation of article 27. The latter would take the form of a presidential decree authorized by Congress, or a Supreme Court ruling. Pesqueira had agreed to this action, but he and Creel thought that it could be done after recognition to avoid the "appearance of unconditional surrender." Colby and Davis expected prerecognition action and the unexplained delays in negotiations—which provoked Creel's anger—were due to their waiting for President de la Huerta to act.[108]

Neither Colby nor Davis had to be informed about the issue of protecting investments in foreign countries. The secretary had done legal work for Standard Oil of New Jersey in 1919 and was a close friend of such investors as John Hays Hammond. The latter helped push Colby's appointment through the Senate Foreign Relations Committee (March 1920) by informing Senator Philander C. Knox of his high opinion of Colby's knowledge and judgment, especially in regard to Russia and Mexico. Hammond did express the fear that Wilson would either pressure Colby to adopt poor policies or dismiss him if he displayed independence. According to Hammond, the secretary told him not to worry: "I've taken my house for only six months." Colby had switched from Roosevelt to Wilson in 1916, but his appointment surprised most observers. The reasons for his selection are not clear, but once in office he displayed that peculiar ability to use the lofty rhetoric of good neighborhood while twisting a neighbor's arm.

107. Creel to Morgenthau, 13 May 1921, Morgenthau MSS.
108. Creel to Secretary of State, 23 October 1920, SD 812.00/24746½; "Memorandum of Conversation between Secretary Colby, the French Ambassador, and Mr. Norman Davis," 10 February 1921, Davis MSS. A member of Senator Fall's staff reported that the proposed protocol was "entirely harmonious with your report excepting religious matters"; C. V. Safford to Fall, 6 November 1920, Fall MSS.

Wilson could well appreciate such a talent. E. L. Doheny also appreciated Colby's talents. The oilman and Franklin K. Lane— former Secretary of the Interior and part of Doheny's collection of former members of the Wilson administration—visited the State Department in July 1920. Lane later informed Colby, "You have hypnotized Mr. Doheny who believes you can work miracles."[109]

Norman H. Davis, formerly associated with J. P. Morgan and Company and the Ports Company of Cuba, had served during the war as financial adviser to the Treasury Department in charge of loans to the Allies. In this capacity he had pushed the move to use Cuba's application for a loan to force the Republic to make a favorable settlement of the claims of the Ports Company and the Cuba Railroad. He was also a loyal Wilsonian Democrat. As undersecretary, Davis handled most of the negotiations with Mexican officials, as his predecessor Polk had done. President Wilson thought very highly of Davis's views on Mexico and on occasion wrote directly to him for advice. Several weeks after submitting the Morgenthau nomination as ambassador to Mexico, Wilson confided to Colby that his "own choice" was Norman H. Davis. This was prior to Davis's appointment as undersecretary.[110]

Wilson's physical and mental condition helped to strengthen the influence of Colby and Davis. Lacking the vigor of his pre-stroke career, the president was visibly weary of dealing with Mexico—a seemingly perennial problem of his presidency. He had become quite suspicious of all Mexican officials; none seemed really to appreciate his self-image as a friend of Mexico. But as a paternalistic Southern liberal, Wilson had displayed the same irritation toward other nonwhites—such as the leaders of the NAACP —who had talked back to him and questioned his leadership. In late September 1920 Robert H. Murray, newspaperman and

109. *Autobiography of John Hays Hammond*, 2:664–65; Lane to Colby, 30 July 1920, SD 711.12/340. One source reports that Wilson selected Colby because he was a gifted speaker and able to write beautiful prose; Thomas A. Bailey, *Woodrow Wilson and the Great Betrayal* (Chicago, 1963), 251. Lane was vice-president and counselor for Pan American Petroleum and Transportation Co.; William Gibbs McAdoo was retained by Doheny, and George Creel had been hired to write Doheny's biography as an inspiration for young Americans (his employment lasted three months). Frank Polk represented the American Metals Co. in 1921.
110. Wilson to Colby, 13 April 1920, Colby MSS.

former CPI agent in Mexico, dined with Wilson and then wired Morgenthau:

His condition most distressing. At first while measurably receptive [he] was not especially interested [in the] subject [Mexico] but interest grew as conversation proceeded. He is strongly inclined to do nothing but leave problem as [a] legacy to [his] successor. Fears that southerners [Mexicans] will not play fair [and] ask [sic] "are you sure they will deal honestly with me and keep pledges if I do this" [He] seemed saddened disillusioned suspicious [as a] result [of] his experience with former elements in government.[111]

Wilson's suspicion and distrust of the Mexicans aligned him more with Colby and Davis than with Daniels and Creel. The advice of the State Department officials was extremely cautious, and they presented it with much deference and tact. This made it even easier for Wilson to adopt their policies. Colby's letters to the president often concluded with phrases such as "I would not think of taking this important step without your explicit authorization" or "will report to you immediately any significant change in the situation, of course taking not the least action which has not your prior sanction." The secretary rarely, if ever, disagreed openly with Wilson, and he handled Creel's indignation with such tact that he retained the full confidence of the president. As a result of this combination of factors, Wilson became a staunch advocate of the use of recognition to obtain firm guarantees for the protection of U.S. economic interests.[112]

Colby and Davis also developed reservations concerning negotiations between private interest groups and the Mexican government. In late July 1920 General Salvador Alvarado requested an appointment with officials of J. P. Morgan and Company. Thomas Lamont notified the State Department, and Davis told him that the department's conversation with Mexico's representative had not gone far enough to warrant the bankers committee's having any discussions with Alvarado, who was described as "very radical." Officials of the Morgan Company did meet with the

111. Murray to Morgenthau, 21 September 1920, Morgenthau MSS.
112. Colby to Wilson, 28 October 1920, SD 812.00/24757a; Colby to Wilson, 6 November 1920, SD 812.00/26464; Colby to Wilson, 20 November 1920, SD 812.00/24782½; Wilson to Colby, 27 September 1920, Wilson MSS.

general, but informed him that little could be done about a possible loan until recognition had been extended.[113]

By the summer of 1920, however, the British and French sections of the International Committee were beginning to show signs of impatience. At a meeting held 11 August, the British section decided that some member of the group should informally suggest to the Mexican government the formation of an advisory commission to help in the reorganization of national finances. In addition, this section agreed that the contact man should not be an American, owing to the Mexicans' fear of possible intervention, and the decision was made to suggest the name of Sir William Wiseman to the other sections. The French section concurred with these proposals, with the suggestion that Wiseman be accompanied by one representative each from the French and American sections.[114]

Lamont informed the State Department of this "considerable pressure" and warned, "My private opinion to you is that we ought, within a reasonable time, find a *modus vivendi* or else we shall not be able to hold our five-power team in hand to the end." Davis was not at all enthusiastic over the Wiseman trip, but after some consideration he finally decided that Lamont's assessment was correct and that Lamont should accompany Wiseman. President Wilson did not like the proposal and recommended that it be "discouraged."[115] He did not want the loan question discussed prior to recognition because he believed that such a display of eagerness would make the Mexican government less conciliatory.

In spite of these doubts, tentative approval for the Lamont trip was given with the understanding that the mission would only be

113. Lamont to Davis, 27 July 1920, Davis MSS; "Memorandum of a Conversation between Lamont and General Alvarado (Minister of Finance of Mexico)," 29 July 1920, and "Memorandum of a Conversation between General Alvarado, Mr. Desvernine, and Mr. Cochran (J. P. Morgan & Co.)," 13 August 1920, Lamont MSS.

114. "Minutes of a Meeting of the British Section of the International Committee, August 11, 1920," sent to the State Department by Thomas Lamont, 28 September 1920, SD 812.51/619; Minutes of the French Section were enclosed in Ira H. Patchin to Davis, 19 October 1920, SD 812.51/601.

115. Lamont to Davis, 25 and 28 October 1920, Davis MSS; Davis to Wilson, 2 November 1920, SD 812.51/598a; Wilson to Davis, 3 November 1920, Wilson MSS. Wilson to Colby, 24 September 1920, and Colby to Wilson, 25 September 1920, Colby MSS.

exploratory in nature. Shortly thereafter the Pesqueira negotiations were terminated and the State Department now advised
Lamont not to make the trip.[116] Sir William Wiseman went to
Mexico as a private citizen and returned with a letter from the
minister of finance formally inviting the committee to open negotiations in 1921. Earlier in the month, the minister of foreign
relations had extended such an invitation to Lamont. He considered it "a little queer to decline," but the State Department
officials made it very clear that they did not want him to go under
any circumstances. So, the invitation was declined.[117]

E. L. Doheny also wanted to go to Mexico to confer with the
new Obregón administration. Davis sent word that such a visit
might confuse rather than clarify the "general situation." He
indicated that the State Department wanted to settle all issues at
once by treaty and not have outside agencies playing around with
piecemeal settlements. Secretary Colby made a similar argument
to the French ambassador and advised against recognition until
article 27 was either revoked or completely reinterpreted by a
treaty.[118]

The Wilson administration left office on this strong note of no
recognition without a treaty. It is one of the supreme ironies of
this period that Senator Fall was in complete agreement with the
administration. As Fall told Lamont in early 1921, "I want to
have you know I consider the policy of the present administration,
in the last six months or a year, on Mexico, to have been 100
percent good. We Republicans are in entire accord with it." The
senator had discussed the issues with Colby and Davis and expressed the conviction that they were all in "thorough agreement
with reference to Mexican matters." This agreement included the

116. Lamont to Davis, 19 November 1920; J. P. Morgan & Co. to
Morgan, Grenfell & Co., 14 December 1920, Davis MSS.
117. Lamont to J. P. Morgan, 9 February 1921, Lamont MSS.
118. "Memorandum of a Conversation between Mr. Branch and Mr.
Johnston (Division of Mexican Affairs)," enclosed in Harold Walker to
E. L. Doheny, 31 January 1921, Fall MSS; "Memorandum of Conversation
between Secretary Colby, the French Ambassador, and Norman Davis,"
10 February 1921, Davis MSS. William Gibbs McAdoo went to Mexico to
confer with Obregón on behalf of Doheny. The officially stated reason
was to see about setting up a commission for rehabilitating the railroads;
McAdoo to Obregón, 21 December 1920, and McAdoo to Doheny, 14
and 17 February 1921, William Gibbs McAdoo Papers, Library of Congress.

disapproval of private negotiations by outside agencies or persons.[119]

Woodrow Wilson took office in 1913 with the inherited problem of Mexican recognition. For the next eight years he grappled with the problem of Mexican revolutionary nationalism, but was unable to direct it along the path of private enterprise liberalism which he believed to be desirable. Until 1920 leading Republicans had constantly criticized his Mexican policies. Perhaps Wilson left office in 1921 feeling a sense of poetic justice in bequeathing the legacy of Mexican recognition to the new Republican administration.

Wilson might change secretaries of state, but he remained a consistent opponent of article 27 and all it implied for the future of U.S. investments and influence in Mexico and other underdeveloped countries. When the Harding administration was on the verge of recognizing the Mexican government in 1923, Wilson wrote to Creel: "I dare say you think as I do that the present administration is finding it too easy to rely on promises of the present Mexican government. It seems to me they are still upon the quicksands."[120]

119. Lamont to J. P. Morgan, 9 February 1921, and Fall to Lamont, 11 February 1921, Lamont MSS; Fall to William E. Brigham (*Boston Evening Transcript*), 10 February 1921, Fall MSS; Fall to Colby, 26 February 1921, SD 711.12/317.
120. Wilson to Creel, 28 August 1923, Creel MSS.

8   "Normalcy," Recognition, and the First Rapprochement, 1921-1924

You could lead them around the world with a lump of sugar but could not drive them an inch.
—Thomas W. Lamont, 1922

Nonrecognition, 1921

Contrary to some Democratic predictions, President Harding did not nominate Senator Fall to be secretary of state. The new president selected the distinguished lawyer and jurist Charles Evans Hughes to fill the post, and Henry P. Fletcher was appointed undersecretary. These officials accepted the view that Mexico must sign a treaty interpreting article 27 in a nonconfiscatory, nonretroactive form prior to recognition. According to Hughes, nonrecognition was the only weapon short of force which would enable the U.S. government to protect nationals and national interests in Mexico. The "rights" of investors constituted a paramount element in this conception of national interests, and these views were concisely expressed in the State Department's official statement of 7 June 1921 on U.S.-Mexican relations.[1] Secretary Hughes summarized the relationship between contracts, property rights, international relations, and national interests in these words:

Another fundamental question at this time is the preservation of the essential bases of international intercourse through the demand for the recognition of valid titles acquired in accordance with existing law and for the maintenance of the sanctity of contracts and of adequate means of enforcing them. Intercourse,

1. SD 711.12/350a; see also Memorandum on Mexico by the Undersecretary, 27 April 1921, SD 711.1211/213 (a discussion of the property issue by Fletcher, Summerlin, and Hughes).

from the standpoint of business, consists in the making of contracts and the acquisition of property rights . . . and the most important principle to be maintained at this time with respect to international relations is that no State is entitled to a place within the family of nations if it destroys the foundations of honorable intercourse by resort to confiscation and repudiation. . . . This is in the obvious interest of business, and thus is merely a way of saying that this course is vital to the prosperity of all peoples for the activities of business are those of production and exchange upon which the welfare of peoples inevitably depend.

The proposed Treaty of Amity and Commerce was presented to the Mexican government on 27 May 1921. Several weeks later Hughes modified U.S. policy, and stated recognition would be accorded automatically when Obregón initially signed the treaty.[2]

Undersecretary Fletcher was a staunch advocate of nonrecognition, and he encouraged his personal friend President Harding not to accept what he regarded as Mexican attempts to compromise the basic issue. The Supreme Court of Mexico ruled in September 1921 (the Texas Company case) that owners of oil-bearing lands acquired prior to 1 May 1917 had complete rights, provided they had performed some positive act indicating intention to exploit the subsoil resources. Fletcher informed Harding that this was the Russian "property concept" and further advised: "The problem is not, as many would have you believe, one of approach, but rather one of fundamental differences with respect to the inviolability of private property."[3] Harding concurred, and agreed that the administration should resist efforts by some U.S. interests to promote the recognition of Obregón. During 1921, and into 1922, the administration firmly held to this position. As former oil company representative James R. Garfield noted in his diary after conferring with Harding, Hughes, and Fletcher on 12 November 1921: "Great good fortune see them all today—and very truely no recognition of Obregon until American interests are fully safeguarded. . . . A most satisfactory day."[4]

2. Hughes Speech of 18 May 1922, SD 711.1211/223; see also "Relations with Mexico," Beerits Memo, Hughes MSS; Lamont to J. Ridgely Carter (Morgan Harjes & Co.), 10 June 1921, Lamont MSS (reporting a conversation with Hughes).
3. Fletcher to Harding, 11 November 1921, Fletcher MSS; Fletcher to Harding, 14 November 1921, SD 812.6363/1028c.
4. Garfield MSS; see also Harding to Fletcher, 19 November 1921, SD 812.6363/1042½.

The nonrecognition policy almost ran into some difficulty in June 1921 owing to a breakdown in communications between Secretary Hughes and the British ambassador, Sir Auckland Geddes, which threatened to disrupt U.S.-British cooperation on Mexican policy. The problem developed when Hughes did not find out about the arrangements which former Secretary Bainbridge Colby and former Undersecretary Norman H. Davis had made with the British Foreign Office in 1920. The British had decided to extend recognition to Obregón, but changed this decision at the request of Colby and Davis. At that time the British ambassador and Davis agreed upon a policy of complete reciprocity of information and "cordial cooperation" on matters concerning Mexico.[5] Davis informed Thomas Lamont that he had prepared a memorandum on these arrangements and called it to Fletcher's attention when the State Department changed hands in March 1921. Hughes, however, did not see the memorandum, and formulated his own recognition plan—the signing of a Treaty of Amity and Commerce—without consulting the British ambassador. Geddes read about the proposal in the newspaper and immediately went to see the secretary of state. According to Geddes, Hughes was "not particularly communicative" and would not show him a copy of the note which had been sent to the Mexican government.

The ambassador was quite upset and mentioned the cooperative arrangement. After the conference Hughes communicated with Davis and was fully informed of the earlier understanding. Then the secretary arranged another conference with Geddes. During this conversation he gave more information to the ambassador, but "not to the extent of satisfying Geddes." Hughes still would not show the recognition demand note to the British ambassador.

Geddes then told Lamont that this was the "gravest thing that had happened in the last two years between the United States and Great Britain." Lamont had a "good frank talk" with Secretary Hughes, who agreed to talk over the matter with Geddes, and Lamont gained the impression that he would try to soothe the ambassador's feelings and get back to a basis of cooperation. As

5. Lamont to Vivian Smith (a partner in the firm of Morgan Grenfell & Co., London), 10 June 1921, Lamont MSS.

Lamont noted in his letter to Vivian Smith, "The situation called for good nature and pleasantry on both sides."[6]

Hughes must have done a skillful job of soothing, since Geddes later told Lamont that "the atmosphere had been very much cleared up and everything was going very smoothly."[7] Once again, Lamont had helped to smooth the paths of diplomacy and had helped to maintain the "undivided front" which he and Hughes believed was vital for the settlement of Mexico's problems with foreign interests.

When other rifts in the front began to appear in 1921, Lamont went to England "for the purpose of co-ordinating the foreign interests," both for this reason and for the purpose of negotiating a settlement of Mexico's external debt. Leading exporters and bankers in London had prepared a memorial calling for the recognition of the Obregón government which they intended to present to the British Foreign Office. Lamont helped to rewrite this memorial so that the second draft was less insistent in its tone. He also suggested that the presentation of the memorial be delayed. Not only was this advice followed, but the British interests finally decided not to present the memorial at all.[8] These activities of Lamont were also part of what Carl Parrini has described as the Morgan policy of "Americanizing the British banking system." The House of Morgan's leadership of the International Committee of Bankers on Mexico reflected this, and the

6. Ibid. Lamont wrote to E. C. Grenfell (senior partner in the London firm) suggesting that he privately show the letter to Smith of 10 June to Sir William Tyrrell (assistant undersecretary of the British Foreign Office). Lamont feared that Geddes might have exaggerated the incident in his reports; Lamont to Grenfell, 10 June 1921, Lamont MSS.

7. Lamont to Smith, 23 June 1921, Lamont MSS. In a debate in the House of Lords (27 February 1924) The Marquess Curzon of Kedleston said that during his five years in the Foreign Office the question of recognition came up no less than eight or ten times and that constant pressure for *de jure* recognition was applied by those who had large financial interests in Mexico. He added that the continuation of nonrecognition was not based on a desire to cooperate with the United States; pages from *Parliamentary Debates* (House of Lords), 27 February 1924, 384, SD 712.41/11.

8. Lamont to Hughes, 9 June 1921, Lamont MSS. The French and Belgian governments were also under pressure to recognize Mexico, and Lamont presented the arguments for nonrecognition to his "old friend" J. J. Jusserand, the French ambassador, and to his friends in the Belgian Foreign Office; Lamont to Jusserand, 3 November 1921, enclosed in Lamont to Hughes, 10 November 1921, SD 812.00/25809.

related effort of advancing the New Yorkers' role in the international financial structure of Latin America.[9]

The adherence to nonrecognition prompted various critics to charge that Hughes was interested only in the oil question. Yet Hughes—as did his predecessors—viewed the oil question as one part of a larger spectrum of economic interests, legal principles, and ideological suppositions. The secretary was prepared to use military force as a final measure to protect the totality of U.S. interests in Mexico, but not to defend the claims of any one group.[10]

Several individuals presented Hughes with schemes for various kinds of military solutions. Judge F. J. Kearful (former counsel for the Fall committee) recommended the establishment of a protectorate over Mexico. He believed that such an arrangement could be made with dissident Mexicans "as might come into power for that purpose." As Kearful described the rather cold conclusion of the interview: " 'I get your thought,' said Secretary Hughes. 'I am glad to have met you: good-bye.' And I suddenly found myself standing alone, feeling like a fool on a fool's errand."[11] A Mexican opponent of Obregón, Manuel Calero, visited Hughes and suggested that the U.S. government help to foment insurrection in Mexico, or at least do nothing to discourage it. The secretary replied that the government "could not countenance" any such actions.[12]

Some U.S. citizens and officials did try to promote the overthrow of the Mexican government. William F. Buckley, a businessman with extensive investments in Mexican resources, reported to Secretary of the Interior Fall concerning his involvement with groups which were organizing to take Lower California. He wired:

Agents of the Department of Justice have worked with Captain Hanson [one of the organizers in the United States] throughout.

9. Carl Parrini, *Heir to Empire: United States Economic Diplomacy, 1916–1923* (Pittsburgh, 1969), 112; see also 56–59, 63, 113–14.

10. 12 August 1922, Memorandum on Mexico by the Undersecretary, 27 April 1921, SD 711.1211/213.

11. "Memorandum of a brief conference between Secretary Hughes and F. J. Kearful," n.d. (probably April or May 1921), Fall MSS. Kearful had been recommended to Fall by Harold Walker; Walker to Fall, 27 August 1919, Fall MSS.

12. "Memorandum of an interview with Mr. Manuel Calero," 29 June 1921, Hughes MSS. Calero had letters of introduction from Elihu Root and Secretary Fall.

The capture of the arms was a mere accident, made by a custom guard who thought shipment was whiskey.

Department Justice agents did everything possible to help release the men and are anxious to release the arms and only await an intimation from Washington, which they feel they must have.

Please see Senator and ascertain whether he thinks such order can be obtained without delay.[13]

Fall, however, was most cautious in such matters and I have found no evidence of his cooperation or of any high-level government support for such activities. In fact, Fall had very little contact with the State Department, and by 1922 he had to request leading Republican senators to approach Hughes for interviews with hardline advocates such as Buckley.[14]

President Obregón began his administration with various displays of good will toward the United States. He was generally viewed as a moderate, and even Senator Fall had tried to arrange a private conference between Harding and Obregón when the general made his 1920 preinaugural visit to the United States. This had failed—as did Fall's attempt to go to Mexico to deliver a personal letter from Harding. But Obregón, both in public and private, stated his desire to settle the outstanding issues between the two countries. The Mexican president's more relaxed attitude in regard to foreign business provided the background for recognition demands from various U.S. groups.[15]

Pressures for Recognition, 1920–23

After mid-1920 the pressure for recognition of Mexico steadily increased as the opposition forces declined. These trends were apparent prior to the Republican ascendancy in 1921.

In spite of the organization of various protective associations, U.S. interest groups did not effect a truly unified force. The

13. Buckley to Fall, 28 October 1921, Fall MSS. See also Hanson to Buckley, 19 April 1921, ibid.

14. Fall to Senator George H. Moses, 8 April 1922, Fall MSS.

15. For proposed trips by Obregón and Fall see Elias Torres (first secretary of legación) to Fall, 16 November 1920; Fall to Torres, 20 November; Torres to Fall, 24 and 25 November; Fall to Cutbert Hidalgo, 27 November; all in Fall MSS. For statements by Obregón concerning good relations see Summerlin to Secretary of State, 21 January 1921, SD 812.00/24851; McAdoo to Doheny, 14 February 1921, McAdoo MSS; President Obregón, "Statement on Mexican Policy for Distribution to the Foreign Press," 2 April 1921, SD 712.00/3.

National Association for the Protection of American Rights in Mexico was stricken with internal divisions almost from its inception. Representatives of some of the small oil companies and the landowners did not trust Doheny and other executives of the major oil companies. The periodic efforts of the latter to work out private arrangements with the Mexican government for their primary benefit provoked much anger among these other members. The charges of duplicity on the part of the major companies were reinforced by their tacit refusal to send witnesses to testify before the Fall committee in 1920. The mining companies did not cooperate with the committee either, but the oil companies stimulated most of the anger as a result of their control of the protective association.[16]

In January 1921 the most dissident elements left the group and formed the American Association of Mexico. Under the provisional leadership of William F. Buckley, this new group endorsed a very militant policy toward Mexico, calling "for a restoration of rights under which Americans became the dominating influence in the development of Mexico's resources in the promotion of the welfare of her people." The immediate cause for the rupture was the refusal of the National Association to publish a letter written by Fall which outlined a more vigorous policy for the protection of American interests. But the underlying cause was frankly stated:

Its [the Petroleum Producers Association which dominated the National Association for the Protection of American Rights] methods have been those of intrigue and have consisted largely in sending numberless representatives to Mexico City for the purpose of reaching a compromise with the Mexican government for the settlement of the difficulties of the oil companies. At any time since May 1, 1917 . . . the oil companies would have compromised with the Mexican Government on the basis of respecting their own properties acquired previous to that date, which

16. Attitudes of small producers in Sidney A. Smith to F. J. Kearful, 30 December 1919; William Buckley to Chester Swain, 6 February 1920; Buckley to Fall, 5 February 1920 and 10 February 1921; General Invitation to membership in the American Association of Mexico, 31 January 1921; all in Fall MSS. Kearful told Fall that he had been "grossly deceived" by the oil companies and that all (with the possible exception of Huasteca) had secretly acquired properties by denouncement; Kearful to Fall, 2 February 1922, Fall MSS.

would have resulted in the confiscation of the oil-bearing subsoil of all other American-owned properties.[17]

The charge that the large companies were "playing with the hare and running with the hounds" was oversimplified. But they would have been willing to accept a settlement which removed the application of article 27 from the oil industry only and shifted the tax burden to other interests.[18]

The policies and actions of the major oil companies were attacked by some small producers for other reasons. A number of U.S. companies in Mexico believed that they were more threatened by their large competitors than by the government. For the most part these were newer companies which were trying to compete with the giants who not only controlled most of the fields and pipelines in Mexico but also dominated the refining and marketing facilities in Mexico and the United States. Many of the smaller companies accepted Mexican regulations and cooperated with the government because such actions strengthened their position vis-à-vis the large companies and provided them with specific benefits as well.[19]

17. General invitation to membership in the American Association of Mexico, 31 January 1921; see also Buckley to Fall, 10 February 1921, Fall MSS. J. P. Morgan and Company contributed to the National Association in 1919 and 1920 but resigned in August 1921 because the oil companies were using the group; undated memorandum in Lamont MSS. Royal Dutch Shell (which had acquired El Aguila in 1919) left the Petroleum Producers Association in December 1920 and applied for federal zone concessions; "Memorandum: Action of the Principal English Companies (Royal Dutch, Aguila, Corona) with regard to Petroleum Concessions," by Harold Walker, enclosed in Walker to Norman Davis, 10 December 1920, SD 812.6363/756.

18. American Association of Mexico, *The Status of Americans* (New York, 1921), 59.

19. E. Dean Fuller, "The Oil Situation in Mexico in Relation to American Investments: An Argument on Behalf of Various Independent Interests," 19 December 1916, SD 812.6363/255; Fuller estimated that 90 percent of the companies did not own transportation facilities, refineries, or marketing units. Eleven companies belonged to the National Association; in 1927, out of 147 companies, 125 abided by the Petroleum Law of 1925. Guffey accused Doheny of causing 90 percent of the troubles between the United States and Mexico, and blasted Doheny for attempting to get the Shipping Board to curtail the allotment of tankers to AGWI; Interview with Joseph Guffey (AGWI) as published in *El Excelsior,* 5 February 1920. Guffey quoted Doheny's letter almost verbatim; Harold Walker to Capt. Paul Foley (U.S. Shipping Board), 30 December 1919. Guffey later accused the Wall Street interests of taking revenge by driving him into bankruptcy through stock market manipulation; *Seventy Years on the Red Fire Wagon* (Lebanon, Pa., 1952), 58–60.

In 1920 the vice-president of the Mid-Continental Mexico Company attacked the Petroleum Producers Association and vigorously defended article 27. He made the following points, which illustrate some of the elements of conflict between the different types of producers. The first step taken by Mid-Continental and its associated companies in 1917 was to investigate the titles of ownership in the Huasteca district; not even 10 percent (either of ownership or rental) were legal according to laws in force prior to 1917.

We discovered an agreement between the old companies by virtue of which they mutually compromised themselves to respect their faulty titles without reference to the law, in this manner practically creating a monopoly, so that only the companies which had pipelines, ships and a market could produce and sell oil, preventing the small new companies, both Mexican and foreign from being able to develop.

Mid-Continental, and others such as AGWI, moved into these leasehold territories after 1918, acquired denouncement titles, and bought the surface rights of the owners. The vice-president's conclusion went to the heart of the Mexican doctrine of retroactivity and positive acts:

If Article 27 is suppressed or is changed as the Association desires many millions of pesos created under the protection of this law will be lost. Enormous interests have sprung forth under the protection of Article 27, and they would be automatically ruined.

The Petroleum Law gives to the companies sufficient lands to operate and to have their reserves, and at the same time it prevents the companies from holding immense useless and unproductive reserved areas.[20]

The titles of the large companies were questioned by various smaller businessmen working in Mexico. One wrote to the secretary of agriculture: "There is so much of this kind of manipulation here that one becomes cynical whenever a piratical company

20. *El Heraldo de México,* 16 August 1920. See also Summerlin to Secretary, 18 August 1920, SD 812.6363/717 (reporting on statements of E. W. Marland of the Marland Oil Co.); Arthur Williams (representing Atlantic Lobos Oil Co.) to Hanna, 9 December 1922, SD 812.6363/1307½ (reports conflict with AGWI over leases); Eben Richards (Pierce Oil Co.) to Joseph W. Folk, 28 September 1920, enclosed in Folk to Colby, 30 September 1920, SD 711.12/324 (defends Mexican claims to subsurface oil).

voices objection to a strict interpretation of Article 27." After receiving letters from small producers, Senator Morris Sheppard commented: "Most of these companies [engaged in shady practices] are American companies, and I am sorry to say their methods . . . are not very commendable and are calculated to get us into disputes with Mexico." Even the "old Mexico hand" Judge Delbert J. Haff wrote the State Department to defend the Mexican assertion of control over the federal zones; the company he represented had obtained a concession in such a zone in 1912.[21]

Small producers in the United States also expressed their opposition to the attempts of the large companies to interfere with Mexican domestic legislation and to obtain the support of the U.S. government for their efforts. These oil interests wanted to defend their domestic marketing situation from the competitive assaults of the larger companies. They heartily endorsed the higher taxes levied by the Mexican government and called for higher U.S. duties on Mexican oil. In a letter to Secretary Hughes, A. B. Butler, the vice-president of the National Oil and Development Company (Oklahoma City), lashed out at the large companies:

We can't conceive that it is for the best interest of our people that our government should take sides with the interest which is represented by E. L. Doheny, Walter C. Teagle and H. F. Sinclair, all closely allied together against the tens of thousands of independent oil operators of the United States. . . .

If the selfishness of the oil interests can be regulated and positively dealt with, many of us feel that this business between our country and Mexico is capable of being settled between the two governments.

This attack was carried on in Congress by Representatives Carl Hayden of Arizona and Tom Connally of Texas in their campaign for recognition of the Mexican government.[22]

---

21. R. W. Baily (engineering sales, Tampico) to John Wallace (secretary of agriculture), 21 May 1921, enclosed in Wallace to Secretary of State, 4 June 1921, SD 812.6363/846; I. T. Pryor to Senator Sheppard, 25 September 1918, and E. A. Hutchins to Sheppard, 25 September 1918, enclosed in Sheppard to Lansing, 3 October 1918, SD 812.6363/413; Haff to Fletcher, 7 April 1921, SD 812.6363/814.

22. A. B. Butler to Hughes, 26 August 1921, SD 600.127/241. See also Gulf Coast Oil Producers Association of Louisiana and Texas, North

The impact of the dissenting position of the small oil producers is difficult to measure. They publicized their opposition to the anti-Mexican position of other groups, and this at least destroyed any idea of a unity of viewpoint among U.S. oil interests.

From 1920 on, a large number of chambers of commerce, trade associations, and small businessmen agitated for the recognition of Mexico. These groups were especially interested in selling goods to Mexico and wanted to take advantage of the growing internal stability to increase their business. In September 1919 W. F. Saunders, the secretary of the American Chamber of Commerce of Mexico, had criticized the "red head-line business in the newspapers" which he said had chilled their campaign to attract as members more than a thousand U.S. manufacturing firms. By early 1921, however, the situation had changed almost completely.[23]

At the invitation of Mexican authorities several chambers of commerce organized tours of Mexico for U.S. businessmen. The composite report of a trade commission of sixty men organized by the San Antonio Chamber of Commerce commented enthusiastically on the very friendly reception given to them by Mexican officials and private citizens. The group also reported its enthusiasm over the stable conditions they found and the great prospects for trade.[24] The attitude of most of these business groups was

Texas Oil and Gas Producers Association, Oil Mens Protective Association of Oklahoma and Kansas, Kansas Oil and Gas Association to Secretary of State, 10 June 1921, SD 600.127/177; Samuel H. Smith (Atascosa Oil Co.) to Senators Fall and M. A. Smith, 1 January 1924, Fall MSS. For the domestic oil problems of this period see John Ise, *The United States Oil Policy* (New Haven, 1928), 105–22. Speeches by Connally and Hayden are in *Congressional Record,* 67th Cong., 2d sess., 1922, 62, pt. 3: 2974–75, 3019, pt. 5, 5125–26. Buckley called Connally the spokesman for the recognition element; Buckley to Connally, 15 April 1922, Fall MSS.

23. William F. Saunders to Fletcher, 8 September 1919, Fletcher MSS. For changed situations see "Mexican Good Will Commission Entertained by Merchants' Association," *Commercial and Financial Chronicle,* 9 April 1921, 1478 (Bruno Newman of the Confederated Chambers of Commerce in Mexico spoke to 300 members of the Merchants Association of New York).

24. Memorandum on Mexican Conditions, n.d. (probably 1921), Lamont MSS; see also W. F. Carter (president, St. Louis Chamber of Commerce) to President Harding, 30 April 1921, SD 812.00/24968; Lewis L. Clark (president, American Exchange Bank, New York) to Joseph Tumulty, 26 November 1920, SD 812.00/24789 (reports a trip organized by the Houston Chamber of Commerce; the American Exchange Bank

well summarized by a business journal, the *Mississippi Valley Magazine*:

In view of the urgent need for additional markets to absorb the surplus of our fields and [factories] it would seem but good business judgement to foster friendly relation[s] with a market whose indication of stability is evidenced by prevailing rate of exchange which is practically on an even basis with our own.[25]

These business demands for recognition made an immediate impact on state governments. Governors and legislatures sent letters and resolutions to the president, the secretary of state, and congressmen. Several border state governors were also leaders in the recognition campaign. When General Obregón visited the United States in the fall of 1920, he was met in El Paso, Texas, by the governors of New Mexico, Arizona, and Texas. By the end of the year six states had officially requested recognition. This number increased to fourteen by mid-1922. All these efforts were reflected in congressional arguments for recognition.[26]

Several leading industrialists added their support to the campaign. Samuel M. Vauclain of the Baldwin Locomotive Works, Judge E. J. Gary of U.S. Steel, and A. B. Farquhar, a manufacturer of farm machinery, were three of the more prominent. Farquhar told Hughes that Obregón was "by far the best ruler Mexico had had since Díaz . . . and in some respects is superior

circulated thirty thousand copies of the report made by the group); Speech by Representative James O'Connor (La.), *Congressional Record,* 68th Cong., 2d sess., 66, pt. 2: 1894–96 (tells about a trip to Mexico by the New Orleans Association of Commerce in 1924).

25. "Recognition of Mexico," *Mississippi Valley Magazine,* July 1923, 6. See also Chester W. Hansen, "American Business Men on Mexico," *Mexican Review,* September 1921, which contains excerpts from letters of businessmen who had recently visited Mexico; Hansen's article was also published as a brochure. From September 1920 through February 1921 the State Department received letters or resolutions in favor of recognition from the chambers of commerce of Laredo, Brownsville, and Beaumont (Texas), Nogales and Tucson (Arizona), and San Francisco, and from the Young Men's Business League (Waco, Texas), and the Arizona Merchants Association; file numbers SD 812.00/24600–24800. During the spring of 1922 still more organizations wrote in support of recognition, such as the Tri-State Association of Credit Men, the New Orleans Association of Commerce, Quaker City Rubber Company, and the American Vulcanized Fibre Company of Wilmington, Delaware; file numbers SD 711.12/380–500.

26. Gov. W. P. Hobby (Tex.) to President Wilson, 11 September 1920, SD 812.00/24633. Dillon, *President Obregón,* 245–46.

to Díaz." Vauclain arranged a private loan for the Mexican government so that railroad equipment could be purchased from U.S. manufacturers.[27]

The hardline opponents of recognition expressed much anger and concern over counter efforts by U.S. businessmen. Harold Walker of the Doheny oil interests bitterly criticized the "Pollyanna talk of those who would sell large crates of socks and suspender buttons."[28] And William F. Buckley expressed amazement over the actions of the border state governors, and wondered "how patriotic Americans could advocate the recognition of a government in Mexico . . . under which Americans are placed in the same category as Japanese in California."[29] Fall, Doheny, and other hardliners also tried to persuade Thomas Lamont and the International Committee of Bankers that recognition should be granted only after the ratification of a treaty. The nonrecognitionists realized that their position was being eroded steadily, both politically and economically, by stability in Mexico and by calculations of business and political interests in the United States.

Secretary Herbert Hoover and the Department of Commerce tended to take a moderate position on the recognition question. The pressure from export interests led to an interesting exchange at the 1922 National Foreign Trade Convention. Dr. Julius Klein, head of the Bureau of Foreign and Domestic Commerce, was asked: "Is there any possibility of the Government recognizing Mexico and in that way making the stability of business relations there more secure?" Klein replied: "I would like to hand that question over to some of my good friends in the State Department. Some of them are here but just now they are rather making themselves scarce, I am afraid." The attitude of the convention had been distinctly pro-recognition.[30]

27. A. B. Farquhar to Hughes, 17 June 1921, Hughes MSS; Lamont to Gary, 15 February 1922, Lamont MSS. Vauclain data in Fletcher to Summerlin, 9 September 1921, SD 812.00/25169A; Summerlin to Hughes, 9 December 1921, SD 812.51/691.

28. Walker to Fall, 17 December 1920, Fall MSS.

29. Buckley to Fall, 4 November 1920, Fall MSS, ibid.

30. Session on "Market Conditions Abroad," *Ninth National Foreign Trade Convention* (New York, 1922), 349. See also Carlton Jackson (commercial attaché, Mexico City) to director, Bureau of Foreign and Domestic Commerce, 31 March 1921, enclosed in Herbert Hoover to Hughes, 15 April 1921, SD 812.00/24978.

The promise of the Mexican market provided a consistent bond for the various individuals and groups agitating for recognition. Senator Edwin Ladd (N. Dak.) pointed to the widespread business support for recognition of the country which he said was "still the treasure chest of the world" and:

Mexico is one of our best customers. Last year she purchased $267,200,366 worth of products from the United States and in return sold us commodities . . . valued at $154,993,154. This is but a small percentage of the trade that could be developed if we recognized the Government of Mexico and established friendly relations which would encourage greater development.

Ladd also stressed the stability of the Obregón government and argued that the reforms of the revolution did not threaten "legitimate interests." The same arguments were presented by the Foreign Policy Association in its campaign for recognition.[31]

It is difficult to measure the impact of these pressures. But the State Department felt them, and Hughes was required periodically to defend his position. In June 1921 interest-group attorney Frederic Watriss suggested to Undersecretary Fletcher that a fellow lobbyist, Judge Parker, call on President Harding to "enlighten" him on certain aspects of the Mexican question. Fletcher asked Hughes if he had any objection to this visit and explained his hope that some of the Mexican propaganda could be "offset by a little American propaganda at the White House." The secretary had no objection. As he told the president a few months later, "I have been silent under much provocation in order to avoid difficulties in Mexico, but there is a limit to the extent to which misrepresentation can go uncorrected particularly when voiced in the Senate."[32]

31. *Congressional Record*, 67th Cong., 2d sess., 1922, 62, pt. 10: 10425; Foreign Policy Association, "In the Matter of the Settlement of Disputed Questions between Mexico and the United States: Memorandum to Hon. Charles Evans Hughes, April 18, 1921" and "Memorandum from Mr. James G. McDonald of the Foreign Policy Assn. for Thomas Lamont," 25 July 1921, both in Lamont MSS. Some stressed the threat of radicalism if Obregón fell; Judge Stebbins R. Wilfley to Hughes, 3 August 1921; "Memorandum of Conversation between George Young (Cananea Consolidated Copper Co.) and the Undersecretary," 21 June 1921, both in Hughes MSS.
32. Watriss to Fletcher, 23 June 1921, SD 812.00/25418: Fletcher to Hughes, 24 June 1921, SD 812.00/25169A; Hughes to Harding, 24 July 1922, SD 812.51/812. Hughes mentioned the "unfair attack" by Senator Ladd.

Oil and Debt Problems, 1921–22

The negotiations with Mexican leaders and other activities of Thomas Lamont and the International Committee constituted one of the more important elements in U.S.-Mexican relations during this period. Lamont quickly established a close relationship with Secretary Hughes. The International Committee continued to act as an unofficial instrument of U.S. policy, especially in its efforts to keep the major European banking interests unified behind a common policy. But the activities of the committee entered a new phase after March 1921. Lamont believed that the Wilson administration had not given the committee enough freedom of action in its dealings with Mexico; he told Hughes:

I, myself, have some doubts as to the complete wisdom of judgment expressed by Mr. Norman Davis in the matter. . . . In other words, I think it inexpedient that too much of an official cast should be given to the committee. It should never fail to work in harmony with the Department but should not be the creature of the Department, for if it is its usefulness is destroyed.[33]

Lamont and other committee members believed that making any debt negotiations contingent upon the settlement of the article 27 controversy, particularly in regard to oil, created a major problem for continued unified action of all the banking interests. The Obregón administration had openly stated its desire to negotiate a settlement with the foreign bondholders, and European bankers were clearly impatient with the "no negotiation" policy. Lamont wanted more flexibility, but he did agree with the continuation of the policy that no loan should be made to Mexico until after recognition. The State Department viewed the integration of private loans with recognition as an important tool for achieving its goals in Mexico.[34]

During its deliberations in March-April 1921 the International Committee dropped most of its proposals for international super-

33. Lamont to Hughes, 29 March 1921, SD 812.51/724.
34. Lamont to Hughes, 13 September 1921, SD 812.51/793; Lamont to Hughes, 27 June 1921, SD 812.51/726; "Confidential Memorandum of Interview with Mr. Paul D. Cravath (Blair & Co.), May 26, 1923," Hughes MSS; President Obregón, "Statement on Mexican Policy . . . April 2, 1921," SD 712.00/3. The Mexican recognition issue was one of the reasons why the State Department issued its general policy statement of 3 March 1922 requesting bankers to submit all foreign loan proposals to the department.

vision of Mexican finances. The members did agree on a plan to internationalize the board of directors of the old Banco Nacional, a private bank largely owned by French interests. The committee's plan called for the bank to be the depository for all funds of the Mexican government and the agency which would make payments on the national debt. As one member suggested, "This would make it more difficult for the Government to break faith with its bondholders than if it collected the taxes itself." Sir William Wiseman wanted to redistribute the capital of the bank so as to reduce French influence, but Lamont and other Morgan partners thought that control of the board was more advantageous to their interests than holding "doubtful assets." The French members of the committee and the bank officials agreed to this proposal, and Lamont hoped that he could persuade the Mexican government to "invite" the Banco Nacional to perform these functions.[35] Even this suggestion of control marked a distinct retreat from the earlier plans of the committee.

Secretary Hughes did not completely abandon the hope that negotiations for a settlement of Mexico's foreign debt might be predicated upon some action by the Mexican government which would make article 27 nonretroactive. Lamont suggested such action to Mexican officials, but they ignored it in their next invitation to Lamont. At this point, Lamont stressed to Hughes the urgency of debt negotiations without preconditions and the secretary finally agreed in July 1921 that Lamont should accept the offer and go to Mexico.[36]

The question of oil taxation once more emerged as a complicating factor in U.S.-Mexican relations and in the negotiations for settlement of the foreign debt. The Mexican government raised the oil export tax in June 1921 with the idea of using the new funds to resume payments on the foreign bonds. Some bankers had quietly encouraged this move. The oil companies again screamed "confiscation" and "bankruptcy." In a quieter vein they responded to a State Department suggestion and asked the depart-

---

35. "Memorandum 'National Bank of Mexico': Conversation of March 16 [1921], T. W. Lamont, William Wiseman, Mr. Anderson, and E. C. Grenfell," Lamont MSS.
36. Lamont to Hughes, 27 June 1921, SD 812.51/726; Lamont to Manuel C. Téllez (chargé d'affaires, México), 30 June 1921, and Téllez to Lamont, 20 July 1921, SD 812.51/787; Lamont to Hughes, 26 July 1921, SD 812.51/832.

ment to propose direct negotiations to the Mexican government. This was done and a committee of leading oilmen left for Mexico. It was composed of the presidents of Jersey Standard, Mexican Petroleum, Atlantic Refining, Texas, and Sinclair.[37]

The negotiations became quite urgent owing to the fact that the production stoppage by the major companies had failed and they would soon need oil to fill their contracts. Nelson Rhoades had lunch with the committee and observed afterward, "They come in a very chastened mood and I think the probabilities of a favorable conclusion are promising."[38]

The State Department placed one restriction on the negotiations. The oil representatives were told that they should not "discuss or consider" the matter of a loan. Undersecretary Fletcher also told them to deal as private businessmen and "not wrap the Embassy about them." As to the objections voiced by the American Association of Mexico, Fletcher noted that the oilmen should be grateful. After all, any group attacked by William F. Buckley must look moderate to Mexicans, and such attacks "could be turned to decided advantage."[39]

The committee of oil company presidents reached an agreement with the Mexican government in early September 1921. Several taxes were eliminated or lowered. The heart of the agreement led to new controversies. It provided that the companies would have the right until 25 December 1921 to pay the export tax imposed by the decree of 7 June. They could pay in cash at the rate of 40 percent of the amount decreed, or in bonds of the Mexican government issued before 1910. These bonds (with coupons attached) would be accepted at par value for payment of taxes. To obtain these bonds the oilmen agreed to try to organize a bankers' syndicate which would go into the market and buy all the outstanding bonds. The syndicate would then sell the bonds to the oil companies at 40 percent of par. The bankers would profit, since the defaulted bonds had little market value, and the

37. Watriss to Fletcher, 26 July 1921, SD 600.127/217; Hughes to American Embassy, Mexico, 6 August 1921, SD 600.127/222a; Hughes to Watriss, 10 August 1921, SD 600.127/226.
38. Rhoades to Garfield, 29 August 1921, Garfield MSS.
39. Lamont to Hughes, 17 August 1921, SD 812.51/790 (warning about a possible loan); Memorandum of interview with Undersecretary Fletcher, 24 August 1921, by H. N. Branch (Committee of Oil Executives), SD 812.6363/1231.

oil companies would still pay only 40 percent of the tax rate.[40]

The oil executives returned to the United States and requested Thomas Lamont, and the American section of the International Committee, to form the syndicate. Lamont refused on the grounds that such action would be impractical, illegal, and unethical. The investment bankers, he declared, could not betray the interests of the bondholders. Lamont also noted that the oil export taxes were already pledged to the "senior" bonds (i.e., the major bond issues of the Mexican government floated by the investment bankers). The syndicate scheme would divert these pledged revenues to redeem all types of bonds. The oil companies accepted this refusal and asked to be released from these clauses of the agreement.[41]

In the midst of this discussion (September 1921) Lamont went to Mexico to begin negotiations for a settlement of the foreign debt. Mexicans attached great importance to this trip, since the House of Morgan was considered to be "the most powerful bank on earth."[42] Mexican officials went to great lengths to make Lamont welcome. When he first called on President Obregón, the chief executive ordered champagne, whiskeys, and liqueurs, declaring, "I want you to know, Mr. Lamont, that you are at last in a free country!" Shortly thereafter some American "adventurers" who had talked to Lamont on the train (and had their names put in the newspapers as being in his party), went to Obregón and said that the banker wanted a special train prepared so that he could take a "mixed party" to the Isthmus of Tehuantepec. The president was bewildered by the request but, wanting to please Lamont, ordered a special train with "ladies" aboard to be readied. Lamont was able to stop the enterprise just as it was preparing to leave.[43]

Lamont's negotiations with Adolfo de la Huerta, now minister of finance, were not as successful. The minister insisted that the bond redemption plan, worked out with the oil executives, become

40. "Committee Understanding of Agreement Submitted at the Fifth Conference, September 3, 1921," SD 812.6363/1231.
41. Lamont to W. C. Teagle, 19 September 1921; Lamont to Hughes, 23 September 1921, SD 812.51/794; Lamont to J. P. Morgan & Co., 20 October 1921, SD 812.51/665.
42. *El Universal,* 5 August 1921.
43. "Remarks before the Dutch Treat Club, Lincoln, March 14, 1922," Lamont MSS.

the main element in the settlement of the foreign debt. When he refused to consider the plan developed by the International Committee, Lamont terminated the negotiations.[44]

During the talks in Mexico, de la Huerta had informed Lamont that James Speyer, of the banking firm Speyer and Company, was willing to undertake the bond purchase plan with unspecified modifications. Because of his connections with German banking firms Speyer had not been invited to participate in the International Committee. Faced with this threat to the negotiating position of the committee, the American section very quickly voted to admit the Speyer firm and Hallgarten and Company of Germany. Simultaneously, Speyer notified the Mexican government that he was now working with the International Committee.[45]

Lamont remained in contact with Minister de la Huerta even though the Mexican government continued its push for the redemption plan. In January 1922 de la Huerta sent Eduardo Yturbide, a banker, to New York to make a last attempt to effect this plan. If this failed, he was instructed to begin discussions with the committee on the principles presented by Lamont the previous fall. Lamont was encouraged by the fact that the Mexican government had turned to a member of an old, conservative family, and he asked Secretary Hughes to polish Yturbide's image by granting him an interview. This was done, and Yturbide returned to Mexico to encourage further negotiations based upon the committee's plan. De la Huerta expressed some anger over this turn of events and threatened to go into the market and buy bonds at reduced value. Lamont countered with the threat that such action would constitute repudiation and would ruin any chance for a debt settlement or a loan. The minister relented and accepted the invitation to come to New York in May 1922 for negotiations.[46]

The Obregón government wanted to settle the debt question and obtain loans for a national bank of issue and for agricultural development, especially for irrigation projects. But Obregón also wanted to scale down the accumulated interest and avoid commit-

44. Lamont to de la Huerta, 10 October 1921, Lamont MSS; Lamont to Summerlin, 10 October 1921, SD 812.51/663; Lamont to J. P. Morgan & Co., 20 October 1921, SD 812.51/665.

45. Lamont to Dept. of State, 30 November 1921, SD 812.51/865.

46. Lamont to Hughes, 13 January 1922, SD 812.51/779; Lamont to de la Huerta, 18 February 1922, and Lamont to Fletcher, 21 February 1922, SD 812.51/719; Lamont to Hughes, 24 March 1922, SD 812.51/837.

ting too large a portion of annual national revenues to debt service. Above all he wanted to maintain an autonomous country free from foreign tutelage.[47] His priorities were not those of the bondholders.

The national debt of Mexico owed to foreigners could be calculated in various ways. After agreeing to eliminate the bonds issued by Huerta in 1913, the International Committee calculated the direct debt as $508,830,321; of this, $243,734,321 was for railroad bonds (see table 1). In addition, accumulated interest amounted to $207 million. Eighty percent of the bonds were held by Europeans.[48]

TABLE 1

THE FOREIGN DEBT OF MEXICO, 1921
(excluding Huerta Bonds of 1913)

Secured Debt:	
Mexican government 5%, 1899	$ 48,635,000
Mexican government 4%, 1910	50,949,000
Mexican government 6%, 1913	29,100,000
Total	128,684,000
Unsecured debt:	
Mexico City municipal 5%, 1899	6,769,000
Mexican government 4%, 1904	37,037,000
Caja de Prestamos 4½%, 1908	25,000,000
Total	68,806,000
Interior debt:	
Mexican government 3%, 1885	21,151,000
Mexican government 5%, 1895	46,455,000
Total	67,606,000
Railroad debt (total)	243,734,321
Grand total	508,830,321

SOURCE: Draft of the Agreement between the Mexican Minister of Finance and the International Committee, 16 June 1922, SD 812.51/775.

47. Ministerio de Relaciones Exteriores, *Documentos oficiales relativos al Convenio de la Huerta–Lamont* (México, D.F., 1924), 13, 42, 52.
48. "Draft of the Agreement between the Mexican Minister of Finance and the International Committee," 16 June 1922, enclosed in Cochran to Hughes, 7 July 1922, SD 812.51/775.

Some members of the International Committee believed that Mexico could afford the cost of complete resumption of debt service if the Mexican government practiced frugality in other areas. As a result, the negotiations almost terminated in early June 1922. The following exchange between a French member of the committee and Minister de la Huerta reveals the difference in views. The Frenchman asserted that even if it were a case of life and death, "certain revenues are already destined to the different bonds."

Mr. de la Huerta: Above all Mexico must live first. . . . If a family is in financial straits bread and milk should be the first consideration and then after that will come the creditors.

Mr. Chevalier: The remedy is to cut down expenses which are not essential.

Mr. de la Huerta: That has already been done.

Mr. Chevalier: What do you understand then by the phrase of "full recognition of contracts."

Mr. de la Huerta: The family has not failed to recognize the debts of the grocer.

Mr. Lamont: Thus the Minister wants the negotiations to break down at this point?[49]

Neither side wanted to end the negotiations. De la Huerta believed that an agreement with the bankers would produce recognition. Therefore he desperately wanted to return with both feathers in his cap. Obregón wanted funds for the Banco Unico and irrigation projects. The bankers wanted some remuneration for the bondholders. An agreement was worked out in late June, but Obregón instructed de la Huerta not to sign unless it contained the basis for such loans for the rehabilitation of the economy of Mexico.[50]

Some confusion developed over the "assurances" for loans. De la Huerta stated that he had "A-SE-GU-RA-DO" (insured) the establishment of the bank. On this basis the president authorized him to sign the agreement. But the bankers had not promised any loans. They had generally stated that they would support the economic development of Mexico and that loans might be possible when Mexico showed evidence of making good her obligations to foreign creditors. De la Huerta interpreted these general remarks

49. "Memorandum of Conference with de la Huerta, June 5, 1922," Lamont MSS.
50. *Documentos oficiales relativos al Convenio de la Huerta–Lamont,* 42.

quite literally. As a result, Obregón thought that definite assurances had been given.[51]

The Lamont–de la Huerta Agreement of 16 June 1922 included these provisions: (1) the bondholders agree to waive the payment of interest on all arrears of interest; (2) the coupons for interest due prior to 2 January 1923 will be deposited and certificates for their face value will be issued, and beginning on 1 January 1928 the Mexican government will begin to redeem these in proportionate annuities over a forty-year period; (3) all sinking funds will be postponed for a period not to exceed five years; (4) all matured obligations will be extended for a "reasonable length of time"; (5) payment of current interest will be based on a fund created by annual payments beginning with $30 million a year to reach $50 million for the fifth year; any annual arrears in this fund will be met with scrip issued by the Mexican government, which will be due and payable in twenty years with a 3 percent annual interest after the first five years; (6) after the expiration of a five-year period the Mexican government will resume the full service of the debt. The agreement was ratified by President Obregón on 7 August, then confirmed by the Congress, and it became law on 29 September.[52]

From the beginning the debt agreement was entangled with the oil question, since the entire proceeds of the oil export tax were pledged· to the current interest fund. The oil executives had been negotiating with the Mexican government over the tax issue, as well as the overall problem of article 27, since late April and had shown some antagonism toward the bankers and their conception of bondholder interest. Minister de la Huerta explained that be-

51. Ibid., 55–56, 49–52; "Memorandum for Mr. Vernon Munroe, November 19, 1929," by Lamont, Lamont MSS.
52. "Draft of the Agreement between the Mexican Minister of Finance and the International Committee," 16 June 1922, SD 812.51/775; Patchin to Hughes, 5 August 1922, SD 812.51/839. Background of Mexican finances in Jesús Romero Flores, *La Constitución de 1917 y los primeros gobiernos revolucionarios* (México, D.F., 1960), 180–81; Alberto Pani, *La política hacendaria y la Revolución* (México, D.F., 1926), 11–14. The committee requested the individual bondholders to deposit their bonds, and within a year 92 percent of the bonds had been deposited. Of the 20 percent held in the United States the largest interests were insurance companies such as Equitable Life Assurance, Mutual Life, New York Life, and the Traveler's Insurance Company. The Washington Trust Company of Westerly, Rhode Island, held $12,610, and the Rockefeller Foundation $50,000; Lamont MSS (exchange rate: two pesos to the dollar).

cause of his forthcoming negotiations with the International Committee he could not pledge to maintain the 40 percent rate on the export tax. Walter C. Teagle of Standard Oil of New Jersey replied that many members of the International Committee wanted to collect 100 percent of the June 1921 export tax and that they had no interest in the oil industry. The Standard Oil executive declared that the interests of the Mexican government and the oil industry were practically identical insofar as there was a limit beyond which either could not pay.[53]

Some bankers did feel that the oil companies could afford to be more cooperative on the tax issue. Even Thomas Lamont—who was on very friendly terms with the oil executives—believed that the committee "could properly urge the oil companies pretty strongly to pay a little extra on this first payment and get the committee's agreement really started."[54] Minister de la Huerta requested the oil companies to pay the export tax in New York with U.S. gold dollars. When oil executives complained to Lamont, he bluntly informed them: "I do not think the Secretary is hard on you at all. In fact he is dead right." Lamont noted that in order to meet the U.S. gold payments in the debt agreement, the Mexican government might have to require more than 40 percent payment of the export tax.[55]

De la Huerta hoped to obtain a loan or advance on taxes of at least $25 million in return for guaranteeing the 40 percent rate. The oil companies at first refused to consider such action. By early July 1922 some oil executives were ready to agree to an advance if they could obtain Mexican agreement on the creation of a development corporation which would control almost the entire oil industry of the country. Secretary Hughes expressed his disapproval of any loan, and the oilmen abided by his decision. Thus, de la Huerta returned to Mexico with agreements on the export tax and the foreign debt, but no loan and no recognition. It was an exceedingly embarrassing situation for the finance

53. "Papers Relating to Conferences between Secretary de la Huerta and Committee of Oil Executives, April 24th–May 3rd, 1922," enclosed in Teagle to Hughes, 25 May 1922, SD 812.6363/1135.
54. "Memorandum on Mexico by AMA [Arthur M. Anderson of J. P. Morgan & Co.], August 28, 1922," Lamont MSS.
55. Lamont to Amos L. Beaty (Texas Co.), 9 October 1922, and Lamont to Ryan, 13 October 1922, both in Lamont MSS. The oilmen preferred to buy pesos in Mexico at special rates for tax purposes.

minister, who had staked his political career on arrangements for the development of his country.[56]

Lamont and the Background to the Bucareli Conference

The negotiations of 1922 played an important role in preparing the way for the Bucareli Conference in 1923 and for recognition. Thomas Lamont was one of the most influential persons involved in the attempt to resolve the differences between Mexico and the United States by private negotiations and the cultivation of person-to-person diplomacy.

The role played by Lamont cannot be characterized as lobbying or pressuring either for or against recognition. Perhaps it can best be described as a quiet process of trying to induce both sides to be less dogmatic and ideological in their approach to the issues. In a letter to Judge E. H. Gary, Lamont said that his attitude on recognition was "absolutely neutral," and he discussed his activities in the United States in these words:

I have felt that it [recognition] was such an important question that it would be unfortunate for the financial interests to take sides upon [it]. On the other hand I have made every possible effort to make known my opinion that conditions in Mexico were on a stabler basis and that in general the government there was endeavoring to do the right thing. I have endeavored to build up the general standing of the Obregón government.[57]

In speeches and private conversations Lamont stressed the point that the disagreements between Mexico and the United States were over practical, economic problems and not over ideological differences. In a speech to a group of businessmen in March 1922, he stated that he had been informed by the British Intelligence Office that the present cabinet of the Mexican government was composed of members of the Third International, "but when I got down there, while I found them somewhat radical,

56. "Minutes and Memorandums of the Conference between Committee of Oil Executives and Secretary de la Huerta, June 1922," SD 812.6363/ 1200; Hanna to Hughes, 10 July 1922, SD 812.6363/1227 (proposal for advance); "Memorandum of a Conference between H. N. Branch and the Secretary, July 11, 1922," SD 812.6363/1228; Hanna to Secretary of State, 14 July 1922, SD 812.51/901.
57. Lamont to Gary, 15 February 1922, Lamont MSS.

they were not at all Bolshevistic or anarchistic." To the American Bankers Association meeting in October 1922 Lamont presented a justification for the Mexican Revolution and said that the constitution of 1917 could be criticized more for its "unworkableness" than for its radicalism. In addition, he urged the bankers to have patience and sympathy for a neighbor which was slowly trying to solve its problems.[58]

Lamont was concerned over the effects of harsh rhetoric on relations between Mexico and the United States. In the first draft of a letter to Secretary of State Charles Evans Hughes he wrote:

I am much disturbed over this writ of attachment against the Mexican government and [I am] against the attempt to class that government in with the Soviets. The logical conclusion, if such attachments are to be permitted, is to nullify all the work that we have been building up for months past, with such Mexican government as exists today, which, on the whole, in my opinion (when its difficult political position is recalled) has done pretty well and made progress.[59]

Since this statement was a rather blunt criticism of some State Department pronouncements, Lamont eliminated it in the final draft. He did, however, incorporate the basic idea into other sections of the letter.

On the other side of the Rio Grande, Lamont urged Mexican officials to take a more pragmatic position on the issues involved in the recognition controversy, and tried to convince them of the friendly sentiments of the State Department. He tactfully encouraged Mexican officials to cooperate with the oil companies and the State Department. Lamont was also adept at the art of flattery.[60]

In 1921, W. P. Hobby, former governor of Texas and a personal friend of Alvaro Obregón, was working for the unqualified recognition of Mexico. D. E. Pomeroy of the Bankers Trust Company (New York) sent Lamont a copy of a letter from Hobby which stated that it was impossible for Obregón to sign a treaty in order

58. "Remarks before the Dutch Treat Club, Lincoln, March 14, 1922"; "The American Bankers' Responsibility Today," 3 October 1922; Lamont MSS; Lamont to Hughes, 19 October 1922, SD 812.51/893.

59. Lamont to Hughes, 31 October 1922, Lamont MSS.

60. Proposed Telegram to Minister de la Huerta, 19 October 1922, enclosed in Lamont to Hughes, 19 October 1922, SD 812.51/893.

to gain recognition. Lamont's reply, obviously intended for Hobby, said that the Treaty of Amity and Commerce proposed by Secretary Hughes was not a sine qua non. "Now," Lamont continued, "if Obregón says it is politically very hard for him to adopt this course, but he can adjust the matter by independent initiative with his Congress or Supreme Court, I should think that that would make no difference to the State Department." Pomeroy was additionally informed that any such action by Obregón would accomplish an "immense step in the rebuilding" of Mexico since this would be of major importance in convincing the great investment interests of the world of the validity of future credits and loans.[61]

Although Lamont was in basic agreement with the goals of the State Department, he took a less dogmatic and legalistic position concerning the kind of "declaration" (or "course of action") which Obregón should adopt. The bankers wanted the Obregón government to survive, and Lamont's decision, in 1921, to accept Obregón's invitation to come to Mexico for discussion of the external debt was largely based on his—and other committee members'—evaluation that such action would help to strengthen Obregón's position vis-à-vis possible rivals. The visit would also provide an opportunity for Lamont to "make very clear to the Mexican authorities that there is an earnest desire on the part of the Committee to be of service to Mexico." He hoped this would also encourage Obregón to move closer to the State Department's concept of international economic relations.[62]

In the course of the negotiation over the external debt during 1921–22, Lamont established friendly relations with several officials; the most significant such contact was with Adolfo de la Huerta. The fact that Lamont was able to negotiate a formal agreement for the settlement of the external debt and that this agreement was accepted in toto by President Obregón is an indi-

61. Hobby to Pomeroy, 22 June 1921, and Lamont to Pomeroy, 29 June 1921, both in Lamont MSS. Prior to this Lamont had a conference with Secretary Hughes.
62. Lamont to Hughes, 27 June 1921, Lamont MSS. For details of invitation see Memo (Lamont) for Martin Egan, 2 September 1921; Ira Patchin to Lamont, 17 July 1922, Lamont MSS. Patchin was a member of the staff of J. P. Morgan and Company and was assigned to work with Lamont on Mexican matters; Lamont to Hughes, 31 December 1923, Lamont MSS.

cation of the nature of these relationships. In mid-1922, when de la Huerta was invited to visit Washington to meet with President Harding and Secretary Hughes, he informed several people that he regarded Lamont "as a prophet." As General James A. Ryan of the Texas Company expressed it, "I have the highest respect for your splendid work with Secretary de la Huerta and I know that he has the highest esteem for you; and your efforts in New York will have a far reaching effect upon the ultimate recognition of Mexico."[63]

On 19 June 1922 Lamont had suggested to Secretary Hughes that he extend an invitation to de la Huerta to visit the State Department. Lamont believed such action would strengthen the finance minister in his dealings with other factions in the government and would break down the barriers of pride. As he explained, "These Mexican people ought not to be proud and peculiar, but they are, and we can't change them overnight into Anglo-Saxons." In summary the banker noted the relationship between economics and diplomacy:

To have it [the debt agreement] worked out, gradually improving economic conditions are essential. Such improvement can be brought about only by improving political conditions, and by taking every friendly opportunity for showing to the Mexicans just what our principles are, why we stand for them, and how they themselves are able to meet the situation.[64]

Hughes extended the invitation but it was "stepped on" by a ranking official in Mexico, probably by the minister of foreign relations, Alberto Pani, a political rival. General Ryan, representing the Texas Company in Mexico, called on President Harding and the invitation was renewed. Obregón instructed de la Huerta to accept, and the minister immediately informed Lamont of his impending visit. With "evident delight" and expectations of recognition, de la Huerta went to the White House on 18 July 1922.[65] The meeting between Harding and de la Huerta was most cordial. The minister invited the president to dinner in his private railroad car and mentioned that he had whiskey, cognac, and even champagne. Harding probably licked his lips but declined for

63. General Ryan to Lamont, 27 July and 4 October 1922, Lamont MSS.
64. Lamont to Hughes, 19 June 1922, SD 812.51/914.
65. Patchin to Lamont, 17 July 1922, Lamont MSS.

reasons of public relations; several senators did accept and arrived early enough to be "a little high" when de la Huerta returned.[66]

Minister de la Huerta also visited Hughes at the State Department. The Mexican official stated that article 27 was retroactive but that his government was willing to confirm the rights acquired prior to 1917 so as not to prejudice foreign investments. Hughes expressed his objection to various aspects of the agrarian laws such as the "worthlessness" of bonds issued for compensation, arbitrary procedures, and the "insufficiency" of indemnity. He also pointed out that the "more important things" promised had not been accomplished; the bankers' agreement had not been approved, nothing definite had resulted from the conferences with the oil executives, the decision in the Texas Company case did not solve the question of the "confiscatory" and "retroactive" character of article 27, and the four supplementary court decisions had not yet officially been published. Hughes reiterated the need for "positive acts" by Mexico and concluded: "Come back when all those matters are settled and we will talk things over again."[67]

General Ryan and Minister de la Huerta were quite optimistic after these meetings. Both were impressed by the fact that Hughes did not mention the treaty as a precondition of recognition, and de la Huerta believed that he could obtain the necessary acts on the part of his government. Lamont and his colleagues at J. P. Morgan and Company were immediately informed of these optimistic views. In their discussions with the State Department, the bankers learned that a substantial gap still existed between U.S. expectations and the interpretations of Ryan and de la Huerta.[68]

General Ryan periodically reported to Harding, Hughes, and Lamont on the progress the Mexican government was making in fulfilling what he considered to be the agreement between Hughes and de la Huerta. Hughes was not satisfied with any of the actions except the debt agreement, and in October he told a Morgan official: "We do not want promises from Mexico; we want

66. Guzmán Esparza, *Memorias de Don Adolfo de la Huerta,* 208–13.
67. "Memorandum of a Conference between Adolfo de la Huerta and Secretary Hughes, July 18, 1922," SD 711.12/525. The oil companies did not accept the Texas Company decision as a settlement of the article 27 issue; Watriss to Fletcher, 6 September 1921, SD 812.6363/951.
68. Patchin to Lamont, 20 July 1922; "Memorandum of conversation between Legorreta and Cochran, July 19, 1922"; Patchin to Lamont, 21 July 1922; all in Lamont MSS.

'things.' " In part, the secretary was influenced by a proposed
Organic Law on Petroleum, drafted by "old Carranza types,"
which he considered to be "entirely inadequate" for the protection
of American rights.[69] Recognition seemed to be stalled by the
latter part of the year. De la Huerta thought that all had been
accomplished and asked Lamont to convey this information to
Hughes. Lamont encouraged the secretary of state to work to
strengthen the position of de la Huerta, since "he is, I know, most
anxious to carry out your ideas."[70]

Under the impact of pressures and events, Hughes's attitude
on the recognition question began to moderate. President Obregón
had demonstrated his willingness to settle some of the questions
and had expressed his acceptance of most forms of foreign investment. The apparent log-jam over recognition began to break after
General Ryan visited the State Department on 27 February 1923
and advised Hughes that Obregón had assured him that he would
be glad to have the question between the two countries considered
by a commission composed of representatives of the United States
and Mexico. The secretary replied that he would "welcome" this,
as he had been thinking about such action. On 5 March, Hughes
informed Ryan that the president viewed the situation favorably
and was ready to appoint the two U.S. representatives.[71]

The developments since 1921 prompted a rethinking of the
U.S. position inside the State Department, and the formulation of
a less dogmatic policy. In March 1923, Matthew E. Hanna, of
the Division of Mexican Affairs, analyzed the basic dilemma involved in the previous policy. Mexico had achieved considerable
internal stability—the most since Díaz according to Hanna—but
this might be jeopardized if the United States continued to insist
upon rigid requirements for recognition. According to Hanna,
these conditions "would appear not only to justify this Govern-

69. "Memorandum of a Conversation with Secretary Hughes, Mr. Hanna
at State Department, October 16 and 20, 1922," by Ira H. Patchin, 21
October 1922; Ryan to Lamont, 27 July and 11 August 1922; all in Lamont MSS; Ryan to Harding, 30 September 1922, SD 711.12/475; Ryan
to Hughes, 22 August 1922, SD 812.6363/1176.

70. De la Huerta to Carlos R. Felix (financial agent of Mexico), 10
October 1922, message to be delivered to Mr. Lamont, SD 812.51/892;
Lamont to Hughes, 13 October 1922, ibid.

71. Hughes to American Embassy (Mexico), 7 March 1923, SD
711.1211/61a; letter from Obregón to Ryan in Alberto J. Pani, *Las conferencias de Bucareli* (México, D.F., 1953), 88–91, 111.

ment in accepting much that it could not accept two years ago but to compel it in justice to do so." This official also pointed out that claims of deprivation of property had been exaggerated grossly. The department was not defending a theory, he wrote, but had to consider whether changed conditions meant that American interests now could be protected better by "conciliatory concessions."

With a kind of racist pragmatism, Hanna noted: "Mexico is and will continue to be governed by an Indian race of low civilization, and it would be a fundamental error to deal with such a government as with that of a highly civilized white race, or to expect to obtain justice by the mere force of logic when justice conflicts with national aspirations." His conclusion reflected the various pressures from U.S. interests:

There should be general satisfaction with such a settlement of the Mexican question. The American public would certainly rejoice; all the miscellaneous American interests in Mexico whose property depends on the prosperity of Mexico are, I believe, patiently hoping and waiting for something of the kind; it would have the support of American business interests in the United States with Mexican connections; it would promise relief for the small army of claimants against Mexico who apparently have not yet taken note of the fact that the absence of recognition is preventing the settlement of their claims under the two conventions which Mexico is ready to sign; and, finally, there is no good reason why the American owners of petroleum interests and large landed estates should complain when they understand that the Department is improving its position for their protection.[72]

Secretary Hughes also had accepted the fact that, barring military coercion, the only way for the United States to maintain and expand its trade and investment role in Mexico was through accommodation with the Obregón government.

President Obregón formally and "eagerly" communicated his acceptance of the conference to General Ryan on 9 April 1923. Ryan forwarded the news to Hughes, and shortly thereafter the secretary appointed John Barton Payne and Charles Beecher Warren as U.S. representatives.[73]

72. Hanna to Secretary of State, 23 March 1923, SD 711.12/541.
73. Ryan to Hughes, 13 April 1923, SD 711.1211/114.

Hughes's instructions to them stated: "It will be observed that the fundamental question at issue has been the safeguarding of American property rights in Mexico, especially as against confiscatory application of the provisions of the Mexican Constitution of 1917." U.S. representatives were given considerable flexibility in regard to settling this issue. Hughes outlined three basic questions for discussion: (1) "the obtaining of satisfactory assurances against confiscation of the subsoil interests in lands owned by American citizens prior to May 1st, 1917"; (2) "the restoration or proper reparation for the taking of lands owned by American citizens prior to May 1st, 1917"; and (3) "the making of appropriate claims conventions."[74]

Lamont discussed with Warren his experiences and the personalities of the Mexican leaders. Armed with some knowledge of the bankers' negotiations, Warren and Payne departed for Mexico. The conferences began on 14 May 1923 at No. 85 Bucareli Street. The Mexican commissioners, Ramón Ross and Fernando González Roa, extended a hearty welcome to the North Americans. Warren, in reply, emphasized the principles of international law, which "are essential as the basis of economic cooperation between nations."[75]

For the most part the conferences proceeded with cordiality even in the midst of some disagreements. On one occasion, however, the talks were disrupted. Warren mentioned a law which applied in Panama. Ross had imbibed a little too much wine at lunch, and when he heard the reference to Panama he struck the table with his fist and shouted, "No nos comparen con Panamá" (Do not compare us with Panama). The Mexican commissioners

74. "Memorandum of the Draft of Instructions Prepared by Secretary Hughes for the American Commissioners meeting in Mexico," 30 April 1923, Hughes MSS; Hughes to Payne, 5 May 1923, SD 711.1211/86a. The land reform issue came to the fore only after 1920. From 1916 through 1920, 172,799 hectares of land were distributed; during 1921, 178,814 hectares were distributed; Clarence Senior, *Mexico in Transition* (New York, 1939), 15. Contrary to the claims of the various hardline groups, most of the American-owned lands taken for agrarian reform were held by land development companies, not by widows and orphans; "Résumé of the Most Serious Agrarian Expropriation of U.S. Citizens, April 1923," SD 712.11/223.

75. Lamont to Hughes, 29 April 1923, Hughes MSS; U.S.-Mexican Commission, *Proceedings of the United States–Mexican Commission Convened in Mexico City May 14, 1923* (Washington, D.C., 1925), 3–5.

then accused the United States of wanting to make Mexico into another Panama. The meeting adjourned on this angry note, but General Ryan went to Obregón and corrected the misunderstanding. Minister de la Huerta was asked to confer with the U.S. commissioners and successfully calmed them. The conference resumed on a friendly note, and Ross was instructed not to visit the Club Sonora-Sinaloa during the remainder of the negotiations.[76]

The Bucareli Conference produced two treaties: a Special Claims Convention covering losses sustained between 10 November 1910 and 31 May 1920, and a General Claims Convention covering all other losses from 1868 on. The most controversial aspect of the conference was the so-called "extraofficial pact," consisting of the completed minutes signed by the four commissioners. Both sides had stated their positions in regard to the agrarian and subsoil issues. Some modifications were made, but no firm agreements as such were recorded. Warren did state, although not in the form of an agreement, that the U.S. commissioners would recommend to their government the proposal that Mexican federal bonds be accepted as payment for land expropriated for *ejidos* "of an area not substantially exceeding seventeen hundred and fifty-five (1,755) hectares [about 4,000 acres] in any one case." But he attached various reservations concerning types of landholding and valuation. The General Claims Commission was to be the bridge between the reservations and the Mexican land reform program; the issue of expropriation of lands owned by U.S. citizens would be settled on an individual basis.[77]

The question of subsoil oil rights was left in an even more vague condition. The Mexican commissioners declared that their government would "respect and enforce" the principles of the Supreme Court decision in the Texas Company case, as reinforced in four subsequent decisions. The basic element in these decisions was the declaration that paragraph IV of article 27 was not retroactive "in respect to all persons who have performed, prior to the promulgation of said Constitution, some positive act which would manifest the intention of the owner of the surface

76. Miguel Alessio Robles, *Historia política de la Revolución* (México, D.F., 1938), 280–89; Manuel González Ramirez, *Los llamados Tratados de Bucareli* (México, D.F., 1939), 193–94; Guzmán Esparza, *Memorias de Don Adolfo de la Huerta,* 238.
77. U.S.-Mexican Commission, *Proceedings,* 37–44.

. . . to make use of or obtain the oil under the surface." A rather broad definition of positive acts was included. The commissioners also declared that those who had not performed positive acts would be granted "preferential rights" to the exclusion of third parties. The U.S. commissioners entered a broad reservation for "all" the rights of American citizens.[78] What can be said of this legalistic sparring? Several years later, Ambassador Dwight Morrow tried to give an explanation:

At the time of the Warren-Payne agreement the Mexican commissioners made a definite statement based largely upon the Texas oil company cases. It is not clear that this was accepted by the American commissioners. On the contrary, they made a reservation and the Mexican commissioners then made a statement that they recognized the right of the United States to make a reservation. . . . If this be true was an agreement or even an understanding reached?[79]

The precise meaning of the so-called Bucareli Agreement has been debated for years by diplomats and historians. Whatever the legalities—and I do not propose to settle them—the immediate result was a *modus vivendi* whereby U.S. officials could approve recognition and still point to Mexican guarantees in the form of two treaties and an "agreement." The U.S. position had been read into the minutes and could be used as a legalistic basis for diplomatic action. The State Department was dealing primarily with "principles" which might lead to future action. The oil companies had not been touched, and the losses of landowners were slight. Hughes chose to consolidate the status quo rather than demand the settlement of potential issues. Hanna had discussed this course of action in his March memorandum. He had argued that the United States could lose nothing by setting aside the technical issues and recognizing Obregón. In turn this action would in all probability strengthen him and protect American interests. Since Obregón had consolidated the power of the revolutionary leader-

78. U.S.-Mexican Commission, *Proceedings*, 47–49; Gómez Robledo, *Bucareli Agreements*, 15–18.
79. "Confidential Memorandum for Mr. Olds from the American Embassy in Mexico City, November 30, 1927," Dwight W. Morrow Papers, Amherst College Library, Amherst, Mass. Ambiguities discussed in Person, *Mexican Oil*, 43–44; Meyer, *México y Estados Unidos*, 140–45.

ship, continued stability and growing commercial ties clearly out-weighed paper guarantees and legal debating points.[80]

The major oil companies were not satisfied with the agreements and tried to put pressure on Hughes, through Secretary of the Treasury Andrew Mellon, for guarantees on the tax question. This failed, but the hardliners were successful in forcing the removal of General Ryan. Lamont advised General Palmer Pierce of Standard Oil of New Jersey that such action might possibly give the impression that the oilmen wanted the conference to fail. This opinion was indeed correct, and Ryan paid the price for his inde-pendent initiative on behalf of Mexican recognition.[81]

De La Huerta Rebellion and Financial Problems, 1923–24

The United States formally recognized the Mexican government and, with the support of Ryan and Lamont, Charles Beecher Warren became the new ambassador to Mexico in September 1923. Shortly thereafter the issue of stability was raised by the de la Huerta rebellion. Obregón's political opposition used the Bucareli settlement as a rallying cry to charge the government with selling out to the Yankees. De la Huerta resigned his cabinet post to run for the presidency against the official candidate, Plutarco Calles, and the former minister became the titular head of the various dissident groups. Since de la Huerta had staked his political future on obtaining recognition without any agreement with the U.S. government, he was probably justified in viewing the Bucareli settlement as a political defeat. The disgruntled generals and politicians who formed the base of the rebellion were motivated by issues more related to the pocketbook.

80. Hanna to Hughes, 23 March 1923, SD 711.12/541. Pani, in *Conferencias de Bucareli*, 111, 139, 198, argues that Mexico made no new concessions to the United States; Aarón Sáenz, in *La política internacional de la Revolución: Estudios y Documentos* (México, D.F., 1961), 50–72, argues that Obregón saved article 27 through this *modus vivendi*; while Trujillo, in *Adolfo de la Huerta*, 139–48, and Guzmán Esparza, in *Memorias de Don Adolfo de la Huerta*, 219, 263–65, both argue that Obregón bowed to the United States.

81. Memorandum: Hanna to Phillips, August 27, 1923, SD 812.6363/1440; Guy Stevens (Association of Oil Producers) to Secretary Hughes, 24 August 1923, SD 812.6363/1438; Lamont to J. P. Morgan & Co., 7 August 1923, and Patchin to Lamont, 9 August 1923, both in Lamont MSS.

Opposition exploded into open rebellion in late 1923. Secretary Hughes decided that support for the recognized government offered the only hope for stability, and the Mexican government was permitted to purchase arms in the United States. The Department of Justice cooperated with Mexican officials by sending the reports of FBI agents to Mexico. These concerned such rebel activities in the United States as meetings, arms purchases, and the possible hiding place of de la Huerta in San Antonio.[82] When Mexican government forces moved against the rebel stronghold in Yucatan, Secretary Hughes did request that they not blockade the port of Progreso or interfere with U.S. commerce, particularly the sisal trade. But he refused Chandler Anderson's request for armed intervention on behalf of the sisal trade and said the United States could not interfere with the action of government forces to defeat the rebels.[83]

Lamont and the International Committee supported the Hughes policy and refused to meet with the de la Huerta agent who was trying to raise funds in New York. As Lamont wrote to Hughes: "I believe, too, as Dwight Morrow, I think, expressed it to you in his talk the other day, that in the policy which has been adopted no occasion should be lost to follow the situation up and to give the present Mexican Government all the backing that can possibly be given to it at the present time."[84]

Lamont was quite upset over the rebellion and feared that it might "unsettle conditions in Mexico for years." Members of the International Bankers Committee suggested that the group con-

82. SREM, 809, Leg. 12; reports are in English and Spanish and most are from the consulate in Los Angeles; they were sent throughout 1924.

83. Chandler P. Anderson Diary, 12, 18, 24 March 1923, Anderson MSS; Anderson represented International Harvester Company.

84. Lamont to Hughes, 15 January 1924, Hughes MSS; John Barton Payne (chairman, American Red Cross) to Hughes, 30 January 1924, SD 812.34/72 (relayed a request from the representative of the Wells-Fargo Express Company in Mexico that the United States sell torpedo boats to the Obregón government); "Memorandum of December 14, 1923, by Ira H. Patchin," Lamont MSS. The Mexican Petroleum Company refused to loan money to de la Huerta ("Memorandum of December 19, 1923, by Ira H. Patchin," Lamont MSS), but some oil companies may have offered support; J. A. Sáenz to Secretaría de Relaciones Exteriores, 19 August 1924, SREM, 809, Leg. 12; Meyer, *México y Estados Unidos*, 146–47 (n. 197). A report from agent Kosterlitzky (U.S. Intelligence) on 3 November 1924 stated that there was no truth to the rumor that Standard Oil of New Jersey was plotting to send arms to rebel groups; SREM, 809, Leg. 12.

sider some possible means of mediation. As a result Lamont went to Washington to confer with Secretary Hughes on 30 January 1924. Hughes stated that the U.S. government could not become involved in such a project but that "the International Committee strikes me as the only possible vehicle of mediation." Lamont then related the general outline of a rather complex undercover plan to maneuver de la Huerta into asking for the mediation of the International Committee. A representative of one of the oil companies could be sent to Veracruz to talk to de la Huerta about the oil situation. In the course of the conversation the representative should link the oil problem to the Lamont–de la Huerta agreement of 1922 and urge that de la Huerta meet with Lamont and a representative of the Obregón government to discuss ways of carrying out this agreement. It was hoped this conference would quickly move from discussion of the bankers' agreement to the issue of the rebellion.

Lamont was not overly optimistic about the success of the plan, but he thought it worth a try and Hughes agreed. The secretary asked Lamont to go at once to the Mexican embassy and discuss the plan with the minister, Manuel C. Téllez, and Ramón Ross. After listening to Lamont, these officials commented that it was worth trying even though they shared Lamont's doubts concerning its eventual success. The next day Téllez and Ross met with Hughes and Lamont at the State Department, and that evening (31 January 1924) Ramón Ross departed for Mexico to communicate the plan to the government.[85]

At this point the written record ends, and there is no material in the Lamont papers concerning the reaction of the Mexican government. By the time the mediation proposal reached Mexico it was already apparent that the government forces had the upper hand. They had won a major victory at Esperanza on 28 January, and on 12 February Veracruz was occupied. After this the conflict was largely a matter of mopping up the remaining pockets of rebel resistance, and this was gradually completed by early March.

The suppression of the de la Huerta rebellion left the Mexican government with severe financial problems. The resulting economic

85. "Memorandum of Thomas Lamont's Conference in Washington, D.C., January 30, 1924," Lamont MSS. This memorandum and the stenographer's notebooks were in a heavy brown envelope secured with three wax seals.

crisis created some tension between the bankers and the Mexican government. Faced with salary arrears for government employees, diminished revenue for social and economic programs, and a growing clamor for repudiation of the debt agreement, President Obregón ordered a cutback on funds being paid into the current interest account. *El Universal* declared on 6 May 1924:

It is evident that while the Government pays its foreign creditors it leaves unpaid its national creditors, and reduces its public employees to the point of starvation. . . . the salaries of the servants of the nation and those small debts which the domestic creditors still have outstanding, are more sacred than the debts to the foreign millionaire bankers.

But towering [over] this argument . . . there is the moral, the fundamental, the biological principle that first is to live and then how to live.[86]

Mexican officials also informed the bankers that a $20 million loan or advance was needed if they were to comply with the 1924 deposit requirements of the debt agreement. The oil executives, however, convinced Lamont that the limit in taxation had been reached. At this point Lamont allowed his creditor orientation to overshadow his diplomatic aplomb. He informed Finance Minister Pani that as a result of waiving the "interest on the interest," postponing the payment of the principal, and reducing interest on current interest scrip, the bondholders had suffered an economic loss of $1.25 million, a sum equal to two and one-half times the amount of the principal. Lamont also complained to Hughes: "What . . . the Mexican Government overlooks is this: that the foreign widows and orphans who hold their bonds have for ten or twelve years been deprived of all revenue from their investment and have probably suffered a good deal more in the long run than the civil employees have suffered from their brief arrearages of salary."[87] Lamont rarely used the bankers' argument about widows and orphans owning the finance capital of the

86. Pani to Alberto Mascarenas (financial agent of the Mexican government), 6 May 1924, enclosed in Patchin to Hughes, 10 May 1924, SD 812.51/1048.

87. Lamont to Hughes, 2 June 1924; Teagle to Lamont, 15 May 1924 (oil company advice); Lamont MSS; Lamont to Pani, 18 April 1924, SD 812.51/1036. Lamont also charged that the Mexican government had cut the original export tax on oil (pledged to bond payments) by approximately 60 percent when it levied the production tax.

Western world. But the Mexican government was not repudiating the foreign debt, and Hughes had not been too concerned over the issue.

The bankers informed the Mexican government that a small advance might be arranged to cover a deficit in the current interest fund if the full amount of the export tax was deposited. This offer was refused, and Obregón planned to declare a default on the agreement as of 1 July 1924. Ambassador Warren persuaded him not to make this statement, and the bankers agreed to make an announcement that "the fulfillment of the Agreement was deferred rather than broken off."[88]

The Mexican government spent the next few months attempting to secure a loan from various small financiers. J. L. Arlitt of Austin, Texas, signed an agreement to float a $50 million bond issue, but the contract was canceled because of Arlitt's failure to provide the guarantee bond of $100,000 and to deliver the bonds. The State Department did convince some Mexican officials that Arlitt's lack of success was not due to governmental action.[89]

The oil companies continued to make periodic complaints about the meaning of positive acts, concessions in the federal zones, taxation, and labor union demands. In September 1924 a committee of oil executives went to Mexico to discuss a list of seven demands which the companies had issued in April. The Mexican government refused to accept these, but a temporary compromise was signed in October. This very general agreement did not really settle any of the issues. It did provide a kind of stopgap arrangement pending the submission of a petroleum code by the next Mexican administration.[90]

In Hughes's official memoir the period after recognition is summarized very simply: "For the remainder of Secretary Hughes' term of office very cordial relations existed between the United States and Mexico." President-elect Calles visited Washington in October 1924 and was given a warm welcome. Various issues had not been resolved, but none seemed to threaten to lead to an

88. Lamont to Hughes, 23 June 1924, SD 812.51/1073; Lamont to Pani, 26 May 1924, SD 812.51/1059.
89. Thomas Cochran to Hughes, 1 October 1924, SD 812.51/1092; Memorandum for Mr. Grew from Division of Mexican Affairs, 12 December 1924, SD 812.51/1136.
90. Guy Stevens to Hughes, 29 February 1924, SD 812.6363/1489; Stevens to Mascarenas, 7 April 1924, SD 812.51As7/orig.

official crisis. This new harmony was largely due to the willingness of Harding and Hughes to give up dogmatic demands for absolute settlements, demands which in the past had produced crises having little to do with real threats to U.S. interests. Thomas Lamont and the International Committee helped to promote these more flexible tactics. In 1922 Lamont wrote to Hughes about the lesson he had learned from de la Huerta. In dealing with Mexicans "you could lead them around the world with a lump of sugar but could not drive them an inch." This was a bit simplistic, but it was a lesson the next U.S. administration would have to learn anew.[91]

91. "Relations With Mexico," Beerits Memo, Hughes MSS; Lamont to Hughes, 31 October 1922, ibid.

9 The Temporary Triumph of Finance Diplomacy, 1925-1932

> *The great powers are partisans of peace, on condition that they continue to enjoy the privileges and advantages which they have succeeded in winning for themselves.*
> —El Universal (1929)

Calles and National Reform

Plutarco Elías Calles became president of Mexico on 30 November 1924. Obregón's main task had been the consolidation of the political control of the new revolutionary elite. Calles intended to continue this, and to begin an active program for the industrial and financial development of the country. In pursuit of political consolidation the new president assumed several guises: laborite, agrarian, and middle-class entrepreneur. His early speeches and actions appealed to all these groups.[1]

Calles also stressed the secularization of education and the development of a national consciousness based upon the emergent mythology of the Mexican Revolution. *Indianismo,* red flags carried by parading labor unions, a socialist catechism, and murals of Diego Rivera all provided a radical dimension for the first years of Calles's administration. The Confederación Regional Obrera Mexicana (CROM), under Luis Morones, became the dominant group in the labor movement and supplied Calles with political clout and rhetorical color. In fact, many foreigners regarded CROM as the radical essence within the Calles govern-

1. Robert Hammond Murray, *Mexico before the World: Public Documents and Addresses of Plutarco Elías Calles* (New York, 1927), 6–16; Carleton Beals, *Glass Houses: Ten Years of Free-Lancing* (Philadelphia and New York, 1938), 228–30.

ment. In part this was due to its strikes against foreign enterprises and to the Marxist rhetoric of its publications. The *Catecismo de las doctrinas socialistas* proclaimed a new prayer in 1926:

Hail Socialism! Thou art full of love, fraternity is with thee, and thou art powerful among all the oppressed, and therefore great shall be the fruit of thy doctrinal womb.[2]

Foreigners reading such items could only see red, and the hand of Moscow. But diamond-bedecked Morones was not the ideological brother of Marx and Lenin. He and CROM served a useful purpose for the new revolutionary elite. For a time they co-opted enough of the laborite left to relieve radical pressure on the leaders as these officials worked for a national consensus designed to promote economic development, centralize political power, and tolerate rather lavish rewards for these efforts. Calles and his colleagues would pursue agrarian and other reforms to a limited degree; they were more concerned with building the economic infrastructure. The "revolutionary family" could be characterized as men on the make and as serious nationalists, with enough social reformism to season the mixture gently. Radicals in the economic sense they were not.

During his first three years in office Calles pushed a variety of programs to stimulate economic development and promote national unity. The national fiscal and monetary system was strengthened and consolidated. This involved the creation in 1925 of a national bank (Bank of Mexico, the only bank permitted to issue money), the reform and consolidation of the private banking system, and the reorganization of the taxation system. Road construction became a priority function and the National Road Commission was organized. Rail and telephone communications were promoted also. Land redistribution was accelerated and a National Bank of Economic Credit was formed. The government also gave active encouragement to investments in various industries. The electric power industry received some priority, and a National Electricity Code was enacted to give direction to its development.[3] In 1925 the first steps were taken to establish an assembly plant

2. Elfego Lugo, *Catecismo de las doctrinas socialistas* (México, D.F., 1926), copy in archives, SD 812.00.S.
3. For details see Pani, *Política hacendaria*, 70–83; Wionczek, *Nacionalismo mexicano*, 72–73, 67–68. During the first three years of Calles's administration 2.6 million hectares of land were distributed.

of the Ford Motor Company. The company manager and Calles negotiated an agreement which provided for concessions in matters of freight rates, customs duties, and taxes. The president also indicated that the company would have no problem with labor unions, and operations commenced in 1926. In other areas Calles promoted the development of a national school system and the reduction in size and professionalization of the army.[4]

Calles and his associates reinvigorated the campaign to assert national control over resources. In December 1925 the Mexican Congress passed legislation to implement article 27. Such acts had been considered on several occasions since 1917, but the Petroleum Law and the Alien Land Law constituted the first real enabling legislation. Both acts clearly embodied the Calvo Doctrine and articulated provisions of the constitution. The Land Law stated that foreigners could not own land within fifty kilometers of the coast or within one hundred kilometers of any border and that aliens or foreign companies could not own a majority interest in land development companies. Foreign corporations were given ten years to dispose of their lands; individual holdings had to be liquidated within five years after death. The Petroleum Law required foreign corporations to apply for "confirmatory concessions." Fifty-year concessions would be given for properties acquired prior to 1 May 1917 if positive acts had been performed. The beginning date of the concession would be the date that exploitation works had begun or from the date of the contract made with the surface owners (in the case of leases). Failure to apply for concessions within a year (until 1 January 1927), obey other provisions of the law, or perform positive acts would result in forfeiture of all rights. Claims could be filed for thirty-year "preferential concessions" on undeveloped holdings. These measures were designed to insure proper development and conservation of Mexico's natural resources. In order to promote governmental participation in developmental activities on federal lands, Calles authorized the creation of the Control de Administración del Petróleo Nacional in December 1925.[5]

4. Mira Wilkins and Frank E. Hill, *American Business Abroad: Ford on Six Continents* (Detroit, 1964), 147; Brandenburg, *Making of Modern Mexico*, 75.
5. Meyer, *México y Estados Unidos*, 151–60; Antonio J. Bermudez, *The Mexican National Petroleum Industry: A Case Study in Nationalization* (Stanford, Calif., 1963), 9.

Sheffield and the Deterioration of Relations, 1925–26

Prior to the enactment of these measures in December 1925, various U.S. officials and businessmen had decided that Calles was a radical, if not an out-and-out Bolshevik. In a speech given in October 1923 Calles had referred to foreign opposition to his candidacy and replied:

Others have said that my candidacy is not regarded favorably in the United States and in Europe. That is a matter of indifference to me. I have to render an account of my acts only to the people of Mexico.

Chargé Summerlin immediately reported that this speech "contains certain very startling anti-American and anti-European utterances." Such hypersensitive judgment helped to set the stage for the deterioration in relations which began in 1925.[6]

The new ambassador, James Rockwell Sheffield, rapidly emerged as the leading proponent of a hardline, no-compromise policy. This former corporation lawyer represented the worst aspects of the American corporate elite. After his selection as Warren's replacement, he wrote to Hughes: "I did not explain to you that I have practically no knowledge of Spanish." He hoped to learn some before his appointment became effective in October 1925, but this was the least of his defects.[7] He was a determined racist who considered the Mexicans to be "Latin-Indians who," he wrote Nicholas Murray Butler, "in the final analysis recognize no argument but force." In the same letter, he evaluated the Mexican cabinet:

There is very little white blood in the cabinet—that is it is very thin. Calles is Armenian and Indian; León almost wholly Indian and an amateur bullfighter; Saenz the Foreign Minister is Jew and Indian; Morones more white blood but not the better for it; Amaro, Secretary of War, a pure blooded Indian and very cruel.[8]

6. Murray, *Mexico before the World*, 15; Summerlin to Secretary of State, 26 October 1923, SD 812.002/170.
7. Sheffield to Hughes, 3 July 1924, Hughes MSS. Illness prevented his departure until March 1925.
8. Sheffield to Butler (president of Columbia University), 17 November 1925, James R. Sheffield Papers, Yale University Library (suggests burning this letter); Sheffield's personal memorandum on his experiences in Mexico, n.d., ibid.

Sheffield also personified the closed-minded self-righteousness of the American elite in its more virulent form. He rarely, if ever, had anything good to say about Mexicans or Mexico. Basically he regarded Mexicans as barbarians who needed to be taken over and civilized by sons of "Mother Yale." The Mexicans were tough opponents, but Sheffield wrote to Professor William Lyon Phelps of Yale:

Somewhere within us all dear Mother Yale has planted that spirit of struggle against odds shown in the last half of the Pennsylvania game and throughout the Army game . . . shown in the race at New London last June against a very fine Harvard crew one and one half length in the lead with more than a third of the course covered. I do not know just what it is but that it exists there can be no doubt and I hope that I have accumulated enough of it to carry me through down here.

The ambassador yearned for class reunions so that he might leave his Mexican purgatory and revel with the good chaps at the tomb of Skull and Bones. Indeed, the almost windowless home of this secret society was a proper symbol for the mind of the ambassador.[9]

Sheffield certainly would have had a more pleasant experience if Mexico had been controlled by Anglo-Saxon "Old Blues" from Yale, or even by men who accepted his views concerning property rights and their protection. He explained to Calvin Coolidge, through his secretary of state:

This principle is at stake not alone in Mexico but in other Latin American countries, and perhaps elsewhere, and it will become increasingly important as the surplus of capital for investment in the United States compels our citizens to seek new outlets for such investments; in short with our development as a creditor nation. Of the total of American investments abroad in 1924, 44% were made in Latin America. Any weakness in our attitude here is certain to be reflected almost immediately in other foreign countries.[10]

9. Sheffield to Phelps, 12 November 1925, Sheffield MSS. Beals records that during a Labor Day parade, when the streets were closed to traffic, Sheffield insisted on driving the embassy auto back and forth through the ranks of the marchers; *Glass Houses,* 260.
10. Sheffield to Kellogg, 5 April 1926, SD 711.12/744.

The ambassador went to his post convinced that the Mexican leaders were plotting the confiscation of foreign investments. He had read George Agnew Chamberlain's *Is Mexico Worth Saving?* and stated that he was in perfect agreement with the characterization of Mexicans and the forceful solutions set forth in the conclusion. The legislation of December 1925 added to Sheffield's fears, but as far as he was concerned the labor and tax laws enacted earlier amounted to "practical confiscation."[11]

In June 1925 the ambassador convinced Secretary Kellogg that Mexico needed a stern warning. Sheffield believed the time was ripe because Calles's political position "was becoming more precarious." A note written by the two of them, and released to the press, concluded: "The government of Mexico is now on trial before the world."[12] From this point until mid-1927 the United States and Mexico engaged in a veritable duel of diplomatic correspondence. The State Department issued a vigorous protest against the petroleum and land laws before they were enacted and proposed the negotiation of a treaty of amity and commerce. The Mexican government replied that there was absolutely no reason to perceive any cloud on the horizon of friendship between the two countries. The Mexicans further stated that they would look upon the proposed treaty negotiations with "great enthusiasm" if such a treaty protected the "legitimate interests" and respected the sovereignty of both nations.[13]

The atmosphere of crisis intensified after the enactment of the Petroleum and Alien Land Laws. In the ensuing correspondence, Minister of Foreign Relations Aarón Sáenz ripped apart the U.S. arguments and clearly exposed the double standard of internal

11. Sheffield to Anderson, 5 June 1926, Sheffield MSS.

12. Secretary of State to the Chargé in Mexico (Schoenfeld), 12 June 1925, *Foreign Relations of the United States, 1925*, 2 vols. (Washington D.C., 1940), 2:517–18. For conversations with Sheffield, and his claim of authorship for the ending, see memorandums by Ira Patchin of 11 and 13 June 1925, Lamont MSS; L. Ethan Ellis, *Frank B. Kellogg and American Foreign Relations, 1925–1929* (New Brunswick, N.J., 1961), 247 (Joseph C. Grew wrote that the statement had not been seen by "the rest of us").

13. Memorandum, Minister of Foreign Relations of Mexico to the American Ambassador, 27 November 1925, Ministerio de Relaciones Exteriores, *Correspondencia oficial cambiada entre los gobiernos de México y los Estados Unidos con motivo de las dos leyes reglamentarias de la fracción primera del Artículo 27 de la Constitución Mexicana* (México, D.F., 1926).

sovereignty advocated by the United States. He cited the various laws of states of the United States regulating the "property rights" of foreigners, the prohibition legislation of the United States which destroyed "rights legitimately acquired," and even had the audacity to quote the great Chief Justice John Marshall:

The jurisdiction of the nation within its own territory is necessarily exclusive and absolute. It is susceptible of no limitation not imposed by itself. Any restriction upon it, deriving validity from an external source, would imply a diminution of its sovereignty.[14]

According to the laws of logic the Mexican government had the most consistent argument.

During 1926 and early 1927 the hardliners, in and out of the State Department, pushed for more aggressive policies. The perennial lobbyist for investment interests, Chandler P. Anderson, proposed to his friends at the State Department an international embargo on oil shipments from Mexico. Secretary Kellogg would not consider the plan, but Sheffield, Anderson, and H. F. Arthur Schoenfeld, counselor of the embassy, continued to push for a showdown with Mexico. They insisted that Mexican officials would intuitively realize the pure determination of the United States and concede all its demands before a war actually started. Yet they admitted that in the event Mexico did not give in, war was the logical terminal point of this policy. In fact, early in 1926 Sheffield asked the department to send some revolvers and provide funds for digging a storage place in the basement of the embassy.[15]

Various State Department officials, including the secretary, were reluctant to follow a too militant policy, not only because they feared a war, but because they were afraid of repudiation by the American people. Schoenfeld argued the matter with Assistant Secretary Robert Olds in June 1926. Olds raised the question of the impact of a war on relations with the rest of Latin America. Schoenfeld replied "that Latin American opposition to alleged American imperialism was a figment of our own imagination and

14. Notes and Memorandum to the United States of 5 December 1925, 20 January, 12 February, and 27 March 1927, ibid.

15. Anderson Diary, 18 February to 14 March 1926, concerning trip to Mexico, Anderson MSS; Anderson to Kellogg ("My Dear Frank"), 21 February 1926, Frank B. Kellogg Papers, Minnesota Historical Society, St. Paul, Minn.; Harold Williamson to Arthur Bliss Lane, 9 January 1926, Lane MSS.

that if you chose to call our manifest destiny imperialism then the anti-American propagandists in Latin America who saw the trend of that destiny had a clearer vision than ours."

Schoenfeld believed that Hugh Wilson, an assistant secretary, was close to conversion. Wilson was worried about public reaction to the occupation of Mexico and commented that "the annexation of northern Mexico would become a pressing question." Schoenfeld then noted: "I asked him if he did not think, after all, that the country from the Rio Grande to Panama was lost to any but American sovereignty; he said he thought so and agreed that for geographical reasons our direct control would permanently rest at Panama."[16] In spite of the efforts of Schoenfeld, Sheffield, Anderson, and Consul General Alexander Weddell, State Department officials continued to be divided severely over tactics. But "nervous Nellie" Kellogg seemed to be unable to make up his mind which way to go.

In spite of the fact that Ambassador Sheffield believed that Secretary Kellogg had been undermining his militant position, the hardline policy seemed to be gaining strength in late 1926. Sheffield, Anderson, and Schoenfeld were diligently working to establish a link between the upheaval in Nicaragua and the ambitions of Mexico. They argued that the Mexican government was determined to undermine U.S. prestige and influence in Central America, increase its own external power, and thereby spread the doctrines of nationalization of foreign property and Bolshevism. Anderson was interested in obtaining U.S. protection for various Nicaraguan interests which he represented, but he was convinced also that military action in Nicaragua would lead to a tougher policy toward Mexico (in January 1927 several major oil companies also employed his services as a State Department contact). Because of Calles's campaign to establish national control of the Roman Catholic Church, some members of the U.S. hierarchy and the Knights of Columbus supported this hardline policy.[17]

16. Schoenfeld to Sheffield, 28 June 1926, and Sheffield to Kellogg, 1 July 1926, Sheffield MSS.

17. Sheffield to Anderson, 3 September 1926, Anderson MSS (Sheffield reported that he did not want to stay in Mexico for long unless "our policy changes very decidedly"); Chandler P. Anderson Diary, 6, 29, 30 October, 14 November 1926, 26 January 1927, ibid. (on 14 November, Sheffield and Anderson spent an hour conferring with Coolidge; the president had agreed to publish a statement about the participation of Mexico in the

The Mexican government did send arms to the Liberal forces of former Vice-President Juan Sacasa during the Nicaraguan civil war of 1926–27 and tried to build support for Mexico's internal policies throughout Central America. The nation can hardly be blamed for wanting friendly neighbors and some international support in its contact with the United States. To many U.S. officials, however, it was unthinkable that any nation except their own should have influence in Central America. Mexican influence was especially anathema because it might promote revolutionary nationalism in other underdeveloped countries. Conservative property-owning groups in Central America agreed and asked for U.S. efforts to block Mexican "radicalism."[18] In a memorandum written in late 1926, Arthur Bliss Lane discussed the activities of the Mexican government and the reports from Central America. He noted that there was little tangible evidence that Mexico was "subservient to Moscow," but he believed that the two held similar views on property and religion. And he concluded: "The evidence that Mexican territory is being used as a base for subversive propaganda and material assistance to promote revolutionary activities in Central America is conclusive." In a similar vein, Schoenfeld informed Stokeley W. Morgan, chief of the Latin American Division, "the Nicaraguan outbreak is merely the symptom of a trouble the seat of which is in Mexico, at which point it should be attacked."[19]

Crisis of 1926–27 and the Forces of Moderation

By late 1926 the United States and Mexico seemed to be on the collision course advocated by the hardliners. In mid-October the State Department learned that the Transcontinental Petroleum

Nicaraguan Revolution, and Sheffield believed that his position had been "much strengthened" by Anderson's efforts. See also Knights of Columbus, *Mexico?* (New Haven, Conn., 1926); Sister M. Elizabeth Rice, *The Diplomatic Relations between the United States and Mexico as Affected by the Struggle for Religious Liberty in Mexico, 1925–1929* (Washington, D.C., 1959).

18. Memorandum by Arthur Bliss Lane, 1926, Lane MSS; Memorandum from Legation in Guatemala to Department, 10 February 1927, SD 712.14/91; Roy Davis (legation, Costa Rica) to Secretary of State, 29 October 1926, SD 712.13/2.

19. Memorandum by Arthur Bliss Lane, 1926, Lane MSS; Schoenfeld to Sheffield, 12 February 1927, Sheffield MSS.

Company had given notice of application for confirmatory concessions on its pre-1917 holdings. The department objected and
the company agreed to postpone such action. The U.S. Marines
returned to Nicaragua in strength during late 1926. Shortly thereafter Secretary Kellogg sent to the Senate a memorandum entitled
"Bolshevik Aims and Policies in Mexico and Latin America."
The secretary appeared to be a convert to the militant "red-scare"
tactics of Sheffield, Anderson, and Schoenfeld. Possible war with
Mexico became one of the hottest issues of the day. President
Calles ordered General Obregón, in the event of a U.S. intervention, to retire to the interior to set up defenses after setting fire to
the oil fields, "making a light which they will be able to see in
New Orleans."[20]

But the Coolidge administration was not at all happy over the
possibility of war with Mexico. Stokeley Morgan told Schoenfeld
that "the Secretary is 'scared' and we had done the wrong thing
so often that the Secretary feared this course [intervention in
Mexico] might prove wrong again!"[21] The great concern over
lack of national support for a militant policy was voiced again
and again by Olds and Kellogg. Chandler Anderson offered to
conduct a private public relations campaign to build support for
State Department militancy, but Kellogg could only bemoan the
fact that he was being attacked by the *Brooklyn Eagle* and the
New York Times: "He [Kellogg] also spoke of the American
Federation of Labor and indirectly of the sympathy which the
Ku Klux Klan had shown for the Mexican attack against the
Church."[22]

Various groups across the country were attacking both the
Nicaraguan and Mexican policies of the State Department. Racist
southern congressmen supported Mexico, partly for reasons of
partisan politics—they were Democrats—and partly because of
Roman Catholic opposition to the Mexican government. These
congressmen made strange bedfellows with Senators Burton K.
Wheeler (Montana), William Borah (Idaho), George Norris
(Nebraska), Lynn J. Frazier (North Dakota), and Robert M.
La Follette (Wisconsin). Senator Norris, in a parody of a popular
poem, ridiculed Kellogg's statement about Bolshevism:

20. Sáenz, *Política internacional,* 131.
21. Schoenfeld to Sheffield, 12 February 1927, Sheffield MSS.
22. Chandler P. Anderson Diary, 29 October 1926, Anderson MSS.

Once't there was a Bolshevik who wouldn't say his prayers,
So Kellogg sent him off to bed, away upstairs;
An' Kellogg heerd him holler, and Coolidge heerd him bawl,
But when the turn't the kivers down he wasn't there at all.
They seeked him down in Mexico, they cussed him in the press,
They seeked him round the Capitol, an' ever'where I guess.
But all they ever found of him was whiskers, hair and clout;
An' the Bolsheviks 'll get you ef you don't watch out.

A number of congressional critics stressed the problem of maintaining good relations with all of Latin America and the relationship of friendship to U.S. commerce. Representatives Ralph Lozier (Missouri) and Tom Connally (Texas), and Senators Joseph T. Robinson (Arkansas) and Duncan U. Fletcher (Florida) avoided the religious issue and hammered on the theme of promoting exports through goodwill.[23]

Robinson also introduced a resolution in January 1927 calling for the arbitration of all differences with Mexico. Acting on behalf of the oil companies, Chandler Anderson tried to get the Foreign Relations Committee to postpone action on this resolution. He failed in this attempt, in part because Kellogg did not want to ask for hearings "on behalf of the oil interests." The Robinson resolution was passed rapidly and the hardliners vehemently denounced this demonstration of congressional opposition to a militant policy.[24]

At least nine resolutions calling for investigations of U.S. relations with Nicaragua and Mexico were introduced in the House of Representatives. Hearings held by Senate and House committees provided further documentation of the opposition to intervention.[25]

For the most part the news media were hostile to militant poli-

23. *Congressional Record,* 69th Cong., 2d sess., 1927, 68, pt. 2: 1291–1330, 1445, 1691 (poem), 1706–7, 1844–45, 2144, 2202–3; pt. 3: 2823; pt. 5: 5580, 5796, 5528; letter from the Lansing, Mich., Chamber of Commerce, enclosed in Representative Grant M. Hudson (Michigan) to Kellogg, 2 December 1926, SD 711.12/795 (protests policy which may hurt market for automobiles).

24. Chandler P. Anderson Diary, 20, 21 January 1927, Anderson MSS.

25. U.S. Senate, Foreign Relations Committee, *Relations with Mexico: Hearing before a Sub-Committee of the Committee on Foreign Relations,* 69th Cong., 2d sess., February 1927; U.S. House of Representatives, Committee on Foreign Affairs, *Conditions in Nicargua and Mexico,* 69th Cong., 2d sess., January–February 1927.

cies. Kellogg's declaration about bolshevism, for example, produced a loud chorus of denunciations. *Commerce and Finance*
said that he was seeing "Bolshevist spooks." And the *Commercial
and Financial Chronicle* urged the administration to avoid intervention "scrupulously" and to maintain a conciliatory attitude
toward Mexico. The *New York Times,* the *Baltimore Sun,* the
Boston Daily Globe, and other prominent papers issued similar
warnings. In fact, Chandler Anderson complained that the only
two major newspapers which consistently supported the administration's policy in Nicaragua and Mexico were the *Washington
Post* and the *Chicago Tribune.*[26]

Attacks on intervention, present and future, came from church
groups, labor unions, and the academic world. Frank Tannenbaum, Ernest Gruening, Samuel Guy Inman, and Robert H.
Murray had been persistent defenders of Mexico and critics of
Sheffield. The ambassador believed that these men had played a
"sinister part" in spreading anti-American propaganda in Mexico
and the United States. Concerning Tannenbaum, Sheffield wrote:
"He is far more Mexican in sympathy than he is American, a
dangerous man for American interests. . . . He is a graduate of
Columbia, a Phi Beta Kappa man, with a distorted view of society
and government." A State Department official called Inman "an
uplifter of note of the parlor bolshevist type, a leader of 'teachers
and preachers.' " The articulate criticism of men such as Tannenbaum and Inman struck a very sensitive nerve in U.S. official-
dom.[27]

26. *Commerce and Finance,* 19 January 1927, 176; 1 December 1926,
2435; 2 March 1927, 461; *Commercial and Financial Chronicle,* 15 January 1927, 276–77; 30 April 1927, 2504; *New York Times,* 5 January
1927, 1, and 13 January 1927, 24; excerpts from various editorials, *Congressional Record,* 69th Cong., 2d sess., 1927, 68, pt. 2:1649–53; Chandler
P. Anderson Diary, 1 January 1927, Anderson MSS.
27. Sheffield to Morrow, 1 August 1929, Morrow MSS; Sheffield to
Kellogg, 16 February 1926, SD 711.12/685 (on Tannenbaum); F. M.
Gunther to Mr. Beck, 28 April 1927, SD 711.12/1070 (on Inman); Sheffield to Kellogg, 31 January 1927, SD 711.12/951 (denounces labor and
the Methodist clergy). Tannenbaum was a scholar who worked in the
areas of labor problems and the Mexican agrarian situation and later
joined the history faculty at Columbia University. Gruening was a writer
and former managing editor of *The Nation,* who became one of the first
U.S. senators from Alaska. Inman was head of the Protestant missionary
Committee on Conciliation with Latin America, professor at Columbia,
and editor of *Nueva Democracia.* Murray was a newspaperman who wrote
the critical reports on Ambassador Henry Lane Wilson (1912–13) and
worked for the Creel committee during the war. Carleton Beals was often
included in this group; see his *Glass Houses,* 362–65.

The apparently interventionist trend of early 1927 provided some encouragement to the advocates of a militant policy. Sheffield informed William Howard Taft that the marines in Nicaragua "are better than all the diplomatic notes that could be written to the Mexican Government." He and Taft were pleased with the growing firmness of U.S. policy. The oil companies also were encouraged by these developments. An official of J. P. Morgan and Company noted: "The oil taxes are getting smaller very rapidly and each month Harold Walker calls me up and congratulates me on the fact that they are going to disappear in the next month. He is getting a great deal of pleasure out of these dark days."[28] Coolidge and Kellogg did not want armed intervention in Mexico. Both realized that such a move would have little national support. But neither seemed to know how to overcome the impasse which had developed. An important element in the resolution of the difficulty was provided by the New York bankers.

Negotiations over the Foreign Debt, 1925

In spite of the deterioration in official relations, Thomas Lamont and his colleagues had been able to reach an agreement with the Mexican government and to preserve relatively open communications. The bankers desperately wanted to preserve the debt agreement and avoid repudiation. Members of the International Committee of Bankers on Mexico repeatedly communicated with the new minister of finance, Alberto J. Pani, during 1925. But Mexican officials believed that de la Huerta had accepted excessively stiff terms in 1922 and they were in no hurry to rush into a new agreement or resume payments under the old agreement. The bankers even offered to try to raise a $20 million loan in return for resumption of the debt service and return of the railroads to private ownership.[29]

28. Taft to Sheffield, 19 February 1927, and Sheffield to Taft, 5 March 1927, Sheffield MSS. (Taft was on the U.S. Supreme Court); Vernon Munroe to Graham Ashmead, 6 May 1927, Lamont MSS.
29. "Memorandum of informal and unofficial conversation between his Excellency, Alberto J. Pani, Mexican Minister of Finance, and the members of the Sub-committee of the American Section of the International Committee of Bankers, on Mexico . . . January 29, 1925," Lamont MSS; F. M. Gunther (Division of Mexican Affairs) to Secretary of State, 24 January 1925, SD 812.51/1158, /1159, /1161.

The Mexican government did not intend to repudiate the foreign debt, and communications with the bankers were generally cordial. After the State Department's "on trial" note of June 1925, committee representative E. R. Jones (also of Wells Fargo) expressed some concern as to whether Pani would receive him on his arrival in Mexico. According to Jones: "He smilingly assured me that the Secretary's note would not be sufficient cause to refuse to discuss their debts which they intended to meet."[30]

In June 1925 the International Committee prepared a memorandum outlining a modified agreement. Some bankers considered proposing to the Mexican government a plan for a kind of customs receivership which would be sweetened with a $25 million loan for railway rehabilitation. But even Sheffield doubted that this would be accepted.[31] The memorandum noted that the bankers would "conditionally" accept the separation of the railways debt from the national debt and would agree to some modification of payments, including the postponement of the payment of the 1924 notes until 1928. Minister Pani waited until late August to answer the proposal. In large part the delay was due to the Mexican government's organization of the new bank of issue. The bankers expressed severe opposition to the new bank and the Mexican officials wanted to postpone any negotiations until funds had been accumulated and the bank was in operation.[32]

On 20 August, Pani sent to the International Committee a proposal for a new agreement. This included the separation of the railways debt from the national debt, the incorporation of the obligations of the agricultural loan bank Caja de Préstamos into the national debt through the exchange of the mortgage bonds on the properties of the Caja for new bonds, and the postponement of payment of the maturities for 1924 and 1925. In return the Mexican government would agree to return the railroads to private management, to appoint a board of directors composed of persons acceptable to the committee, to entrust the appraisal of reparations for railroad damages to a three-man technical

30. Memorandum by E. R. Jones, 30 June 1925, Lamont MSS.

31. Memorandum on Mexico, 10 June 1925, Lamont MSS (attached to this was a memorandum on the Platt Amendment and other forms of U.S. fiscal supervision in Central American and the Caribbean); Memorandum by Ira Patchin, 11 June 1925, ibid.

32. Memorandum by E. R. Jones, 30 June 1925, and Lamont to Jones, to be presented to Pani, 26 August 1925; both in Lamont MSS.

commission, to maintain existing taxes on the railroads for debt service, and to allocate oil production taxes for payment on the foreign debt.[33] The committee was not entirely happy with the Mexican proposal, but E. R. Jones informed Lamont that Pani would not come to New York unless he was "practically assured" that his plan would be accepted. Jones urged acceptance and noted that Pani sincerely desired to renew payments. Pani had warned him that the government would use all of the oil taxes for irrigation purposes unless a new arrangement was formulated.[34]

The bankers realized that the confident determination of the Mexican government placed them in a weak bargaining position. Lamont did not want to lose the opportunity to settle the bond and railroad issues. He informed Jones that the committee could not guarantee advance acceptance of all Pani's proposals. "Nevertheless we believe that most of the points contained in them can, if satisfactorily clarified, be worked through."[35]

Negotiations began in September 1925 and the next month the Pani-Lamont agreement was completed. With some modifications concerning payments, it incorporated the Pani plan of 18 August. Pani also agreed that the National Railways would be returned "in such condition and under such terms as will yield net earnings sufficient to meet all the fixed charges," and that until 31 December 1929 the government would not permit any changes in rates or wages which would affect earnings adversely. The debt included in the new agreement was as follows:

Principal	$302,500,000
Interest	$132,500,000
Total	$435,000,000

Formal payments to the committee would begin in 1926.[36]

During his stay in New York, Pani's extramarital sex life added spice to the negotiations and became a political issue in Mexico

33. Pani to Elias, for Lamont, 20 August 1925, Lamont MSS. The issuance of new bonds for the Caja would free the properties from the old mortgage and allow the Mexican government to utilize them freely, since bondholders would no longer have a priority claim.
34. Jones to Lamont, 28 August 1925; Lamont to Jones, 31 August 1925; Jones to Patchin, 1 September 1925; all in Lamont MSS.
35. Lamont to Jones, 9 September 1925, Lamont MSS.
36. Memorandum of 7 October 1925, and Memorandum to Mr. Morrow by Vernon Munroe, 26 September 1927, Lamont MSS; Alberto Pani, *Tres monografías* (México, D.F., 1941), 114.

which the agrarian party used to attack the Calles administration. In New York, the ultrahardliners hired a private detective to shadow the finance minister. The reports of his comings and goings with Gloria Faure—the daughter of the sixth president of the third French republic, Félix Faure—were sent to Lamont by the group. The bankers did not believe in letting sex interfere with financial negotiations, and the reports were ignored. But they were leaked to the newspapers and the front page of the 14 October edition of the *New York Daily Mirror* was filled with a photograph of a raven-haired beauty posed with dress hiked above the knee under a banner headline, "Señor Pani is a Wonderful Lover."[37]

The young lady was rushed out of the country, and there were rumblings about prosecution under the Mann Act. Nothing developed in the United States, but Pani was bitterly attacked in the Mexican Chamber of Deputies. In a stormy session the agrarians linked the minister's love life to the question of land reform and charged that Pani was selling out to Wall Street. A special committee went to see President Calles, who defended his minister and asked if it would please them to have "a cabinet of eunuchs." The committee reported back and the session ended amid catcalls and general uproar. The turmoil did not last long, and the Pani-Lamont agreement was approved in December 1925.[38] The new agreement removed one basic issue complicating U.S.-Mexican relations and helped to maintain a bridge of relatively harmonious communication during a period of deteriorating official relations. It also preserved the "united front" of international bankers under the leadership of the U.S. investment bankers.

The Ideas of Lamont and Morrow

When Dwight Morrow's appointment as ambassador to Mexico was announced in September 1927, a Mexican newspaper commented: "After Morrow come the marines."[39] To some contemporary observers this may have seemed to present a logical

---

37. Reports sent by Wilbur Bates (former associate of Felix Díaz), in the Lamont MSS. President Faure had died while making love to his mistress in his study.
38. Dulles, *Yesterday in Mexico,* 286.
39. Ibid. 324–25.

progression of events, but in reality the Morrow appointment was a distinct move in the opposite direction. Top-level Mexican officials knew this, since they had been involved for several years in negotiations with Lamont and the International Committee. Lamont and Morrow were colleagues in J. P. Morgan and Company and close friends. Lamont regularly supplied Morrow with information about the activities of the International Committee, and during 1926 Morrow began to work closely with Lamont on the Mexican question.

Prior to 1927 the attitudes and actions of Lamont, Morrow, and some of their colleagues had made a positive impression on several key Mexican officials. Feelings of trust, respect, and even friendship developed on both sides. Lamont and the Morgan Company established a working relationship with Alberto Pani, Alvaro Obregón, Agustín Legorreta, and Manuel Téllez.

Most of these officials were identified with the national development wing of the "revolutionary family." This group generally stressed economic development based upon some degree of national control over the economy, especially natural resources. They were willing to listen to, and even solicit, advice from the outside, provided it came from persons who treated them with respect and displayed some understanding of their national aspirations. Such was the basis of the rapport which developed between these officials and the representatives of the Morgan bank. Disagreements and arguments did take place. At times the relationship was strained because of actions of other groups. In Mexico the national development faction had to compete with other elements for influence in the inner circle of the "revolutionary family." In spite of some complications, the working relationship between the bankers and the development-oriented Mexican officials was cultivated even during periods of deteriorating relations between the two governments. The Morrow appointment and the diplomatic fruits of his ambassadorship were directly connected to this relationship.

The attitudes and actions of Lamont and his colleagues provided an important basis for this working relationship. During the 1920s, Mexican officials had ample opportunity to compare these attitudes and actions with those of other foreign interests. The hard line put forward by the leading U.S. oil companies, combined with the numerous reports that these interests were involved in counterrevolutionary activities, made the investment bankers appear rather mild.

Lamont and Morrow were opposed to armed intervention and to policy tactics which relied on the threat of ultimate force. In January 1925 Pani informed Lamont that Mexico could not resume service on its exterior debt. When Lamont replied that the International Committee might have to declare the 1922 debt agreement (the Lamont–de la Huerta agreement) in "final default," Pani asked if this meant intervention by the governments involved. Lamont emphatically stated "that in his view it meant nothing of the kind and that he felt the time when a debt could be collected by force of arms was past."[40] On another occasion, when asked about government protection of foreign investments, Lamont referred to Dwight Morrow's article in the January 1927 issue of *Foreign Affairs* as the "latest and best answer." He concluded:

I hold with him [Morrow] that good faith on the part of a borrower is far sounder security for a lender than armed forces however great or powerful. The theory of collecting debts by gunboat is unrighteous, unworkable and obsolete. While I have, of course, no mandate to speak for my colleagues of the investment banking community, I think I may safely say that they share this view with Mr. Morrow and myself.[41]

In 1925 Morrow stated that businessmen who had differences with the Cuban government should seek remedies through the ordinary channels in Cuba: "They should not look to Washington."[42]

In his negotiations with the Mexican government, Lamont did not employ threats of retaliation by either the U.S. government or the bankers. Some of his associates on the International Committee considered him to be "soft on Mexico," but as Lamont noted in regard to one committee debate: "Millhauser [Speyer and

40. Memorandum of a Conversation between Finance Minister Pani and Lamont, 21 January 1925, Lamont MSS.

41. Lamont to James E. Sabine, 9 January 1928, Lamont MSS. The article was "Who Buys Foreign Bonds?" *Foreign Affairs* 5 (January 1927): 217–32. For remarks about the Mexican situation see Thomas W. Lamont, "Three Examples of International Cooperation," *Atlantic Monthly,* October 1923.

42. *New York Times,* 23 April 1925; see also Morrow to Mr. Olds, 8 May 1928, SD 812.6363/2563½.

Company] talks glibly about wielding the big stick or kicking them in the stomach. There is no big stick to wield and we have no boot that could possibly reach their remote and very tough stomach."[43]

Lamont and the Morgan bank stressed this type of low-pressure, quiet diplomacy in their dealings with the Mexican government. They were willing to negotiate on a give-and-take basis and emphasized specific issues rather than broad principles or legal technicalities. As Morrow wrote to Lamont in April 1927: "I hope you can see Teagle and Swain [Standard Oil of New Jersey] and get them to see that they can be helpful to themselves by thundering more about *oil* and less about *rights* to oil."[44]

Lamont and the bankers did not insist on winning every point and were even willing to accept defeat on some issues. An excellent example of this took place in 1925 when the Calles administration announced its plans for a central bank of issue and began to accumulate funds for a reserve. At first the International Committee, through Lamont, privately stated its opposition to various Mexican officials and then, on 26 August, sent a formal protest through the U.S. State Department. The bankers listed three major complaints: (1) funds intended for the bondholders under the Lamont–de la Huerta agreement were being used for the new bank; (2) the bank would be a "government controlled institution" which could not "command confidence in international banking centers"; and (3) the head of the bank, Alberto Mascarenas, had made the "grave mistake" of appointing as American agent of the bank the New York labor bank (the Federation Bank) instead of the Federal Reserve Bank of either New York or Dallas. After delivering the protest, H. F. Arthur Schoenfeld, chargé d'affaires ad interim, reported that the New York bankers could wreck the new bank if they so desired.[45]

When the Mexican government proceeded to implement its plans Lamont prepared an advisory memorandum for the International Committee. He stated frankly:

43. Lamont to Vivian Smith and J. R. Carter (Paris office of J. P. Morgan & Co.), n.d. (internal evidence indicates November 1928), Lamont MSS.
44. Morrow to Lamont, 12 April 1927, Lamont MSS.
45. Memorandum by Lamont of a Conversation with Secretary Kellogg, 16 September 1925, SD 812.51/1201; Schoenfeld to Secretary of State, 28 August 1925, SD 812.51/1201.

We have to face the facts: (I) Capital has been accumulated for
Bank of Issue (legally or otherwise) which will open September
1st. To 49 percent of the capital local banks have subscribed.
This shows their confidence. No use in effect bucking them.[46]

Lamont noted Pani's promise to renew full payments to the
International Committee on 1 January 1926 and praised the
"thoroughgoing financial reorganization" of the Mexican government. He advised:

I think they are getting out of the woods and we shall show ourselves unwise if we don't walk out with them.

Now our gesture to prevent their opening the Bank of Issue has
failed. This is a great disappointment and I don't quite see how
we are going to save our face. Yet it is more important to save
our bondholders than to save our face.[47]

The International Committee accepted these ideas, and Lamont
informed the State Department that they did not desire any
further action.[48]

When the Mexican finance minister came to New York to discuss a new agreement, Lamont took him to see Benjamin Strong
of the Federal Reserve Bank of New York. Lamont hoped that in
the future "some sort of relationship could be established between
the Federal Reserve Bank of New York and the Bank of Mexico,"
and he told Strong that "friendliness counts with these people
more than I can say."[49]

Lamont firmly believed that issues between nations should be
kept out of the arena of internal politics. To further this he constantly advocated the use of the "discreet person" who could
privately and quietly negotiate disputes. As he advised Sir William
Tyrrell, the British foreign secretary, in 1925, "send down to
Mexico some discreet, tactful person who will form friendly contacts with the Mexican Government and trade out your situation
with the Government prior to your recognition."[50]

46. Memorandum for Sub-Committee from Thomas Lamont, 31 August 1925, Lamont MSS.
47. Ibid.
48. Memorandum by Lamont of a Conversation with Secretary Kellogg, 16 September 1925, SD 812.51/1201.
49. Lamont to Strong, 23 October 1925, Lamont MSS.
50. Memorandum of a Conversation with Sir William Tyrrell, Permanent Undersecretary of Foreign Affairs, at the British Foreign Office, 7
May 1925, Lamont MSS. The British wanted to recognize the Mexican

In all their contacts with Mexican officials Lamont and his colleagues tried to "educate" (as they called it) them in the ways of
orthodox economics and proper capitalistic behavior. U.S. officials and other interest groups tried the same thing with less
success owing to their more didactic or even strident arguments.
Yet there was a note of paternalism in the attitude of the bankers,
though Lamont and Morrow were eminently successful in adopt-
ing a nonpaternalistic approach in their negotiations. Concerning
the Mexicans, Lamont told Secretary Hughes:

. . . ignorant as they are, unwise as they are, untrusty [*sic*] as they
are, nevertheless, if you once take time and patience, one can
handle them. They need financial advisers very solely [sorely?]
and they need an ambassador whom at the same time they can
respect.[51]

Not all the bankers could handle their paternalism with the diplomatic aplomb and friendliness of Morrow and Lamont. Thomas
Cochran and J. P. Morgan, Jr., were quite virulent in their private
denunciations of Mexicans. Perhaps, the difference between these
bankers was that Lamont and Morrow did not evidence, either in
public or private, racial prejudice or any tendency to condemn
entire groups. They might voice criticism of individuals or groups,
but both generally avoided terminology which stressed inferiority
or absolute venality.[52]

Attempts to "educate" officials were also attempts to exert
influence over the policies of the Mexican government and shape
the direction of the revolution. This kind of tutorial service was
difficult in a country where revolutionary nationalism was still a
strong force. Many Mexicans considered admonitions about orthodox economics to be attempts to halt or limit socioeconomic reforms, especially those that affected foreign investments. And
even those officials who tended to be more economically conserva-

government but wanted some acknowledgment of claims in advance. The
British did follow Lamont's advice; see Sir David Kelly, *The Ruling Few;
or, the Human Background to Diplomacy* (London, 1952), 170.
    51. Lamont to Hughes, 31 December 1925, Lamont MSS.
    52. George Rublee to Morrow, 31 December 1927, Morrow MSS. Ex-
tensive research in the Lamont and Morrow collections has not produced
a single case where either man used terms such as "ignorant Indians" to
describe Mexican officials. On the other hand, Ambassador James R.
Sheffield frequently used these terms.

tive often were men who also insisted that their nation be treated with respect as a fully sovereign, independent entity. Under these conditions, representatives from industrial-creditor nations had to handle negotiations and advice with the utmost skill and tact. Too many representatives did not realize that the old tactics for exerting influence no longer applied. Lamont and his colleagues learned this fact rather early in the game.

Banker Diplomacy and Morrow's Negotiations, 1927–29

During the first half of 1927 Thomas Lamont, Dwight Morrow, and other officials of J. P. Morgan and Company met regularly with several influential Mexicans. Alberto Pani, Manuel C. Téllez, A. L. Negrete, David Montes de Oca, finance minister after February 1927, and Agustín Legorreta, all took an active part in these informal meetings and dinners. In turn, they met with President Calles and presented the views of the bankers. Morrow played a leading role in many of these discussions. In January 1928, Ambassador Morrow wrote to Lamont about the November 1927 oil decision of the Mexican Supreme Court (concerning the retroactive nature of article 27): "It went fully as far as we contemplated last January [1927] in the talks that we had with Pani."[53]

Morrow and Lamont also helped to establish informal contacts between the Mexicans, the oilmen, and the State Department. The emphasis of their approach was one of discussing issues, not theories. Early in April 1927, Morrow reported that Negrete had informed him that the Mexican government would impose no "physical interference" with drilling new wells on lands held prior to 1917, and Harold Walker of the Pan American Petroleum and Transport Company also told him that the companies were "not

53. Morrow to Lamont, 3 January 1928, Morrow MSS. For documents giving the details of these meetings and their effect on the Mexican government, see "Memorandum of the Conversation held when Pani and Negrete dined with Morrow on Tuesday evening, February 23, 1927"; Memorandums by Dwight Morrow, 21 February and 18 March 1927; Memorandum for Mr. Negrete by Thomas Lamont, 25 May 1927; Memorandum, Conversation between Pani, Negrete, Morrow, Cochran, Anderson, and Munroe, 25 February 1927; all in Morrow MSS; Lamont to Agustín Legorreta, 14 January 1927; Lamont to Robert Olds, 16 May 1927; Lamont to Manuel C. Téllez, 16 May 1927; Lamont to Legorreta, 15 July 1927; all in Lamont MSS.

now being interfered with *even in drilling new wells*." Morrow then voiced his belief that "the real crisis is over so far as confiscation of oil rights is concerned." He then suggested that Téllez explain this situation to Assistant Secretary of State Robert Olds.[54]

It should be noted that other interests were also working behind the scenes for a settlement of the oil issue. Paul Shoup, executive vice-president of the Southern Pacific Railroad, held several secret meetings with General Obregón in late 1926 and early 1927. The general proposed a *modus vivendi* with the oil companies, and Shoup passed the word on to the Petroleum Producers Association and the White House.[55] Subsequently Obregón informed Shoup that President Calles would be glad to receive the committee from the Producers Association "as soon as possible for the purpose of reaching an equitable understanding and friendly disposition of the whole controversy." The oilmen, however, were not willing to accept the invitation, and this attempt at private negotiation was frustrated.[56]

In late March 1927, President Calles instructed Ambassador Téllez to deliver a personal message to Coolidge, assuring him of a desire to adjust all differences and telling him that Calles would be pleased if Coolidge would send a personal representative to Mexico to discuss the situation privately, perhaps on his ranch. Secretary Kellogg was present during the Téllez-Coolidge meeting and as a result the Mexican ambassador did not deliver the critical part of the message. Téllez then went to New York to see Lamont, and at a meeting at Lamont's house the details were

54. Morrow to Lamont, 12 April 1927, Lamont MSS. Harold Walker informed Chandler Anderson that the Huasteca Company had obtained a large number of drilling permits for their undeveloped properties prior to January first, and as a result they were "obtaining an enormous amount of new production"; Chandler P. Anderson Diary, 15 April 1927, Anderson MSS.

55. Paul Shoup to Edward T. Clark, 27 December 1926, Edward T. Clark Papers, Library of Congress (Clark was private secretary to President Coolidge); Memorandum by Dwight Morrow, 21 February 1927, Morrow MSS.

56. Shoup to Clark, 2 March 1927, Clark MSS. Shoup also reported that he had had conversations with some of the most important mining interests and two of the largest American landowners in Mexico, and all wanted an amicable settlement of the oil controversy; Harold Walker to Clark, 10 March 1927, ibid. (enclosed the message which he had sent to Shoup). For other details see Meyer, *México y Estados Unidos*, 172, 175–76.

fully presented. Lamont advised the ambassador to explain in detail to Robert Olds the reasons for Sheffield's unpopularity and tell him of Calles's desire to get as far away as possible from the method of negotiating by notes. Téllez took this advice and in all probability Coolidge received the information from either Olds or Morrow.[57]

Lamont himself also established contact with Calles through mutual friends, and the Mexican president informed one American visitor that he wished the U.S. government would let Lamont handle the situation in place of Sheffield and Kellogg, for he had complete confidence in the New York banker.[58] As Lamont told Robert Olds concerning a letter which the former was sending to Ambassador Téllez: "You may think that I lay it on a bit thick about my friendship for Mexico, but that is in line with the repeated messages which I have received from President Calles."[59]

Signs of a possible relaxation of tensions were slightly evident by late April 1927. On 25 April, Coolidge delivered a speech emphasizing the protection of investments and of foreigners engaged in "opening up undeveloped countries." Mexico received considerable attention but the president ended on a friendly note by stating that the issues could be settled by negotiation.[60]

Dwight Morrow was directly involved in this move toward conciliation. In February 1927, he sent to Coolidge a lengthy letter from the international lawyer and former department official J. Reuben Clark, Jr., concerning a proposed arbitration agreement with Mexico over petroleum and land questions. Clark endorsed such an agreement, and raised several questions concerning the legal bases of the State Department's arguments.[61] The

57. "Memorandum of a meeting at Mr. Lamont's house, at 9:30 A.M., March 31, 1927, at which the Mexican ambassador Mr. Téllez, Mr. Lamont, Mr. Negrete, Mr. Prieto, and V. M. [Vernon Munroe] were present," Morrow MSS; Memorandum of a Conversation between Asst. Sec. Olds and the Mexican Ambassador (Téllez), 1 April 1927, SD 711.12/1084.
58. Memorandum from Martin Egan to Lamont, 9 May 1927, Lamont MSS.
59. Lamont to Olds, 16 May 1927, Lamont MSS.
60. "Address Delivered by President Coolidge at the Dinner of the United Press Association at New York, April 25, 1927," *Papers Relating to the Foreign Relations of the United States, 1927*, 3 vols. (Washington, D.C., 1942), 3: 209–21; for Calles's reply see ibid., 221–25.
61. Morrow to Coolidge, 4 February 1927, Morrow MSS. Calles had suggested arbitration in January; Meyer, *México y Estados Unidos*, 172.

editor of the *Christian Science Monitor* wrote in 1928 that Morrow visited Coolidge several times in late 1926 and early 1927 and convinced the president that a break in relations with Mexico would mean revolution and consequently losses to American investors. The editor also stated that Morrow arranged a meeting between Ambassador Téllez, Secretary Kellogg, and President Coolidge in April and that this meeting provided the background for the president's conciliatory statements on 25 April. Walter Lippmann, a close friend of Morrow, has written that Morrow persuaded Coolidge to negotiate a settlement and avoid intervention.[62] Another indication of Morrow's influence comes from the diary of Chandler P. Anderson. At a February 1927 luncheon meeting with oil company attorneys Harold Walker and Chester O. Swain and embassy counselor Arthur Schoenfeld, Anderson suggested that the oil interests should try to get the president to bring Sheffield to Washington in order to prepare for a confrontation with Mexico. Walker then asked Morrow to make this proposal to Coolidge. Walker reported "that Morrow had not been very keen about having Jim Sheffield sent for, perhaps not appreciating its full significance, or perhaps appreciating it too well." Morrow did suggest that the oil association hire J. Reuben Clark, a suggestion which was not received with any enthusiasm.[63]

Although representatives of the oil companies objected to the conciliatory statements and tried to block the various proposals for arbitration, indications of a new flexibility were evident in the State Department. Robert Olds wrote an extensive analysis of U.S.-Mexican relations in which he stated pointedly that the oil companies had suffered very little actual damage. He noted: "They have been coming to us with the same story for decades, and during all of that time they have gone right on operating and taking out oil." Olds also stated that the parties who would like for "us to use the club on Mexico" did not realize that such tactics invariably "made the whole situation worse." His conclusions reveal a new emphasis on practical, nondogmatic tactics.

62. *Christian Science Monitor*, 31 March 1928; Walter Lippmann, "Mexico Keeps a Bridge Open to the Cubans"; *Evening Bulletin* (Providence, R. I.), 22 March 1966; Letter, Walter Lippmann to author, 28 March 1966; Lippmann noted that Morrow did not make written records of his talks with the president.
63. Chandler P. Anderson Diary, 3, 15 February 1927, Anderson MSS.

It is doubtful whether the difficulties are any greater or the conditions, broadly speaking, more acute than they have been at almost any time since 1910. . . . Unquestionably we have a clear duty to protect so far as we can the personal and property rights of our citizens in foreign countries, but the methods we employ, and the extent to which we can go, are dictated by considerations of national policy looking far beyond the private interest of individuals. If anything is plain from our experience with Mexico it is the fact that an ideal solution for all concerned is not to be expected. . . . No such thing as a guarantee of full protection by this Government seems possible.[64]

Olds's evaluation followed the decision of the Mexican government in June 1927 to use the army to prevent the drilling of new wells by companies which had refused to apply, or had withdrawn their application, for "confirmatory concessions" and consequently had been denied drilling permits. Prior to this the Petroleum Producers Association had decided to defy the government and drill without permits. Faced with the decision to use the army to enforce the law, the executives of the major U.S. companies instructed their officials in Mexico to refrain from any drilling attempts. The executives then tried to obtain State Department support for their position. But they ran into the new moderation policy. At a meeting in Washington on 9 August 1927 the secretary informed the oil companies that the United States would not break relations with Mexico or consider armed intervention because of the oil question.[65]

These developments provided the background for Dwight Morrow's appointment as ambassador to Mexico and for the tactics

64. Memorandum on Mexico, 22 July 1927, Lane MSS. After Kellogg's enforced vacation in February-March 1927 Mexican affairs were generally handled by Olds, who became undersecretary in July; Ellis, *Frank B. Kellogg*, 37.

65. Memorandum by J. Reuben Clark, Jr., 9 August 1927, SD 812.6363/2384. Starting in July the Justice Department began sending reports about conspiratorial activities to the Mexican government; SREM, 852, Leg. 6. By February 1927 confirmatory or preferential concessions had been applied for by companies which had supplied 58.4 percent of the 1926 oil production; the nonconforming companies had produced 41.6 percent (most of these companies were controlled by Doheny, Sinclair, and Andrew Mellon). Subsequently, the Petroleum Producers Association tried to enforce an earlier decision for defiance of the law and several major producers (including El Aguila) withdrew their applications for confirmatory or preferential concessions; U.S. Senate, *Relations with Mexico*, 24–31; Ellis, *Frank B. Kellogg*, 46–47.

he used in his dealings with the government. Morrow had urged Coolidge to adopt a conciliatory policy based upon negotiation, and in August 1927 Morrow agreed to accept the task of finding "some *modus vivendi* for getting along with them [Mexicans]." This did not mean a change of policy, and the new ambassador stressed the fact that the primary concern was still the safeguarding of American rights.[66]

Morrow's diplomatic accomplishments in Mexico cannot be separated from the shift in emphasis within the Mexican "revolutionary family" and the decision of the Calles administration to accept the advice of the bankers concerning basic economic strategy. Domestic political conflicts, the struggle with the church (and the related Cristero rebellion), and the deteriorating condition of the Mexican economy, due largely to decreased oil revenues, were directly related to these developments. By late 1926 Calles had probably pushed most programs about as far as the development-oriented faction was prepared to go.[67]

Prior to Morrow's appointment, Calles had accepted the idea of a *modus vivendi* concerning the oil controversy which would maintain some aspects of the principle of national control of resources. Morrow, in fact, had little difficulty in negotiating a compromise with the Mexican president. His major problem was to convince the oil companies to accept what he regarded as a reasonable solution. Earlier, Morrow had told Chester Swain, of Standard, that the Mexican government had a "naturally strong" desire to save its face. Morrow told Lamont that his conversation with Swain had been rather discouraging because of the attitude that the oil companies "must win a victory over the Mexicans."[68] This dogmatic approach complicated Morrow's work and even threatened the rejection of any compromise.

During these negotiations Morrow's relationship with the Morgan bank aided him in his dealings with the oilmen. Lamont, and

66. Morrow to J. P. Morgan, 31 August 1927; Morrow to Lamont, 3 January 1928; both in Morrow MSS.

67. Morrow believed that Calles's increased political strength during the last half of 1927 was of particular importance; Morrow to George Rublee, 2 February 1928, Morrow MSS. For background and interpretations of Calles's policy see Meyer, *México y Estados Unidos*, 178, 186; Stanley Robert Ross, "Dwight Morrow and the Mexican Revolution," *HAHR* 38 (November 1958); 524, 526; Dulles, *Yesterday in Mexico*, 294.

68. Morrow to Lamont, 7 November 1927, Morrow MSS.

other former colleagues of Morrow, worked to convince the oil executives not to "rock the boat," either by harsh public statements or by an uncompromising stand on the legal issues. Morrow did not directly solicit this kind of behind-the-scenes assistance. But, as he wrote to Secretary Olds explaining why he had sent Lamont information on the oil issue, "Lamont's influence on the oil men in New York can be considerable if he desires to exert it."[69] The bankers' efforts did not have to be solicited. They were interested not only in the success of a friend and former colleague but also in the practical settlement of the various issues complicating U.S.-Mexican relations. Vernon Munroe, a Morgan executive, wrote to Morrow explaining why the bankers had arranged a conference between Agustín Legorreta and General Palmer Pierce of Standard: "There was perhaps the feeling that you would be very glad if the oil companies would approach the oil problem from the point of view of a practical settlement rather than of a purely legalistic settlement and undoubtedly Mr. Legorreta called on General Pierce because he and we felt that you would be glad to have him do so."[70]

The new petroleum legislation, which became effective in January 1928, provided that confirmatory concessions, unlimited in time, would be given for all holdings on which positive acts had been performed prior to 1 May 1917. Properties which had not received positive acts ("untagged lands") were still subject to national control, but the owners or lessors would receive "preferential" consideration for thirty-year concessions.

Some of the oil company executives were not pleased with either the November Supreme Court decision or the revisions of the 1925 Petroleum Law passed by the Mexican Senate in December 1927. Early in January 1928, General Pierce told Lamont that the oil executives might file suit for an injunction to block the new compromise measures. Lamont informed the State Department, and meetings were subsequently held between Lamont and Pierce, and Pierce and Secretary Olds. The oil executives finally decided

69. Lamont to Morrow, 22 November 1927; Vernon Munroe to Morrow, 6 January 1928; Morrow to Olds, 3 January 1928; all in Lamont MSS.
70. Munroe to Morrow, 6 January 1928, Morrow MSS; see also Memorandum for Mr. T. W. Lamont (by Vernon Munroe), 13 December 1927, Lamont MSS.

not to complicate the situation through legal action, in part because the oil companies' representatives were sharply divided over the new legislation.[71] Some of the attorneys in Mexico had been converted to Morrow's views and recommended support for his efforts. But Morrow observed that the New York attorneys "show such a complete misunderstanding of even their own cases that I do not expect anything to satisfy them."[72] This was an accurate statement, since some of the companies protested against the new regulations after the State Department announced on 27 March that these appeared to have brought "to a practical conclusion the discussions which began ten years ago."[73] Yet the oil companies grudgingly accepted the compromise, although some of the executives wanted an unconditional victory. The final acquiescence of the petroleum giants was due at least in part to the fact that by 1928 they were no longer contending with Mexico alone, but with a prestigious ambassador backed by both the administration in Washington and J. P. Morgan and Company. In the past the oilmen had counted on the bankers as allies in the fight to protect foreign investments in Mexico. But this fundamental issue had been eliminated for all practical purposes when the Calles administration conceded the point of the nonretroactive nature of article 27. The compromise which the bankers had urged for over a year had been achieved, and the oilmen were left with few allies and almost no supporters.[74]

Some State Department officials, and many oilmen, would grumble for years to come about Morrow's "giving away our

71. Munroe to Morrow, 6 January 1928, and Arthur M. Anderson to Morrow, 15 February 1928, Morrow MSS; Memorandum for Mr. Anderson by Vernon Munroe, 18 January 1928, Lamont MSS. General Pierce seemed at the time to hope that the bankers would "do something through Morrow to pull the wires" for changes in the new regulations.

72. Morrow to Rublee, 2 February 1928, Morrow MSS.

73. Person, *Mexican Oil*, 46–47.

74. W. E. McMahon to Richardson Pratt (both of Standard Oil of N. J.), 11 January 1928, Morrow MSS. McMahon urged acceptance of the new law because he had become convinced that cooperation with Morrow was the only way the oil companies could achieve any satisfactory solution. The oil executives realized how little support they enjoyed in the United States (especially in the press), and they knew that Morrow had become something of a national hero. Perhaps that is the reason they promulgated the rumor that Morrow was encouraging or supporting higher taxes on the oil companies in order to obtain funds for the bankers (especially Morgan & Co.); for rumor see Memorandum by W. R. C. [William R. Castle, Jr., assistant secretary], 11 April 1929, SD 812.51/1496.

national shirt." Walter Lippmann informed Morrow of his discussion with Chester Swain and the perverse self-righteousness displayed by this executive:

I gathered from his discussion that you were all right on the more materialistic and selfish plane, having safe-guarded all the substantial interests of his company, but that you did not fully grasp, or at least had failed to live up to those very high and disinterested ideals which have always characterized the conduct of the oil companies. He shook his head very sadly about the untagged lands.[75]

The ambassador became involved in the church-state controversy because he believed that settlement of this issue was vital for the internal stability of Mexico. Working with the prominent Catholic layman John J. Raskob of the Democratic National Committee and Father John J. Ryan of the National Catholic Welfare Conference, Morrow stretched a diplomatic arm all the way to Rome in an attempt to moderate the policy and utterances of the Vatican. A settlement was finally reached in 1929.[76]

The ambassador also cultivated good public relations by arranging for Charles A. Lindbergh's flight to Mexico City and the visit of humorist Will Rogers. In the last analysis, however, Morrow won acclaim as a successful ambassador largely because of the internal shift in emphasis of the Mexican government. The Calles administration had decided that Mexico should return to the fold of "well-behaved" underdeveloped countries within the international system of the industrial-creditor nations, provided that this could be done with dignity and without completely surrendering all the changes produced by the revolution. In essence, this was what the United States had been trying to accomplish since 1912—the curtailment of the revolution before the process fundamentally altered the status of foreign holdings. The U.S. *quid pro quo* was rather small in price but symbolically important for the Calles administration. It included the acceptance of greater

75. Lippmann to Morrow, 30 April 1928, Morrow MSS; see also Hugh Gibson to Arthur Bliss Lane, 6 December 1928, Lane MSS ,(Gibson had suggested to Herbert Hoover that Morrow be appointed secretary of state but encountered opposition in the department).

76. For details of negotiations see Confidential Memorandum for Mr. Olds from Morrow, 30 November 1927; Morrow to Raskob, 2 October 1928; and P. Pizzardo (secretary of state of the Vatican) · to Raskob, enclosed in Raskob to Morrow, 14 August 1928; all in Morrow MSS.

national regulation of the Mexican economy, and the limited distribution of land; the concession of a few debating points over the theoretical aspects of national control of natural resources; and the official acceptance of the inner circle of the "revolutionary family" as important national leaders. The revised status of the Mexican government was revealingly characterized by Morrow's report in April 1928 that most of the foreign residents believed that "Calles is the best President the country has had since Díaz."[77]

The Period of Calm Relations, 1928–32

During 1928 Morrow became involved in the question of Mexico's foreign debt and the negotiations with the International Committee of Bankers for a revision of the 1925 agreement. Calles confided to the ambassador that he trusted his advice, even though Morrow had been "firmly on the bondholders' side." "The curious result followed," Morrow wrote, "that in the negotiations between Montes de Oca and Lamont, I was in the strange position of having the President send Montes de Oca to me for advice as to how to answer his telegrams." At first the results seemed to be quite satisfactory. Upon Morrow's advice, all agreed that Mexico would pay the amount still owed to the bondholders' committee for 1927 but would make no payments on the 1928 account until a thorough study had been made of the overall financial situation. The Mexican government invited the International Committee to send a team of experts to make this study and the ambassador helped to lay the foundations for the investigation. Morrow also suggested to Lamont that he send Arthur Anderson, of the Morgan firm, to Mexico to coordinate the efforts of the investigators and the International Committee.[78] Lamont was enthusiastic over the prospects for this kind of cooperation. He wrote to J. P. Morgan:

The whole situation hangs together. The Committee can not work out its problems for the long future without a decently prosperous Mexico and revival of the oil business; Dwight can not work out his settlement of the oil and land question, unless there is a chance

77. Morrow to Sheffield, 2 April 1928, Sheffield MSS. In 1930 Mexico ranked second among Latin American countries in number of U.S. branch factories (17); *Congressional Record*, 71st Cong., 2d sess., 1930, 72, pt. 10; 10828–30.
78. Morrow to Rublee, 2 February 1928, Morrow MSS; Morrow to James R. Sheffield, 2 April 1928, Sheffield MSS.

that the external debt question can be handled too. This is the best chance that we have had yet. Heretofore the committee agreements have been temporarily designed to get as much money for the bondholders as could be legitimately secured. Now we have something more permanent to look forward to for the bondholders. It will be of immeasurable value to have Dwight helping along constructively in this way.[79]

Morrow believed that long-range Mexican stability would be achieved only by the complete financial reorganization of the country. The Sterrett-Davis report commissioned by the International Committee reinforced this conviction, since it convinced the ambassador that Mexico was in a condition of virtual bankruptcy (more liabilities than assets). He advised Lamont in November 1928:

I do not think any partial settlement [by Mexico] should be made with the International Committee, with the governments, with the specie banks or with any other group of creditors, because I think such partial settlements will most inevitably break down and delay the real financial reorganization of the country.[80]

Morrow probably wanted a Dawes Commission for Mexico. But even without such an instrument he at least hoped to arrange a consolidation of the entire Mexican debt and a balanced budget which would allow Mexico to make payments to all claimants and at the same time provide funds for essential governmental functions, especially for the army and education. In short, Mexico should be handled as a bankrupt corporation.[81]

Lamont did not entirely agree with the ambassador's views, but he cooperated with Morrow during the latter part of 1928 and early 1929 with the hope that Morrow would support some kind of revised agreement between the International Committee and the Mexican government. Other members of the committee, however, were pressuring Lamont to negotiate for additional funds for the bondholders.[82] Mexico was negotiating *en bloc* settlements

79. Lamont to J. P. Morgan, 16 January 1928, Lamont MSS.
80. Morrow to Lamont, 29 November 1928, Morrow MSS; see also Memorandum for Mr. Cotton [By Morrow], 1 October 1929, SD 812.51/1520.
81. Morrow to Secretary of State, 9 November 1928, Morrow MSS.
82. Lamont to Vivian Smith and J. R. Carter, n.d. (internal evidence indicates November 1928), Lamont MSS. Lamont was informed that a

with several governments which were aimed at consolidating and funding the various claims of each country's citizens. The bondholders represented by the International Committee, rather than by governments, wanted a new agreement to insure that they would not be left out, and Morrow believed that a series of uncoordinated settlements would completely wreck Mexican finances.[83]

On 27 March 1929, Secretary Kellogg formally instructed Ambassador Morrow to register the objections of the State Department to any new agreement between the International Committee and the Mexican government.[84] The bankers believed that Morrow inspired the note, and Lamont decided to "proceed as vigorously as possible despite the Ambassador's attitude."[85]

Yet, all concerned still hoped for a renewal of cooperation. After a series of conferences between the bankers, State Department officials, and Morrow (September–October 1929), Lamont reluctantly agreed to cooperate with the ambassador's effort to work out a general plan for Mexican finances. In return, Morrow was to try to convince the Mexican government to include in the 1930 budget an allocation of ten million pesos for the bondholders. Lamont informed Undersecretary Joseph P. Cotton that the bankers were doing this "against their better judgment," and Cotton remarked, "This represents a marked concession and change of mind." Cotton concluded:

Lamont complained that Morrow is just as nice as he was but that his plans are terribly vague. He thinks Morrow is in an atmosphere of liking the Mexicans and being fond of individuals there and being fooled by them. I think Lamont is expressing

---

member of the House of Commons had intended to raise the issue of Mexican bonds, but had decided not to when informed that Lamont was "doing everything possible" to induce the Mexican government to make a settlement. C. F. Whigham to Lamont, 16 February 1929, ibid.

83. Morrow to Lamont, 3 January and 29 November 1928, Morrow MSS. Bondholder pressure in Memorandum of telephone conversation with Thomas W. Lamont, N.Y. [by Joseph P. Cotton], 18 October 1929, SD 812.51/1529; Lamont to Arthur M. Anderson, 31 May 1929, and Lamont to Morrow, 24 July 1930, Lamont MSS.

84. Department of State to Morrow, 27 March 1929, Morrow MSS.

85. Lamont to J. P. Morgan & Co., 3 May 1929, Lamont MSS. Criticism of Morrow in Frank L. Polk to John Bassett Moore, 24 September 1929, Moore MSS. Lamont had requested Polk's law firm (Sullivan and Cromwell) to prepare a memorandum on the legal points involved in the State Department's case.

genuine affection for Morrow and that it is for that reason very largely that he is changing the position which was stated by him to the Secretary of State.[86]

Morrow did try to influence the drafting of the 1930 budget, and he suggested that the International Committee use its influence to convince Finance Minister Montes de Oca to increase the amount for debt service. He also noted that the committee should communicate with President-elect Pascual Ortiz Rubio. Morrow solicited the aid of Calles, who agreed with the proposed budget. Calles, however, pointed out the difficulties involved. Not only were Mexican revenues decreasing, but agitation from the "agrarian elements" was increasing. To cut the budget for various governmental programs while increasing the amount for debt service would entail political risks which the Mexican leadership was not willing to take.[87]

Morrow continued to press his budgetary plans, especially the idea of sharply curtailing land distribution and paying cash for lands taken in order to limit the growing debt, and turned to a serious consideration of an *en bloc* settlement of all American claims. With growing pressure from the bondholders, Lamont began to push for a new debt agreement. He explained to Morrow that his own influence as head of the International Committee was declining and that the group itself was showing signs of disintegration. In a real sense, Lamont felt that his own prestige, involved as it was in twelve years of committee leadership, was at stake.[88]

Lamont negotiated a revised agreement with Montes de Oca in July 1930. During and after the negotiations, Lamont and his colleagues utilized all the influence they could muster to try to counteract Morrow's advice. One of the ambassador's former aides (the military attaché, Colonel Alexander Macnab) inadvertently contributed to their campaign. In late April, Macnab

86. Memorandum of telephone conversation with Thomas W. Lamont, N.Y. [by Joseph P. Cotton], 18 October 1929, SD 812.51/1529; see also Memorandum of Meeting with Representatives of the International Committee of Bankers on Mexico, 2 October 1929, SD 812.51/1531.

87. Memorandum to T. W. Lamont [by Vernon Munroe], 11 December 1929, Lamont MSS.

88. Lamont to Morrow, 24 July 1930, and Lamont to J. Ridgely Carter, 22 August 1930, Lamont MSS; Morrow to McBride, 10 February 1930, Morrow MSS. Embassy officials hoped to use bondholder pressure on the Mexican government to help expedite a general settlement; McBride to Morrow, 14 March 1930, Morrow MSS.

made a speech in Newark, New Jersey, supporting Morrow's candidacy for the U.S. Senate. In the course of his praise for Morrow's efforts in Mexico, he stated that Morrow "took the Secretary of Finance under his wing and taught him finance." The Mexican government was quite disturbed over the implications of these remarks. A close associate of Morrow told me that it was Lamont who called the statements to the attention of the finance minister and asked him "who really ran Mexico." According to this source, Montes de Oca returned, determined to show Morrow who did run Mexico.[89] Morrow went directly to the president of Mexico to argue against the Lamont–Montes de Oca agreement and received his first major rebuff. Arthur Bliss Lane, first secretary of the embassy in Mexico, believed that the incident ended Morrow's effectiveness in Mexico.[90]

Lamont also tried to utilize the influence of Pani and Legorreta to offset the influence of the ambassador. In late August, Lamont suggested to one of the Morgan officials in the Paris branch that he should ask Aristide Briand to send for Pani and impress upon him the benefits which the French bondholders would derive from the agreement.[91] The Ortiz Rubio administration pushed for ratification of the agreement, but a growing tide of opposition stalled congressional action. The depression was growing worse in Mexico, and the committee was denounced as "a kind of Shylock, that wants its pound of flesh."[92] Lamont also hoped that Joseph Cotton or Secretary Henry L. Stimson might alter the State Department's opposition to the bankers' agreement. These men did not agree completely with Morrow's views, but they did not see any viable alternative either.[93]

89. Harold Nicholson, *Dwight Morrow* (New York, 1935), 382–83; Interview with Richard B. Scandrett, Jr. (Cornwall, N.Y.), 1 January 1966; Beals, *Glass Houses*, 313–15 (provides additional confirmation based on conversations with Morrow).

90. Lane to Cotton, 16 August 1930, Lane MSS (this letter was not sent); Memorandum for Morrow [by Arthur H. Springer] of a telephone call from Arthur Bliss Lane, 7 June 1930, Morrow MSS; Scandrett interview.

91. Lamont to J. Ridgely Carter, 22 August 1930; Lamont to Montes de Oca, 4 September 1930; Memorandum for Arthur M. Anderson from Thomas Lamont, 4 December 1930; all in Lamont MSS.

92. Memorandum for Lamont from V. Munroe, 29 November 1930, Lamont MSS.

93. Memorandum of Conversation with J. P. C. [Joseph P. Cotton] at Mt. Kisco, 30 July 1930 (by V. Munroe), Lamont MSS; Henry L. Stimson to Lamont, 6 October 1930, SD 812.51/1640. On 28 July 1929 George

Morrow returned to the United States to serve in the Senate, and died in October 1931. A month before his fatal seizure he confided to a close associate that he had failed in "the most important part of his mission in Mexico," and he attributed this to his former partners.[94] He believed that real stability for Mexico could be achieved only by a complete financial reorganization which would allocate specific amounts to governmental services and to debt service. Individual settlements would only produce chaos and economic ruin. During 1931, Mexico went off the gold standard as the value of the peso declined; undoubtedly Morrow saw these events as portents of disaster.[95]

In one sense both Morrow and Lamont failed in Mexico. The Lamont–Montes de Oca agreement was not ratified, and when the final settlement was made in 1943, Lamont claimed that the bondholders received only 10 percent of their total claims.[96] In the short run the policies of neither Morrow nor Lamont produced the kind of stability envisaged by these men of finance. The reinvigoration of land reform, new labor legislation, and the oil expropriation of 1938 were certainly not included in their concept of proper development. The depression and the resurging tide of revolutionary nationalism had a profound effect upon the inner circle of the "revolutionary family." These factors were reflected in the policies of the government and in the alteration of established patterns of political influence and individual relationships. In this changing context, neither Lamont nor Morrow could achieve their immediate objectives.[97] Yet in the broad, long-range perspec-

Rublee told Morrow, "About Mexico, Joe [Cotton] said that neither he nor Stimson would specially concern themselves. They were going to leave you to do whatever you thought best and wished only to be kept informed," Morrow MSS. Cotton opposed any agreement which gave some creditors exclusive claim to Mexican revenues; Memorandum of 3 August 1930, Morrow MSS.

94. Scandrett Interview.

95. McBride to Morrow, 22 December 1930, and Lane to Arthur H. Springer, 14 August 1931 ("August, 1931, is at hand and we are fishing in troubled waters!!!"), Morrow MSS; Nicholson, *Dwight Morrow*, 394–95.

96. Lamont to Sumner Welles, 21 October 1942, Lamont MSS. Between 1923 and 1928 the International Committee received from the Mexican government $45,076,558. Lamont's 10 percent estimate was based on reductions in interest. Under the agreement the bondholders received 20 percent of the principal amount. The railways bonds were retired in 1946.

97. Captain McBride wrote about these pressures in late 1930; McBride to Morrow, 22 December 1930, Morrow MSS. Lamont and his colleagues

tive, the policies of these men did produce a kind of success. Today Mexican bonds are sold on Wall Street, and the offices of major U.S. banking firms greet one on almost every corner of Mexican cities. The same cannot be said for the foreign oil companies.

The years 1930–33 represented a calm period before the re-newed storm of revolutionary nationalism led by President Lázaro Cárdenas. Relations between the United States and Mexico were quieter than they had been in years. Morrow's successor, J. Reuben Clark, Jr., continued the "soft-sell" diplomacy, and a Boston banker commented to Arthur Bliss Lane: "I have occasionally had misgivings as to the real efficacy of the come-to-me-my-prodigal-brother policy which we have been recently pursuing towards Mexico, and although actions speak louder than words, the apparent cordiality shown to Mr. Clark on his departure would indicate that the policy is evidently to be crowned with practical success."[98] This was a quasi-paternalistic approach, but disguised enough to be palatable to the men of Calles's group.

Dwight Morrow was perceptive enough to realize that the flexible tactics of one period could become the dogmatism of another. The Mexican Revolution was an integral part of the historical evolution of the nation, and Morrow realized that such developments could never be permanently fixed. The revolution had raised basic issues concerning the economic and political role of the underdeveloped world which were far from settled. Thus, in a letter to General Enoch H. Crowder, Morrow made a succinct evaluation of U.S.-Mexican relations, past and future: "It some-times amuses me when people say 'settle the Mexican question.' You and I know that neither the Mexican nor the Cuban ques-tions will be 'settled' in the life time of any one now living."[99] In an age of nationalistic revolutions in underdeveloped countries, Morrow was a better prophet than he realized.

---

held a very low opinion of Ambassador Josephus Daniels; Lamont to B. S. Carter, 5 August 1937, and Vernon Munroe to Lamont, 14 June 1947, Lamont MSS.

98. John M. Cabot to Lane, 9 March 1933, Lane MSS.

99. 25 February 1929, Lane MSS.

Appendix

Article 27 of the 1917 Constitution (Sections I–VII)

Ownership of all lands and waters comprised within the boundaries of the national territory is vested originally in the Nation. The Nation has had, and has, the right to convey title thereof to private persons, so establishing private property.

Expropriations shall be effected only for reasons of public utility and through indemnification.

The Nation shall have at all times the right to impose on private property such modalities as the public interest dictates, and the right to regulate the use and exploitation of all natural resources susceptible of appropriation, in order to preserve, and to effect an equitable distribution of, the public wealth. For this purpose there shall be taken whatever measures are found necessary for the break up of large landed estates; for the promotion of small land holdings; for the establishment of new centers of rural population provided with such lands and waters as are indispensable to them; for the development of agriculture, and to prevent the destruction of natural resources and to protect property from damage detrimental to the interests of the community. Settlements, hamlets situated on private estates, and lands held communally by peasants resident therein, having no lands or water or not having them in quantities sufficient for their needs, shall have the right to be provided with them from the adjoining estates, always with due regard for small land holdings.

In the Nation is vested the direct ownership of all mineral or other substances which in veins, layers, masses or beds form deposits the nature of which is different from the component elements of the soil, such as minerals from which metals and metalloids used for industrial purposes are extracted; beds of precious stones, rock salt, and salt lakes formed directly by marine waters; products derived from the decomposition of rocks, when their exploitation requires underground work; mineral or organic deposits of matters which may be used for

Reprinted from Gilberto Bosques, *The National Revolutionary Party of Mexico and the Six-Year Plan* (México, D.F.: Bureau of Foreign Information of the National Revolutionary Party, 1937), app. IV.

fertilizers; solid mineral fuels; petroleum, and all hydrocarbons whether solid, liquid or gaseous.

In the Nation is likewise vested the ownership of the waters of territorial seas to the extent and in the terms fixed by the Law of Nations; those of lakes and inlets on shores; those of inland lakes of natural formation which are directly connected with flowing waters; those of principal rivers or tributaries from the sources of their first permanent waters down to their mouths, whether they flow to the sea or cross two or more States; the waters of seasonal streams coursing through two or more States in their main body; the waters of rivers, streams, or ravines, when they bound the national territory or the territory of any of the States; the waters drawn from mines, and the beds and banks of the lakes and streams hereinbefore mentioned, to the extent fixed by law. Any other stream of water not comprised within the foregoing enumeration shall be held as an integral part of the private property through which it flows; but the use of waters when they cross from one landed property to another shall be held as of public utility and shall be subject to the provisions prescribed by the States.

In the cases to which the two preceding paragraphs refer, the ownership of the Nation is inalienable and shall not be liable to loss by prescription; concessions may be granted by the Federal Government to private parties, or to civil or commercial corporations organized under Mexican law, on condition that said resources be regularly exploited through duly established works and that all legal provisions be observed.

Legal capacity to acquire ownership of lands and waters of the Nation shall be governed by the following provisions:

I. Only Mexicans by birth or naturalization, and Mexican concerns, have the right to acquire ownership of lands, waters and their appurtenances, or to obtain concessions for the exploitation of mines, waters or mineral fuels in the Republic of Mexico. The State may grant the same right to aliens provided they agree before the Department of Foreign Affairs to be considered as Mexicans in respect to such property and, accordingly, not to invoke the protection of their own Governments in respect to the same, under penalty, in case of breach of that agreement, of forfeiture to the Nation of the property so acquired. Within a zone of 100 kilometers from the frontiers, and of 50 kilometers from the sea coast no alien shall under any conditions acquire direct ownership of lands and waters;

II. Religious associations known as churches, irrespective of creed, shall in no case have legal capacity to acquire, hold, or manage real estate or loans made on real estate; all real estate or loans on the same which are at present held by the said religious associations either on their own behalf or through third parties, shall vest in the Nation, and anyone shall have the right to denounce property so held. Presumptive proof shall be sufficient for declaring the denunciation well founded. All places assigned for public worship are the property of the Nation, represented by the Federal Government, which shall determine which such places may continue to be devoted to their present purposes. Episcopal residences, rectories, seminaries, orphan asylums or colleges of religious associations, convents or any other buildings built or assigned for the administration, propaganda, or teaching of the tenets of any religious cult shall forthwith vest, as of full right, directly in the Nation, to be used exclusively for the public services of the Federal or of the State governments within their respective jurisdictions. All places of public worship which may later be erected shall be the property of the Nation;

III. Public and private institutions of charity for the needy, for scientific research, for the diffusion of knowledge, for the mutual aid of their associates or for any other lawful purpose, shall in no case acquire any but the real estate indispensable for their true purposes and directly devoted to the same; they may notwithstanding acquire, hold and manage moneys loaned on real estate provided the mortgage terms do not exceed ten years. In no case shall institutions of this character be under the patronage, direction, administration, keeping or supervision of religious corporations or institutions, or of ministers of any religious cult or of their dependents even although either the former or the latter are not in active service;

IV. Commercial stock companies shall not acquire, hold, or manage rural property. Concerns of this nature organized to exploit any manufacturing, mining, petroleum or other industry, excepting only agricultural industries, may acquire, hold, or manage lands only in the area strictly necessary for their establishments, or adequate to serve the purposes indicated, which the Federal or the State Executive Power shall in each case determine;

V. Banks duly organized under the laws governing institutions of credit may grant mortgage loans on rural and urban property in conformity with the provisions of the said laws, but they shall neither own nor manage any real estate other than that absolutely necessary for their direct purpose;

VI. With the exception of the corporations to which clauses III, IV and V hereof refer, and of the population groups that in fact or by law conserve their communal character, or the population groups that have been given lands by the way of endowment grant or by way of restitution, or that have been constituted as centers of an agricultural community, no civil corporation shall hold or manage in its own behalf real estate or mortgage loans derived therefrom, with the single exception of the buildings assigned directly and immediately for the purposes of the institution. The States, the Federal District and the Territories, as well as the Municipalities throughout the Republic, shall enjoy full legal capacity to acquire and hold all real estate required for public services.

The Federal and the State laws shall determine within their respective jurisdictions those cases in which the occupation of private property is of public utility; and in conformity with the said laws the administrative authorities shall make the corresponding declaration thereanent. The amount that shall be fixed as compensation for the thing expropriated shall be based upon the sum at which the said property has been valued for fiscal purposes in the catastral or revenue collection offices, whether this value has been declared by the owner or tacitly accepted by him as betokened by the payment of his taxes on such a basis. The increased or reduced value which the property may have acquired or lost through improvements made in it or deterioration suffered by it after the date when the fiscal value was fixed shall be the only matter subject to expert opinion and to judicial resolution. The same procedure shall be observed in respect to objects the value of which is not recorded in the revenue offices.

The exercise of the rights pertaining to the Nation by virtue of this Article shall follow judicial process; but as a part of this process and by order of the proper tribunals,—which order shall be issued within the maximum period of one month,—the administrative authorities shall proceed without delay to the occupation, administration, sale by auction, or direct sale of the lands and waters in question, together with all their appurtenances, and in no case shall the acts of the said authorities be set aside until final sentence has been rendered.

VII. The population groups which by right or in fact conserve their communal status shall be entitled to enjoy in common the lands, forests and waters belonging to them or given them already by way of restitution or that may be so given them in the future.

Bibliography

Primary Sources: Unpublished

General Records of the Department of State in the National Archives (Record Group 59): the most useful for this study were: 711.12 (relations between the United States and Mexico), 812.00 (Mexico, political affairs), 812.51 (economic affairs), 812.6363 (petroleum), 710.11 (relations with Latin America).

Archivo General de la Secretaría de Relaciones Exteriores de México, Ramo 119, "Revolución Mexicana, 1910–1920." (This was the only record group which I was allowed to see, and these records were screened before they were delivered to me.)

Manuscript Collections: *Library of Congress* (Washington, D.C.), Chandler P. Anderson, Newton D. Baker, Edward T. Clark, Bainbridge Colby, Calvin Coolidge, George Creel, William S. Culbertson, Josephus Daniels, Norman H. Davis, Henry P. Fletcher, James R. Garfield, Leland Harrison, Charles Evans Hughes, Philander C. Knox, Franklin K. Lane, Robert Lansing, Boaz Long, Breckinridge Long, William Gibbs McAdoo, John Bassett Moore, Henry Morgenthau, Woodrow Wilson; *Yale University Library* (New Haven, Conn.), Gordon Auchincloss, Edward M. House, Arthur Bliss Lane, Frank L. Polk, James R. Sheffield, Henry L. Stimson, Sir William Wiseman; *Amherst College Library* (Amherst, Mass.), Dwight W. Morrow; *Baker Library, Harvard Graduate School of Business Administration,* Thomas W. Lamont; *Columbia University Library,* Frank Vanderlip; *Henry E. Huntington Library* (San Marino, Calif.), Albert B. Fall; *Minnesota Historical Society Library* (St. Paul, Minn.), Frank B. Kellogg; *State Historical Society of Wisconsin* (Madison, Wis.), Samuel Gompers.

Primary Sources: Published

Newspapers and Journals

The New York Times.
The Wall Street Journal.
The Commercial and Financial Chronicle.

Commerce and Finance.
The Mexican Review.

Government Publications

Carranza, Venustiano. *Address Delivered by Venustiano Carranza to the Mexican Congress on April 15, 1917.* Comisión de Reorganización Administrativa y Financiera, 1918.

México. Cámara de Diputados. *Diario de los debates del Congreso Constituyente.* 2 vols. 1917.

México. Comisión nacional para la celebracion del sesquicentenario de la proclamación de la independencia nacional y del cincuentenario de la Revolución Mexicana. *Labor internacional de la Revolución constitucionalista de México (Libro Rojo).* 1960 (first published in 1918).

México. Secretaría de Industria, Comercia, y Trabajo. *Legislación petrolera.* 1922.

México. Secretaría de Relaciones Exteriores. *The Mexican Oil Controversy as Told in Diplomatic Correspondence between the United States and Mexico.* 1920.

México. Secretaría de Relaciones Exteriores. *Documentos oficiales relativos al Covenio de la Huerta–Lamont.* 1924.

México. Secretaría de Relaciones Exteriores. *Memoria de labores realizados por la Secretaría de Relaciones Exteriores de agosto de 1925 a julio de 1926.* 1926.

México. Secretaría de Relaciones Exteriores. *Correspondencia oficial cambiada entre los gobiernos de México y los Estados Unidos con motiva de las dos leyes reglamentarias de la fracción primera de artículo 27 de la Constitución Mexicana.* 1926.

U. S. Department of Commerce. Bureau of Foreign and Domestic Commerce. *The Petroleum Industry in Mexico.* 13 September 1920.

U. S. Department of State. *Papers Relating to the Foreign Relations of the United States: The Lansing Papers.* 2 vols. 1940.

U. S. Department of State. *Papers Relating to the Foreign Relations of the United States.* Vols. for 1913 to 1932.

U. S. Department of State. *Proceedings of the United States–Mexican Commission: Convened in Mexico City, May 14, 1923.* 1925.

U. S. House of Representatives. Committee on Foreign Affairs. *Conditions in Nicaragua and Mexico,* 69th Cong., 2d sess., 1927.

U. S. Senate. Committee on Foreign Relations. *Relations with Mexico: Hearings before a Sub-Committee of the Committee on Foreign Relations.* 69th Cong., 2d sess., 1927.

U. S. Senate. Committee on Foreign Relations. *Investigation of Mexican Affairs.* 2 vols. 66th Cong., 2d sess., 1919–20.

U. S. Senate. Committee on Public Lands. *Leasing of Oil Lands.* 65th Cong., 1st sess., 1917.

U. S. Senate. Committee on Public Lands. *Leases upon Naval Oil Reserves.* 68th Cong., 1st sess., 1924.

Vazquez Schiaffino, José; Santaella, Joaquín; and Elorduy, Aquiles. *Informes sobre la cuestión petrolera.* Cámara de Diputados. 1919.

Memoirs

Beals, Carleton. *Glass Houses: Ten Years of Free-Lancing.* Philadelphia and New York: J. P. Lippincott Co., 1930.

Cabrera, Luis. *Veinte años después.* México, D.F.: Ediciones Botas, 1937.

Chamberlain, George Agnew. *Is Mexico Worth Saving?* Indianapolis: Bobbs-Merrill Co., 1920.

Davis, Will B. *Experiences and Observations of an American Consular Officer during the Recent Mexican Revolution.* Los Angeles: Privately printed by author, 1920.

Grew, Joseph C. *Turbulent Era: A Diplomatic Record of Forty Years, 1904–1945.* 2 vols. Boston: Houghton, Mifflin, 1952.

Guffey, Joseph. *Seventy Years on the Red Fire Wagon.* Lebanon, Pa.: privately published, 1952.

Guzmán, Martin Luis. *Memoirs of Pancho Villa.* Translated by Virginia H. Taylor. Austin: University of Texas Press, 1965.

Guzmán Esparza, Roberto. *Memorias de Don Adolfo de la Huerta: Según su propio dictado.* México, D.F.: Ediciones Guzmán, 1957.

Hammond, John Hays. *Autobiography of John Hays Hammond.* 2 vols. New York: Farrar and Rinehart, 1935.

Houston, David F. *Eight Years with Wilson's Cabinet.* 2 vols. Garden City, N.Y.: Doubleday, Page, 1926.

Kelley, David. *The Ruling Few: or, the Human Background to Diplomacy.* London: Hollis & Carter, 1952.

King, Rosa. *Tempest over Mexico.* Boston: Little, Brown, 1935.

Lamont, Thomas W. *Across World Frontiers.* New York: Harcourt Brace & Co., 1951.

Lansing, Robert. *War Memoirs of Robert Lansing.* Indianapolis: Bobbs-Merrill, 1935.

O'Hea, Patrick. *Reminiscences of the Mexican Revolution.* México, D.F.: Talleres Gráficos de Editorial, 1966.

Pani, Alberto. *La política hacendaria y la Revolución.* México, D.F.: Editorial Cultura, 1926.

Pound, Arthur, and Moore, Samuel Taylor, eds. *They Told Barron: The Notes of Clarence W. Barron.* New York and London: Harper & Bros., 1930.

Reed, John. *Insurgent Mexico.* New York and London: D. Appleton & Co., 1914.

Sands, William Franklin, and Lalley, Joseph M. *Our Jungle Diplomacy.* Chapel Hill: University of North Carolina Press, 1944.

Collections and Editions

American Association of Mexico. *The Status of Americans in Mexico: Bulletins of the American Association of Mexico.* New York, 1921.

Baker, Ray Stannard, and Dodd, William E. *The Public Papers of Woodrow Wilson.* 5 vols. New York: Harper & Bros., 1925–27.

Baker, Ray Stannard. *Woodrow Wilson: Life and Letters.* 8 vols. Garden City, N.Y.: Doubleday, Doran & Co., 1927–39.

Blakeslee, George H., ed. *Mexico and the Caribbean: Clark University Addresses.* New York: G. E. Stechert & Co. 1920.

Bonsal, Stephen. *The American Mediterranean.* New York: Moffat, Yard & Co., 1913.

Borchard, Edwin. *Diplomatic Protection of Citizens Abroad, or the Law of International Claims.* New York: Banks Law Publishing Co., 1915.

Bosques, Gilberto. *The National Revolutionary Party of Mexico and the Six-Year Plan.* México, D.F.: Bureau of Foreign Information of the National Revolutionary Party, 1937.

Clark, J. Reuben, Jr. "The Oil Settlement in Mexico." *Foreign Affairs,* July, 1928.

Creel, George. *The People Next Door: An Interpretive History of Mexico and the Mexicans.* New York: John Day Co., 1926.

Cronon, E. David. *The Cabinet Diaries of Josephus Daniels, 1913–1921.* Lincoln: University of Nebraska Press, 1963.

Culbertson, William S. *Commercial Policy in War Time and After.* New York: Appleton & Co., 1919.

Dillon, E. J. *President Obregón—a World Reformer.* Boston: Small Maynard & Co., 1923.

———. *Mexico on the Verge.* New York: George H. Doran Co., 1921.

Fabela, Isidro, ed. *Documentos históricos de la Revolución Mexicana.* 12 vols. México, D.F.: Fondo de Cultura Económica, 1960–68.

Galindo, Hermila. *La Doctrina Carranza y el acercamiento indo-latino.* México, D.F., 1919.

Gibbon, Thomas E. *Mexico under Carranza.* Garden City, N.Y.: Doubleday, Page & Co., 1919.

González Ramírez, Manuel, ed. *Planes políticos y otros documentos.* 5 vols. México, D.F.: Fondo de Cultura Económica, 1954.

Hammond, John Hays, and Jenks, Jeremiah W. *Great American Issues: Political, Social, Economic.* New York: Charles Scribner's Sons, 1921.

Hendricks, Burton J. *The Life and Letters of Walter H. Page.* 3 vols. Garden City, N.Y.: Doubleday, Page & Co., 1923–25.

House, Edward M. *The Intimate Papers of Colonel House, Arranged as a Narrative by Charles Seymour.* 4 vols. Boston: Houghton, Mifflin, 1926–28.

Jones, Chester Lloyd. *Mexico and Its Reconstruction.* New York: D. Appleton & Co., 1921.

Kellogg, Frederic M. "Mexico's Oil Rights." *The Nation's Business,* November 1920.

Knights of Columbus. *Mexico?* New Haven, Conn., 1926.

Lamont, Thomas W. "Three Examples of International Cooperation." *Atlantic Monthly,* October 1923.

Lane, Anne W., and Wall, Louise H., eds. *The Letters of Franklin K. Lane: Personal and Political.* Boston and New York: Houghton Mifflin Co., 1922.

Lippmann, Walter. *The Stakes of Diplomacy.* New York: Henry Holt & Co., 1915.

———. "Vested Rights and Nationalism in Latin America." *Foreign Affairs,* April, 1927.

Lodge, Henry Cabot, ed. *Selections from the Correspondence of Theodore Roosevelt and Henry Cabot Lodge.* 2 vols. New York and London: Charles Scribner's Sons, 1925.

Madēro, Francisco I. *La Sucesión presidencial en 1910.* 3d ed. México, D.F.: Librería de la Viuda de Ch. Bouret, 1911.

Manero, Antonio. *México y la solidaridad Americana: la doctrina Carranza.* Madrid: Editorial-América, 1918.

———. *Que es la Revolucíon? breve exposición sobre las principales causas de la Revolución Constitutionalista en México.* Vera Cruz: Tipografía "La Heroica," 1915.

Marburg, Theodore. *Expansion.* New York and Baltimore: John Murphy Co., 1900.

———. "Backward Nation." *The Independent,* 20 June 1912.

Middleton, Philip Harvey. *Industrial Mexico: 1919 Facts and Figures.* New York: Dodd, Mead, 1919.

Molina, Enríquez, Andrés. *Los grandes problemas nacionales.* México, D.F.: Imprenta de A. Carranza e hijos, 1909.

Morrow, Dwight W. "Who Buys Foreign Bonds?" *Foreign Affairs,* January 1927.

Murray, Robert H., trans. and ed. *Mexico before the World: Public Documents and Addresses of Plutarco Elías Calles.* New York: Academy Press, 1927.

Pani, Alberto. *Cuestiones diversas, contendidas en 44 cartas al presidente Carranza.* México, D.F.: Imprenta nacional, 1922.

———. *On the Road to Democracy.* Translated by J. Palomo Rincon. México, D.F., 1918.

Rosecrans, William S. *Manifest Destiny and the Monroe Doctrine and Our Relations with Mexico: A Letter from Gen. Rosecrans to the People of the United States.* 1870.

Sáenz, Aarón. *La Política internacional de la Revolución: estudios y documentos.* México, D.F.: Fondo de Cultura Económica, 1961.

Sherwell, G. B. *Mexico's Capacity to Pay: A General Analysis of the Present International Economic Position of Mexico.* Washington, D.C., 1929.

Thompson, Wallace. *Trading with Mexico.* New York: Dodd, Mead, 1921.

Vasquez Schiaffino, J. "Mexico." *Petroleum Magazine,* August 1919.

Wilson, Woodrow. "The Road Away from Revolution." *Atlantic Monthly,* August 1923.

Essay on Selected Secondary Works

This essay is not intended as a review of the literature in the field. It covers only those works which I found most useful for this book.

For the general ideological-economic setting of the American open-door world view one should start with the basic works by William Appleman Williams: *The Tragedy of American Diplomacy* (1959) and *The Contours of American History* (1961). My views of U.S.–Latin American relations were also influenced by Charles A. Beard's *The Idea of National Interest* (1934), Arthur P. Whitaker's *The Western Hemisphere Idea: Its Rise and Decline* (1954), and Octavio Paz's *The Labyrinth of Solitude: Life and Thought in Mexico* (1950; translated by Lysander Kemp, 1961). Woodrow Wilson's liberal-capitalistic world order is analyzed in detail by N. Gordon Levin in *Woodrow Wilson and World Politics: America's Response to War and Revolution* (1968). For the objectives of United States international economic policy during this period the basic work is Carl Parrini's *Heir to Empire: United States Economic Diplomacy, 1916–1923* (1969). Cleona Lewis's *America's Stake in International Investments* (1938) is a classic.

James M. Callahan's *American Foreign Policy in Mexican Relations* (1932) contains much material for the period to 1910. This needs to be supplemented by the well-researched volumes (emphasizing Mexican archives) by Daniel Cosío Villegas, *Historia moderna de México: El Porfiriato—vida política exterior* (1960–63), and *The United States versus Porfirio Díaz* (1963). Howard F. Cline's *The United States and Mexico* (1953) combines an introductory survey of U.S.–Mexican relations with a discussion of Mexican internal developments for the period 1910–50. A survey from the Mexican point of view is the fine work by Luis G. Zorilla, *Historia de las relaciones entre México y los Estados Unidos de America, 1800–1958* (1966). Also useful (and more anti-American) is Alberto María Carreño's *La diplomacia extraordinaria entre México y Estados Unidos* (1951). For the revolutionary period, two extensive works are by Isidro Fabela, *Historia diplomática de la Revolución Mexicana* (1959), and (especially for 1913–16) Eduardo Luquin, *La política internacional de la revolución constitucionalista* (1957).

A good starting point for any analysis of American investment in Mexico is David M. Pletcher's *Rails, Mines, and Progress: Seven American Promoters in Mexico, 1867–1911* (1958). Several other works contain material for the post-1910 period as well. Two of the best studies of a Mexican industry and the role of American investment are Marvin D. Bernstein's *The Mexican Mining Industry, 1890–1950: A Study of the Interaction of Politics, Economics, and Technology* (1966), and Lorenzo Meyer's *México y Estados Unidos en el conflicto petrolero (1917–1942)* (1968). The latter has more information on the diplomatic conflicts engendered by investments. Two very useful analyses of foreign investment in Mexico are Chester

Lloyd Jones and George Wythe, *Economic Conditions in Mexico* (1928), and G. B. Sherwell, *Mexico's Capacity to Pay: A General Analysis of the Present International Economic Position of Mexico* (1929). Antonio J. Bermúdez, *The Mexican National Petroleum Industry: A Case Study in Nationalization* (1963) presents some information on foreign oil holdings. George S. Gibb and Evelyn H. Knowlton's *The Resurgent Years, 1911–1927* (1956) contains information about SONJ in Mexico but has little sympathy for the Mexican position. Some interesting information about the copper-mining industry is contained in Harvey O'Connor's *The Guggenheims: The Making of an American Dynasty* (1937). Mira Wilkins and Frank E. Hill's *American Business Abroad: Ford on Six Continents* (1964) has information on the development of the Ford Motor Company in Mexico.

Miguel S. Wionczek's *El nacionalismo mexicano y la inversión extranjera* (1967) is one of the best analyses of the interaction between Mexican nationalism and foreign investment after 1910. The most complete survey of the foreign debt controversy is Edgar Turlington's *Mexico and Her Foreign Creditors* (1930). An able discussion of the various aspects of foreigners, investments, and revolution is F. S. Dunn's *The Diplomatic Protection of Americans in Mexico* (1933). The Bucareli Conference of 1923 represented an important landmark in the diplomatic drive to protect American interests in Mexico, and they have provoked an ongoing controversy in Mexico. Some argue that the "agreements" at Bucareli represented a surrender by the Obregón government to the United States. Others contend that the "agreements" were a needed compromise which aided reform. Several of the more important examples of these positions are: Antonio Gómez Robledo, *The Bucareli Agreements and International Law* (1940): Rafael Trujillo, *Adolfo de la Huerta y los tratados de Bucareli* (1966); A. J. Pani, *Las conferencias de Bucareli* (1953); and Manuel González Ramírez, *Los llamados tratados de Bucareli: México y los Estados Unidos en las convenciones internacionales de 1923* (1939). Some of the results of the conference are discussed in Abraham H. Feller, *The Mexican Claims Commissions, 1923–1934: A Study in the Law and Procedure of International Tribunals* (1935).

For the Wilson administration, the most complete account of U.S.–Mexican relations is in the volumes by Arthur S. Link, *Wilson: The New Freedom* (1956) and *Wilson: Campaigns for Progressivism and Peace, 1916–1917* (1965). Link almost completely ignores economic and ideological factors, and so these volumes should be supplemented by William E. Diamond's *The Economic Thought of Woodrow Wilson* (1943) and Lawrence E. Gelfand's *The Inquiry: American Preparation for Peace, 1917–1919* (1963). On the 1920s, Merlo J. Pusey's *Charles Evans Hughes* (1951) is useful. L. Ethan Ellis's *Frank R. Kellogg and American Foreign Relations, 1925–1929* (1961) is most complete for the diplomatic controversies of the period.

More specialized works which contain much useful material for the Wilson period are: Peter Calvert, *The Mexican Revolution 1910–1914: The Diplomacy of Anglo-American Conflict* (1968); Robert E. Quirk, *An Affair of Honor: Woodrow Wilson and the Occupation of Vera Cruz* (1962); Kenneth J. Grieb, *The United States and Huerta* (1969); Haldeen Braddy, *Pershing's Mission in Mexico* (1966); Clarence C. Clendenen, *The United States and Pancho Villa: A Study in Unconventional Diplomacy* (1961); and Luis Lara y Pardo, *Matches de dictadores: Wilson contra Huerta, Carranza contra Wilson* (1942).

For the 1920s the best study of the religious question (with a pro-Catholic slant) is Sister M. Elizabeth Rice's *The Diplomatic Relations between the United States and Mexico as Affected by the Struggle for Religious Liberty in Mexico, 1925–1929* (1959). Some details are also presented in Harold Nicholson's *Dwight Morrow* (1935).

Milton R. Konvitz's *The Alien and Asiatic in American Law* (1946) provides an excellent analysis of American restrictions on foreigners and illuminates the double standard applied by the United States to Mexico. The real nature of international law in the hemisphere and the interests underlying the legalisms are well analyzed by C. Neale Ronning in *Law and Politics in Inter-American Diplomacy* (1963). Complementing this work is Donald R. Shea's *The Calvo Clause: A Problem of Inter-American and International Law and Diplomacy* (1955). Two excellent analyses of the problem by Mexicans are Isidro Fabela's *Las doctrinas Monroe y Drago* (1957) and Pablo Gonzalez Casanova's *La ideología Norte americana sobre inversiones extranjeras* (1955).

Good surveys of the internal history of the Mexican Revolutions are Daniel James's *Mexico and the Americans* (1963) and Victor Alba's *The Mexicans: The Making of a Nation* (1967). James devotes much more attention to diplomacy. More analytical in terms of the political sociology of the revolution is Frank R. Brandenburg's *The making of Modern Mexico* (1964). A useful work is Miguel Alessio Robles's *Historia política de la Revolución* (1946). John W. F. Dulles's *Yesterday in Mexico: A Chronicle of the Revolution, 1919–1936* (1961) provides a wealth of information on internal developments and foreign relations. Helpful background material is also presented in Stanley R. Ross's *Francisco I. Madero, Apostle of Mexican Democracy* (1955), Charles C. Cumberland, *Mexican Revolution: Genesis under Madero* (1952), Ruben Romero et al., *Obregón: Aspectos de su vida* (1935), John Womack, Jr., *Zapata and the Mexican Revolution* (1969), and Robert E. Quirk, *The Mexican Revolution, 1914–1915: The Convention of Aguascalientes* (1960).

Studies emphasizing agrarian reform are Frank Tannenbaum's *Peace by Revolution* (1933) and *Mexico: The Struggle for Peace and Bread* (1950), and Jesús Silva-Herzog's *El agrarismo mexicano y la reforma agraria* (1959). A good analysis of the reforms stemming from the constitution of 1917 is Jesús Romero Flores's *La Constitución de 1917 y los primeros gobiernos revolucionarios* (1960). For banking and financial developments one should consult Antonio Manero's *La Revolución bancaria en México, 1865–1955* (1957), Alberto Pani's *Tres monografías* (1941), and William P. Glade and Charles W. Anderson's *The Political Economy of Mexico: Politics and Development Banking in Mexico* (1963). The latter work provides a fine synthesis of the politics and economics of the revolution.

As a concluding note, I would recommend, for the essence of the revolution, reading Anita Brenner, *The Wind That Swept Mexico: The History of the Mexican Revolution of 1910–1942* (1943); Oscar Lewis, *Pedro Martinez: A Mexican Peasant and His Family* (1964); and the novels of Mariano Azuela, Martín Luis Guzmán, José Rubén Romero, and Carlos Fuentes.

Index